THE FIGHTING FOURTH

No.4 COMMANDO AT WAR 1940–45

JAMES DUNNING

SUTTON PUBLISHING

This book is dedicated to all ranks of No. 4 Commando who served, trained and fought together during the Second World War from 1940 to 1945.

We were a team held together by our training and shared experiences. No other form of endurance, except great danger at sea or on the mountains, could bring about the same links of comradeship. We were bound to one another – men on the same rope . . .

Lord Lovat, writing of No. 4 Commando
in his autobiography, *March Past.*

First published in the United Kingdom in 2003 by
Sutton Publishing Limited · Phoenix Mill
Thrupp · Stroud · Gloucestershire · GL5 2BU

British Library Cataloguing in Publication Data
A catalogue record for this book is available from the British Library.

ISBN 0-7509-3095-0

Typeset in 10/12 pt Plantin.
Typesetting and origination by
Sutton Publishing Limited.
Printed and bound in England by
J.H. Haynes & Co. Ltd, Sparkford.

Contents

List of Illustrations and Maps

Maps

Author's Foreword

Following the success of a previous book, *It Had To Be Tough*, which dealt exclusively with the story of the origins of the Commandos and their special training in the Second World War, deliberately excluding narratives or accounts of the actions fought by these Special Service troops, it was suggested that I should attempt to write the whole story of No. 4 Commando, of which I had been a founder member.

The idea appealed to me, albeit I appreciated it posed a formidable undertaking, especially as, although I had joined No. 4 Commando in the beginning, I left the unit a couple of months after its successful participation in the Dieppe Raid to become an instructor at the Commando Basic Training Centre at Achnacarry in Scotland. It meant that from January 1943 my account would no longer be based on personal experiences, but dependent on records, accounts, books and the memories of others.

I need not have worried, for my old comrades rallied round and, thanks to the assistance of the Secretary of the Commando Association, Ron Youngman, I soon had contributions, in words and photographs, from a host of ex-members of No. 4. Without their splendid support and help this book would not have materialised; there were so many of them that I have acknowledged their help individually, and that of others on pages xi–xii. I have also been able to quote from books written by ex-members of the Commando.

I must, however, thank my dear wife, Jane, separately, and here, for her help, encouragement and understanding during the months that I have been engaged on this fascinating war story.

Acknowledgements

I decided to make a separate issue of acknowledging all those old comrades, friends and others who have been so generous in their help with the writing of this book, in making contributions, lending photographs or maps, and also allowing me to quote from their books.

Four officers, the late Brigadiers Lord Lovat and Mills-Roberts, the late Capt Gilchrist and the late Lt McDougall all wrote of their experiences in No. 4 Commando, but none of these authors covered its early formative period. Where I have quoted them I mention the source in the narrative.

A further fifty-eight old comrades of No. 4 have also contributed in some way to this story and they are listed below; where applicable I have also mentioned them as the source in the text. Special acknowledgement must be made to the family of the late Bill Bidmead, of No. 4, who kindly sent me the unpublished manuscript of Bill's detailed record and story of his service in the war. Another special word of thanks must be afforded to Col Alastair Thorburn, the sole known surviving officer of No. 4's campaigns in Normandy and Walcheren, who kindly checked the chapters on those actions.

I am grateful for the help and advice received from Leon Gaultier, one of those intrepid French Commandos who stormed ashore with the rest of No. 4 on 6 June, and his comrade Maurice Chauvet, who was there too.

Grateful thanks are also extended to Emyr Jones, who, against all odds, toiled for a couple of years to produce a roll of the members of No. 4 who went on the Dieppe Raid, as there was no official list. He has an encyclopaedic knowledge of that action as a result of this research, so I thank him for checking the chapter on the Raid, and also to Will Fowler for allowing me to quote from his book.

As I was nearing the end of my researches an old comrade of my Commando days at St Ives, Jimmy Pook, kindly sent me a bundle of items connected with the D-Day landings since his uncle, the late Lt Cdr Jack Berry, was captain of LCI 523, which took one of the French troops ashore. I thank him for allowing me to reproduce items from that original source.

I also thank Ron Youngman, especially for helping me track down the following veterans of No. 4, whose contributions and support have been great and are most gratefully acknowledged: Messrs R.J Anderson, 'Curly' Anderson, Norman 'Monty' Banks, Chris Birmingham, 'Ted' Brewer, George Bridges, E.B. Briggs, Ernie Brooks, Joe Burnett, Pete Burrows, R. Buxton, the late D. Clement, L. Cocker, Dennis Cooper, Capt Eric Cross, Johnny Duhig, Frank Farnborough, Len Fraser, J. Givens, Jack Griffiths,

E. Havilland, 'Bill' Hoare, 'Ossie' Hughes, Hugh Hunter, Charlie Jacobs, Bill Johnson, George Jones, Gwyn Jones, Peter Lambert, Frank Lansley, Vic Lessons, the late Les Lilley, Jim Linham, the late Gerry Lynn, Bob Mahan, 'Maxie' Maxwell, Alex Morris, Fred Morris, John Murray, 'Rollie' Oliver, Bill Parker, Malcolm Parr, Larry Phillips, 'JED' Price, Glyn Prosser, Col P.G.B. Pugh, John Skerry, Stan Smith, Milton Smithson, Peter Snook, Joe Spicer, Ken Stoakes, Gerry Swailes, Roy Tarbox, Bob Tout, George Tyreman, Denys Vickers and Doug Webb.

Finally, I wish to thank the staff of the Imperial War Museum, the Public Record Office and the National Army Museum, also the Military Attaché at the Norwegian Embassy, Mr and Mrs Van Asperan and John Martin (the nephew of the late Don Martin) for their kind help, advice and contributions.

Introduction

One of the significant outcomes of the Second World War was the recognition of the strategic and tactical value of Special Forces, but it wasn't until Winston Churchill took over the premiership – and leadership – of Britain that the raising of an elite force of volunteers was contemplated and steps were taken to create such a force.

It was a challenging innovation for the British Army and a breakaway from outdated concepts of warfare that prevailed at the beginning of the war and during the months of the so-called 'phoney war' and in the 'Maginot Line' philosophy that preceded the fall of France.

The first Special Service troops to be formed were the Army Commandos, and it is a salutory thought to reflect that all four of our current Special Forces, namely the Royal Marine Commandos, the Parachute Regiment, the Special Air Service (SAS) and the Special Boat Service (SBS) all share the same origin, namely, the first Army Commandos formed on Churchill's orders in July 1940.

No. 2 Commando became Britain's first unit of paratroopers and as such were the 'founding fathers' of the Parachute Regiment, while the SAS and SBS were founded by two Army Commando officers, David Stirling and Roger Courtney, and although the Army Commandos were disbanded in 1945, their Royal Marine Commando comrades survived and have maintained the traditions and high standards of military excellence established by the first Army Commandos from 1940 onwards.

The story that follows is the history of one such Commando, No. 4, from its first day in Weymouth in July 1940 to its ultimate demise and disbandment in Recklinghausen, Germany in January 1946. It relates how during those years a superb fighting unit was created from 500 volunteers who initially came from many different regiments and corps of the British Army. They all hoped for immediate action, but for a variety of reasons this was denied them. In truth they were not ready to carry out successful amphibious raiding operations. Two early raids by other Commando forces had proved this point – they were dismal failures. These early Commando volunteers had neither the means nor sufficient training for immediate results.

But during those early formative, if frustrating, months all ranks got physically fit, leaders were found, the unfit, unsuitable and unwanted were returned to their unit (RTU'd), new weapons and equipment began to trickle in, the right types of landing craft became available, and new methods, skills, techniques and battle drills were developed, often from scratch, to meet the demands and requirements of the proposed amphibious operations. Consequently many months passed before the men of No. 4 Commando eventually carried out their first raid and won their spurs on the Lofoten Islands. It was a start.

Thereafter, there were many disappointments as operations were planned and rehearsed, then cancelled – often at the last moment. In one such project, a special composite troop was even sent out to West Africa to make preparations for the follow-up of the rest of No. 4 Commando before an amphibious assault on the Canary Islands.

Disappointed, but undeterred, the Commando continued to train hard. This training forged the fighting force that became the only unit to successfully carry out its mission on the Dieppe Raid, where, among other awards for gallantry, one of its numbers, Capt Pat Porteous, won the Victoria Cross.

There followed more months of varied and strenuous training (plus some small raids), undertaken throughout the length and breadth of England, Scotland and Wales. This ranged from cliff climbing in South Wales and rock climbing in North Wales to snow and mountain warfare training in the Cairngorms, from boating exercises in the Atlantic swell of Devon and Cornwall to the more placid waters of the Norfolk Broads, interspersed with street fighting training in blitzed areas of Southampton, London and Glasgow, while one entire troop also qualified as paratroopers. There was no end to the variety of courses attended and innovative training carried out as a prelude to being picked for a place in Montgomery's order of battle to spearhead the invasion of Normandy on D-Day.

No. 4 Commando, by now an integrated British-French Commando, stormed ashore on that momentous day to destroy vital enemy strongpoints that dominated the extreme eastern flank of the Allied landing beaches at Ouistreham. The account of that action on 6 June is recalled by those, British and French, of the Commando who were there. It makes graphic reading.

For the next eighty-three days the men of No. 4 Commando, with their other Commando and Airborne comrades, held the left flank of the Allies' invasion bridgehead, before the capture of Caen and the breakout from Falaise. This was a period when every man in the Commando – even the clerks became front-line soldiers – was involved in daring counter-attacks and patrols in a calculated Commando policy of 'offensive defence'.

After Normandy and a short break in England, No. 4 Commando was soon back in action again, when it took part in what was aptly called 'a perfect little campaign'. It included a night landing and assault to capture the port of Flushing.

From then onwards the Commando was part of the force that had the arduous task of defending the flank of the Allies' advance in Germany by securing the island of Walcheren from enemy incursions. It was a long, cold winter, followed by a rapid move into Germany, to Recklinghausen, for the irksome task of guarding a camp of Nazis whose wartime activities warranted their detention and, ironically, the Commando was called upon to protect the local German farming community from marauding bands of displaced persons.

Sadly, the days of the Commando were numbered, and in January 1946 No. 4 Commando was disbanded. It was an inglorious ending to a distinguished wartime Commando. Fortunately, the deeds and achievements of all ranks of the Commando have been kept alive through memorials, museums, books and films. Indeed, such tributes are widespread and are to be found not only in Britain but also in France, Norway and Holland, and although diverse and varied in their forms, they are there to serve one joint purpose, namely, to honour the memory of all who served in the Fighting Fourth – No. 4 Commando – from 1940 to 1946.

CHAPTER ONE

It All Started in Weymouth

It was one of those glorious summers we all dream about – and hope for. Each morning ushered in a clear blue sky and the promise of yet another warm and sunny day. But – and it was a big 'But' – it was wartime. And even worse, Britain's fortunes were at their lowest ebb, as it faced an imminent enemy invasion. For within the space of just three weeks in June 1940 the armies of France, Britain and the Low Countries had been routed and defeated by Hitler's forces, who had swept on to the Channel ports and forced the withdrawal from Europe of the British Army, by way of evacuation at Dunkirk.

As a result, in July 1940 Britain stood alone, seemingly ill equipped and unprepared to face and repel a threatened invasion by the Nazis, who were now masters of Europe, dominating the western coastline from the Arctic in the north to nearly as far as the Pyrenees to the south.

Indeed, with a plan of invasion (Operation Sea Lion) prepared and in hand, the Germans had already made a start with a series of daylight air raids on targets in the south of England, thus beginning the Battle of Britain.

They were grim days. The fearsome threat of invasion occupied the thoughts and lives of everyone. Nevertheless, it was against this daunting background that the prime minister, Winston Churchill, took the bold decision to look ahead beyond the bleak, immediate future, and, appreciating the potentially vulnerable and extensive European coastline held by the enemy, proposed that an elite force be raised to take the fight to the enemy with seaborne and airborne raids.

In the immediate short term these elite forces, or Commandos, as they were soon to be called, would be available to repel enemy seaborne incursions and parachute descents, but their main purpose was to wage a campaign of 'tip and run' raids on the enemy coastline.

Churchill's audacious and adventurous plan, in the circumstances then prevailing, was soon translated into action, with the result that the Dorset seaside resort of Weymouth became the base of one such unit. By the third week of July some 500 volunteers from close on 90 different regiments and corps of the British Army arrived in the town to form this new unit – No. 4 Commando. On arrival we all quickly found out that even routine life in a Commando was going to be vastly different from what we had been accustomed to in our previous units, when we lived in barracks or wartime camps. One of the features of this new force was the prerequisite that every individual – officers and other ranks (ORs) alike – would be responsible for his own quartering and feeding.

This arrangement was an innovation in the British Army. There were many training, administrative and operational reasons for this novel and unusual arrangement; not least it meant that the Commando had no lengthy 'tail' of cooks, orderlies, fatigue men and other personnel employed on purely administrative duties, as did the rest of the Army. Those irksome and unpopular daily chores could account for as many as 20 per cent of the personnel unavailable for training, contrasting with the Commandos, who, living in civilian billets, could count on almost 100 per cent of their personnel available, all the time, for training and ready for operations. Furthermore, this system of making every man responsible for his own quartering helped to foster self-discipline and self-reliance, important factors in a force of this kind.

To make the system work was simplicity itself. All ranks were paid a daily subsistence allowance and given a ration card. The allowance was 13*s* 4*d* for officers and 6*s* 8*d* for ORs. In both cases it was a flat rate throughout: the subaltern got the same as his colonel, and likewise, the private soldier the same as his regimental sergeant-major (RSM). The ration card, exactly the same as that issued to civilians during the war, was a vital piece of paper; without it none of the basic foods could be purchased. The subsistence allowance adequately covered bed and breakfast, and two other meals per day, and was paid to the landladies on a weekly basis. This added up to 30 bob – £1 10*s*.

All the bases chosen for the new Commandos had to be on the coast, where, *inter alia*, boating and swimming facilities were at hand, and this led to the choice of Weymouth for No. 4 Commando. With so many of the traditional seaside B & B landladies unable to let their rooms because of the war and restrictive regulations applying to coastal areas, these good ladies were only too glad to offer the Commandos accommodation, and they soon became their 'lads', while some of the younger landladies were not averse to welcoming a virile young Commando to her 'bed – and breakfast' establishment!

Most of the Commandos were billeted in traditional B & Bs, and were provided with three daily meals. The ration cards enabled the landladies to buy the basic rationed foods – meat, butter, cheese, tea and sugar. Fortunately, some other foods such as bread, milk, home-grown potatoes, vegetables and fruit were not rationed, enabling the shopkeeper to sell them on a rota basis, or 'under the counter' as depicted by L/Cpl Jones in the popular TV series, *Dad's Army*.

It was ironic that the Commandos, about to undergo the toughest physical training, did so on 'civvy' rations, whereas the rest of the Army living in barracks, many of whom were employed in sedentary jobs, had much larger service rations. However, this didn't worry us. We were often able to supplement our landladies' larders with the odd rabbit, chicken and/or fish obtained during exercises when we were 'living off the land' or during some boating practice or river crossing, when we did a spot of fishing with the odd 36 grenade.

After the first night in their new billets, the whole unit, less one Troop, which arrived later in Weymouth, assembled for the first time. It was 22 July. Close on 100 different regiments, infantry, armoured, artillery, engineers and service corps, were all represented, with each man wearing the distinctive cap badge and flashes of his late parent unit. It presented a motley collection of forage and SD caps, tam-o'-shanters and berets, but would have provided a 'field day' for any military cap badge collector.

The assembly was held in the Weymouth Pavilion, on the sea front, which had been requisitioned as Commando Headquarters. As we waited for the 'welcome' talk from our new commanding officer, there was an unforgettable air of excitement, an exhilarating atmosphere and a babble of animated conversation, which came to an abrupt halt and hush when the newly appointed RSM, 'Jumbo' Morris of the Royal Tank Regiment, from the stage and in full view, bellowed out, 'Parade . . . 'Shun', before saluting and handing over to the commanding officer.

For most of us it was the first glimpse of the CO, Lt Col C.P.D. Legard, of the 5th Inniskillin Dragoon Guards, a tall, lean and fit-looking officer with an elegant, yet dashing, appearance in his service dress uniform, shining Sam Browne belt and the distinctive green trousers of that famous cavalry regiment the history of which went back to the seventeenth century. We later learnt that he was an international sportsman, having represented Great Britain in the Olympic Games of 1932 and 1936, participating in the Modern Pentathlon, finishing eighth in his first Games, but dropping back to nineteenth four years later when they were held in Berlin. Legard apparently liked to recall that during the opening ceremonial march-past, in front of Hitler, he 'gave the bastard a V-sign salute'!

In his opening talk the colonel outlined the intended role of Commandos – 'hit and run raids' on the extended enemy coastline. He warned that the training would necessarily be tough and demanding, and accordingly some might not be able to cope with it. For those who couldn't measure up to the high standards demanded there was only one outcome – RTU. Such military action was again unique, but the subsequent records of the Commandos prove that this seemingly drastic, but obviously necessary, action was one of the major factors contributing to their success. Furthermore, he emphasised that the decision to RTU any officer or man was his, and his alone, and there would be no appeal against it. We were left in no doubt on this important issue. He also mentioned the origin of the designation 'Commando'. At that time most of us had no idea that it belonged to an old enemy, the Boer guerrillas, who had wrought some humiliating defeats on the British Army – and captured Winston Churchill – in the Boer War of 1900–2. Finally, he stressed the need to prepare for action as quickly as possible; he stated that we would have to be ready in weeks rather than months. There was no time to lose.

With high hopes of almost immediate action we left the Pavilion eager to start training and prepare for that first raid. During the next few days as we settled down to our new 'lifestyle', the priority for training was on getting fit and on individual weapon training.

Fortunately, one of the original volunteers, the late Sgt 'Tich' Garnett, later in the war was given the old F Troop Diary that covered the first three months of that Troop's existence. He kindly lent it to me for my previous book, *It Had To Be Tough*, which deals in detail with the origins of all the Commandos and their special training in the Second World War, but does not cover any of the actions fought, so I was able to extract pertinent details of the early days of No. 4 from the diary's pages.

In his introduction to the Troop Diary, Capt Young wrote: 'We have got off to a flying start. There are men from every walk of life, a poacher, Harris (also a reservist who had served in India), a Colonel's son, Addison, a "Wall of Death" stunt rider, Knowles, a farmer, Holgate, an International TT rider, Locke, an artist, Ingram, and many other colourful characters, all of whom have volunteered not only out of a sincere desire to serve their country, but also for fun and adventure.' It is important to add that, although there were 'colourful characters' in F Troop, throughout the whole unit such men were in the minority. Furthermore, contrary to later media reports we had no 'hard cases', men who had received their education in borstal, or who had served prison sentences for such crimes as safe-cracking.

Unfortunately, soon after the Commandos were formed and their existence and exploits made public, the press reports and coverage tended to present them as 'undisciplined thugs and homicidal maniacs'. This was unwelcome and untrue, and cast a slur on all who served in the Commandos at the time. It was even used by the Germans, who made propaganda use of it with statements such as 'England has . . . opened up a non-military form of gangster war!'

Fortunately, forceful steps were quickly taken, with success, to redress the balance with a series of media reports on the background, training and types of men serving in the Commandos. None were supermen. It was their high standards of training, physical and mental stamina, discipline and determination, plus outstanding leadership from officers and NCOs, that produced the high morale and confidence that brought undeniable success in action worldwide.

The range of ages and service is highlighted by mentioning the following extremes. Among the ORs were a venerable trio of 'old sweats'. 'Chalky' Blunden had served as an under-age soldier in the First World War. He was renowned for being the first in his troop to offer to carry the unpopular Boys anti-tank rifle, but, more importantly, he was to win the Military Medal at Dieppe.

Next was 'Dusty' Maund, a rascally character, fearless, outspoken, but loyal and dependable in action. He became the batman/runner/'minder' to a young subaltern, Robert Dawson, at Weymouth, and stayed with him throughout the war, during which time Dawson advanced from Section Officer to Commanding Officer. Maund was one of the first in No. 4 to be decorated, when he was 'Mentioned in Dispatches' for his part in the Lofoten Islands Raid.

The third was 'Private' Donkin, who teamed up with his mate, McVeigh, to make a legendary and inseparable 'team' until a German bullet outside a bunker in Flushing killed the 41-year-old Donkin. But more about this couple later, especially as McVeigh was a tough, courageous, yet also outspoken soldier, who was to win the Distinguished Conduct Medal (DCM).

The RSM, 'Jumbo', Bill Morris, also stands out. A long-serving warrant officer of the Royal Tank Regiment (RTR), he was not one of those swearing, bullying, barrack-square tyrants, but a level-headed and 'firm but fair' RSM, who didn't demand obedience and respect, but earned it from all ranks in No. 4. He was no athlete: he struggled on the speed marches and hated them but never dodged or 'ducked' them. He set an example. We all saw how he kept going, nigh on 'knackered', yet refused to give in. In action, he was always calm, dependable and courageous, and deservedly won a Military Cross – a rare honour for those not commissioned officers – before a serious wound on the Flushing operation ended his Commando days.

At the other end of the age scale were two very young regular soldiers, barely off 'Boy Service', Gunners Pike and Halliday. Great pals, they steadily earned promotion as young dependable NCOs. Both saw action at Lofoten and Dieppe before being commissioned.

Prominent among the early officers of No. 4 was Robert Dawson, whose spectacular rise has already been mentioned. He ultimately won the Distinguished Service Order (DSO), the Légion d'Honneur and the Croix de Guerre. He was a great innovator in training matters and responsible for introducing 'battle drills' based on fire and movement to the Commando, plus some 'hair-raising' schemes for cliff assaults.

Gordon Webb was another 'original' who later distinguished himself in action. A gunner officer, tough, resourceful and always ready to see the funny side of a grave situation, especially in action, he took over B Troop in 1941 and commanded it for most of the rest of the war, earning a Military Cross and a bar to it. He was one of those officers whom the troops were prepared 'to follow . . . anywhere'.

There were many outstanding ORs I should like to mention by name because they played prominent parts in the history of No. 4, but space precludes this. Nevertheless, it is important to record that most of the NCOs who led their sub-sections ashore on D-Day in 1944 were only privates when they originally joined No. 4 at Weymouth in 1940. They became the backbone of the Commando.

After more than sixty years their names spring to mind: Hughie Lindley, John Skerry, 'Tich' Garnett, Frank Major, Danny Holdsworth, 'Darkie' Woodward, Ernie Brooks and Frank Bend, while TSMs Portman, Heaynes, Chattaway and Edwards had likewise climbed the ladder of promotion.

In contrast to these senior NCOs, who were all 'originals' and rose up through the ranks over time, a lot of the best-known names among the officers of the Commando, namely Mills-Roberts, Porteous, Carr, McDougal, Gilchrist, Thorburn, Burt and Menday, did not join the Commando until after the Lofoten Raid and, in the case of the three last named, after the Dieppe Raid.

Now for a few details on the organisation of the Commando when it was formed in 1940 and consisted of Headquarters and ten troops. Each troop had a captain, two subalterns, four sergeants, eight corporals, twelve lance-corporals and twenty-three private soldiers, making a total of fifty all ranks. The organisation of the troop was based on just two in Troop HQ (the troop leader and his batman/runner), two sections (each commanded by a subaltern, who also had a batman/runner) and which in turn consisted of two sub-sections, each led by a sergeant, and was made up of two corporals, three lance-corporals and five private soldiers.

Commando Headquarters – consisting of the CO, second-in-command (2IC), adjutant, medical officer, administrative officer, intelligence officer, RSM, clerks, medical orderlies, intelligence staff and just two drivers – only the CO and the administrative officer had vehicles – plus a very important man, the armourer – totalled just over forty all ranks. Naturally all ranks in HQ were volunteers serving under the same conditions as those in the ten fighting troops.

Col Legard had recruited the medical officer (MO), 'Doc' Wood. It was an excellent choice. Tall, lean and already fit, Wood had been a police doctor before the war, and he took to the physical side of the training with obvious relish and was able to transmit his enthusiasm to all in his section, most of whom had served with him in France and at Dunkirk. They were a great bunch of 'medics'.

The original intelligence section was small, an officer and three other ranks, but over the next few years this number increased in keeping with demands made on its services. Again the Commando was fortunate in having some excellent officers and men who, over the next five and a half years, served in this section. Thanks to them we are all able to follow the fortunes of the No. 4 through the pages of the War Diary of the unit which they compiled on the spot as the events took place. The Diary has been kept and preserved in the Public Record Office, Kew.

Following the CO's talk on that first day, no time was lost in starting the training. Everyone was keen 'to get cracking'. But what kind of training? Unfortunately no unit training directives have survived, if they ever existed, and there is no mention made of them in the Troop Diary. However, one can deduce from the details of training and comments made in the Diary – plus personal experiences – what these priorities were.

The fact that the Commando was expected to prepare for its first mission as soon as possible, rather than in a given time of, say, three months hence, posed limitations and problems which were exacerbated by the fact that the unit was made up of volunteers from such a wide range of military backgrounds and experiences.

With hindsight it would have been better to have made sure that all ranks were proficient in basic individual skills before even starting on the collective training of troop and section movement, tactics and deployment. However, in the circumstances, this was not possible, so we had to start on individual and collective training at the same time, and it wasn't easy, especially in F Troop, with so few infantrymen.

Accepting this situation, the priorities were clearly as follows. First and foremost was the overall need for all ranks to get physically fit, not for the playing of team games on the sports fields, but fit to fight on the battlefield. There is a big difference. Second was the need to set and achieve the highest possible standards of skill-at-arms, in the handling and firing of the Commando weapons. Third was the need to be able to move quickly and quietly, with arms and equipment, over all sorts of terrain, including the crossing of obstacles and the climbing of cliffs. Fourth, for the raiding role envisaged, it was imperative to train in seamanship and the handling of small boats, and to develop the techniques and tactics necessary to carry out amphibious operations successfully. These were the immediate priorities, but there were other subjects to be tackled, such as map reading and compass work, signalling and inter-communications, and explosives and demolitions.

During the first few weeks weapons training was limited. Every man in the Commando was issued with a rifle, if he hadn't brought one with him from his previous unit, and every officer had a pistol. That was it. No automatic carbines, and so the few Bren guns that they had had to be kept in Commando HQ and issued for instructional purposes on a rota basis.

All the rifles were the Short Magazine Lee Enfield (SMLE), with bayonet boss and standard to affix the 18-inch steel bayonet – shades of the famous *Dad's Army* quip, 'they don't like it up 'em'. Although this rifle had been in service with the British Army since 1895, it was both reliable and popular with the troops. It had a nice simple bolt/breech action, making it, in the hands of the well-trained soldier, capable of a relatively high rate of rapid fire – as the Germans had found out in the opening months of the First World War. The SMLE rifle fired a .303 round and the magazine held ten rounds. It could also project grenades (Mills 36) from a special screw-on cup, making it useful as a mini-mortar to engage enemy behind cover.

The early issues of pistols to officers were either Webleys or Enfields, but both types fired a .38 calibre round. There wasn't much difference between them; both were of the same weight and length and the chambers held just six rounds and fired single shots. Pre-war training with the pistol had focused on holding the hand gun in front of the face and taking a deliberate aim, but this method was about to be challenged in the wake of new ideas on close-quarter combat, and the replacement of these pistols with the US .45 Colt automatic.

The Bren Light Machine Gun (LMG), on which all were trained, had been introduced to the British Army in 1935 when it started to replace the old Lewis Machine Gun, although some of the latter were still in service in the Royal Navy, and the men of No. 4 used them when they were later attached to some of the smaller RN ships in the role of ack-ack (anti-aircraft) gunners.

The Bren was relatively light, weighing about 23 lb (10.4 kg). Gas-operated, it fired single rounds or automatic bursts. The magazine, which held 30 rounds (although to prevent undue stress on the spring it was normal to restrict loading to 28 rounds), was fitted on to the top of the weapon. The barrels were air-cooled, but after sustained firing could be changed. This was a simple operation taking only a few seconds, or the barrel could be 'water-cooled' naturally, by pissing on it.

We had our first shoot on the ranges at Lulworth on 2 August, but we only had enough ammunition to zero our rifles and two practice shoots at 100 and 200 yards, a total of 25 rounds per man. However, there were just 50 rounds left over and these were used to let two junior NCOs, earmarked as Bren gunners, fire one mag each. This they did at a 4-foot target, first firing in single shots and then in short bursts – while the rest of us stood by and watched. Obviously no realistic choice of Bren gunners could be made under such conditions, but this does reveal the dire situation in respect of ammunition that prevailed after Dunkirk – and we, supposedly, had priority as we were preparing for offensive operations.

A couple of weeks later we were able to train on the Boys anti-tank (A/Tk) rifle, but these too were initially kept in Commando HQ and only issued for training on a rota basis. This weapon had been developed in the mid-1930s in response to a need for a light anti-tank weapon for the infantry. It was named after its inventor, Captain Boys, who unfortunately died just as his weapon was nearing its final trials before going into production. It was essentially a large-scale version of a service rifle, but able to fire as large an armour-piercing bullet with as large a charge as the average soldier could manage to hold and fire with accuracy, given the help of a spring absorber, a flash eliminator and front support legs to fire from the prone position, or on a resting platform of some sort. But even so it gave a nasty kick.

The magazine held just five .55 armour-piercing rounds. It was a heavy and cumbersome weapon, with an overall length of some 5 feet (1613 mm) and weight of 36 lb (16.33 kg). Unfortunately by the time it came into production the armour of even the lightest tanks had increased and so it was of limited use. Nevertheless, the Commandos did later use it in action against pillboxes, gun emplacements and in street-fighting roles. In 1943 the Boys A/Tk rifle was replaced by the PIAT (an acronym for Projector, Infantry, Anti-Tank), a lighter and more efficient weapon.

Appreciating that raids would almost certainly be carried out at night, all troops started on night training and exercises. The F Troop Diary records that two or three night exercises per week were carried out during the first five weeks or so at Weymouth. They were laid on as proper operations, with written orders, and duly reported on afterwards. What is clear from these records – and my own memories – is that they were not altogether successful for a variety of reasons.

The main faults were attributable to over-ambitious exercises – a case of 'trying to run before we could walk'. Few of the officers, NCOs and men were proficient in moving over unfamiliar ground and maintaining control in the dark. And it was dark too. Under the rigidly enforced wartime 'blackout', the only illuminations came from searchlights, gunfire and the explosions of bombs during an air raid, with Weymouth and the surrounding areas having more than their fair share of them, by day and by night. On the subject of air raids, Sapper Allan, in a letter home, wrote: 'While we were on a night exercise on Friday we saw flashes in the distance where bombs were being dropped, and a member of our Troop arrived back at his billet at 3 a.m. to find a wall of his bedroom completely blown in. . . .'

It soon became clear after starting our training at Weymouth that we were earmarked for seaborne raids and not airborne ones, because all the talk and emphasis was on amphibious operations. In spite of Churchill's grandiose plans of having a force of 5,000 paratroopers, this had been scaled down to just 500 in a single unit, No. 2 (Para) Commando.

Sadly, none of the Commandos preparing for these seaborne raids was able to start training for assault landings using suitable craft. Initially, we all had to improvise and make do with any boats available at the various bases. At Weymouth we were able to obtain the use of some local rowing boats and motor launches – all civilian – although we did also manage to borrow two naval cutters from the RN Dockyard at nearby Portland.

One troop managed to get some 'sea service' aboard one of the smaller unarmed RN boats as ack-ack and anti-E-Boat gunners. John Skerry and Ernie Brooks, both in E Troop, recall such spells of duty on board HMS *Computator*, a requisitioned trawler. On deck with their Bren and Boys A/Tk rifle, without proper sea-going clothing, they got very wet. 'I was under water most of the time,' Skerry laughingly recalls.

The sea landings, for obvious security reasons at this stage of the invasion scare, were restricted to daytime, and it was during one of these, carried out from a requisitioned motor launch, that we nearly suffered our first fatal training accident. On returning to the beach to re-embark, we found that the motor launch was unable to come inshore. There was no alternative but to swim out. It wasn't too far, about 75 yards or so. Halfway across one man got cramp and went under; fortunately his section officer was at hand, saw what was happening, and took quick action, towing the hapless man to the launch. It was a near thing.

This incident prompted Capt Young to increase the number of swimming sessions in full clothes and kit. These swims were carried out in the sea.

Starting from the steps of the Pavilion, we swam parallel to the beach for about 100 yards before turning round to swim back. There were day and night swims. One or two who couldn't make the grade were RTU'd.

The importance of swimming had also been highlighted in a premature and abortive raid carried out by No. 3 Commando in July, when the only casualties were non-swimmers: one man drowned and three were captured because they couldn't manage the swim out to the waiting Eureka boat. This is mentioned because this early raid on Guernsey was almost bound to fail; as the CO, Col Durnford-Slater, later wrote, 'Looking back, I can see that under such rushed conditions, no experience, no proper landing craft and inadequate training, this first operation was doomed to failure.'

About this time our training was interrupted when we were placed under the command of the local area commander, instead of under direct command of the newly formed Combined Operations, for anti-invasion duties. However, our role was limited to that of 'a mobile reserve', and not,

During the invasion scare No. 4 Commando, then mobile on Army bicycles – all 500 of them – often acted as 'Fifth Columnists' to test regular and Home Guard units. Here a group of the Commando, dressed in 'civvies' but armed, are seen returning from one such exercise held in Dorset. (*Author's Collection*)

fortunately, to static beach defences. There was one major problem to our employment as a mobile force: we had no mobility apart from two small Army vehicles and 500-odd pairs of feet!

But there was a happy outcome. Within a week or so, we were all mobile: a supply of bicycles had been discovered in an Ordnance Depot in Tidworth, North Hampshire. So off we went and collected them, vintage First World War models, and the problem of mobility was solved. We had many interesting exercises and schemes using our bikes, including acting as 'Fifth Columnists' to test local regular and Home Guard units, and a memorable six days' troop exercise, based at Clovelly, in North Devon, where we 'lived off the land'. We cycled to and from Clovelly by night, not an easy task in the blackout, with no lights, as it was supposed to be 'operational'. Needless to add there were a few mishaps, but on the whole, as the Diary noted, 'The rides were carried out successfully, although it rained throughout the journey back.'

However, the more orthodox method of mobility was marching, which played an essential part then – as now – in Commando training. Initially, in our troop, with so few infantrymen, we had problems, mostly from blisters. But gradually in the first few weeks we built up from the steady marches of 8 to 10 miles to regular ones of 15 to 20 miles, and it was quite an event when we did the first 15-miler non-stop in just under four hours. This doesn't sound much, and compared with latter-day standards it wasn't, but by regular Army standards of that period it was good going. Furthermore, most marches at this time were with Full Service Marching Order (FSMO), in which we carried all personal needs for protracted action, that is, spare clothing, socks, washing/shaving kit, some rations and groundsheet in the large back-pack, plus a rolled gas-cape, a respirator, personal weapons and ammunition.

But admirable as these fully laden marches were for getting fit and improving stamina – they were often used as a prelude to a two/three day exercise – they didn't meet the concepts of a 'quick in and quick out' mission.

This was a new requirement for which we needed a different approach to traditional route marches. We needed much faster movement, with far less equipment; we had to have a faster rate of marching, combined with steady running – or in Army parlance, 'doubling'. And so were born the 'Commando Speed Marches', which to this day are a special feature of Commando training. Although we made a move in this direction while at Weymouth, we didn't really start to tackle 'Speed Marching' until we left the Dorset town in early October, when the following standards were established:

> 7 miles in under 70 minutes
> 9 miles in under 90 minutes
> 12 miles in under 130 minutes
> 15 miles in under 170 minutes

To emphasise the fact that these marches were not a fulfilment in themselves, but the means for a troop to get to an objective quickly, yet still fit to fight and carry out a mission, each march was followed with a related task – a mock attack, a firing practice on the ranges or a dash over an assault course. More about some memorable marches later.

Much, but by no means all, of the initial training at Weymouth was based on pre-war regular Army training and done very much to 'the book', but although the basic principles of this training were sound, the methods had to be adapted to meet the needs and demands of waging 'irregular warfare'.

Fortunately, just before the formation of the Commandos a special training centre had been set up in the western Highlands of Scotland, around the castle of Lochailort, for this purpose. It was ideally located in isolated and rugged terrain, with a loch alongside for amphibious training.

The story of how this centre happened to be created is a fascinating one; it tells how a few determined and visionary officers can, particularly in wartime, turn ideas into realities – especially if they have access to those in office 'in the corridors of power'. A group of officers, mostly from a special unit that had been raised to fight as a ski battalion against the Russians in Finland in early 1940, but subsequently disbanded without being used, together managed to form this special centre.

The instructors came from a mixed background of soldiers, sailors, polar explorers and ghillies, and their expertise covered a wide range of potential military activities. The team included the Stirling brothers (one of whom later joined the Commandos, then later still founded the SAS), Lord Lovat, 'Mad Mike' Calvert (a demolition fanatic, who later served with Wingate's Chindits), Peter Kemp (who was later an SOE agent), Capt Wally Wallbridge (a King's Medallist for marksmanship on the rifle) and an incredible duo, Capts Fairbairn and Sykes (ex-Shanghai Police officers and martial arts exponents), who introduced unarmed combat to the Commando curriculum. There were other experts who, together, made up a formidable instruction team and succeeded in passing on their knowledge, innovative concepts and ideas on irregular warfare to those enthusiastic Commando officers and NCOs who attended their short, but intensive, courses.

From early August officers and NCOs from No. 4 started to attend these courses and returned to 'spread the gospel'; as a result new methods of weapon handling and firing, unarmed combat and close-quarter fighting, fieldcraft and battle procedures and demolitions were gradually introduced to the rest of the Commando. But it didn't all happen overnight.

In writing the story of the deeds and exploits of the Commandos in the war it would be impossible to exaggerate the importance of the contribution by the instructors of the Special Training Centre at Lochailort; much of the success of the Commandos in action is due to them.

By the end of August a new weapon was issued to the Commando, the famous American Tommy gun. Its arrival caused quite a stir, although once

As a result of officers and NCOs attending the Fairbairn and Sykes' courses at Lochailort, unarmed combat was an early training innovation in all Commandos. Right, a Commando disarms his adversary, and below, using the enemy's own weapon, finishes him off. (*Courtesy of the Imperial War Museum, London*)

again there were so few that they were held in Commando HQ and only issued for allotted training sessions. This excellent and reliable short-range weapon was ideal for our intended role. Firing a snub-nosed .45 round at the rate of 700 per minute, it had great stopping power. It became a very popular and trustworthy weapon, rarely, almost never, guilty of any stoppages. Although it was supplied with two different magazines, a drum or box type, the box magazine, holding 20 rounds, became the normal one used, chiefly because the spares were easier to pack into the equipment pouches.

On the subject of arms and ammunition, it is opportune to mention that soon after arriving in Weymouth and receiving our rifles, we were all issued with a canvas bandolier of 50 rounds of .33 ammunition – for use in the event of an invasion. We were also issued with one Mills 36 grenade and detonator. These we kept in our billets – originally much to the consternation and concern of the landladies, but they soon accepted it, for 'after all', they would say, 'there is a war on'.

Looking back today, when there is so much worry and fear over firearms and security, it is astonishing to think that in 1940 there were thousands of homes throughout the country housing arms and ammunition, sometimes unguarded, with bandoliers of ammo hanging on hooks on bedroom doors and 36 grenades standing, like *bric-à-brac*, on the mantelpieces.

We were placed on anti-invasion alerts on several occasions, when we were confined to billets or restricted training areas. There was, however, one particular 'real' invasion scare. It happened on the evening of 7 September. We were not on an alert at the time and all off duty, scattered throughout the town in pubs, cinemas or in billets listening to the 'wireless'. The orderly officer on duty in the Pavilion received an urgent message from higher authority that the whole Commando was to muster immediately for imminent anti-invasion duties. The only way, at the time, to pass on the message was by word of mouth. There had been no contingency plan for such an emergency. The result was a shambles, compounded by the ringing of church bells at 2300 hours. There was chaos in the town, because under wartime regulations the ringing of church bells was banned except in the event of an invasion!

Within minutes the rumours were spread that 'Jerry had landed'. The mustering of all ranks in the Commando on the municipal car park, with our arms and ammunition, took ages. It wasn't until almost midnight, some four hours after the alarm had been initiated, that all troops reported: 'All present and ready for action.'

In the event, and fortunately, nothing materialised; we sat around all night, and were dismissed early next morning. There followed a 'CO's inquest' on the débâcle, and steps were taken to make sure we weren't caught out again. It had been a salutory experience, with lessons learnt and acted upon. Years later I read in Churchill's memoirs what had happened – similar scenes of confusion and chaos had occurred all over the country that night. We were not the only ones unprepared. The apparent cause of the false alarm was a mistaken interpretation of a codeword in London. Churchill's final words on the whole affair were apt. He wrote: 'As may be imagined, this incident caused a great deal of talk and stir . . . it served as a useful tonic and rehearsal for all concerned.'

We had several mock call-outs after this episode, and also a six days' exercise for six troops to go independently and set up separate troop bases on the Ridgeway, a long high feature just off the main Weymouth to Dorchester road. In these bases the troops would 'fend for themselves, living off the land' and the rations procurable on their ration cards or from their landladies. They would also carry out mock raids and sorties in daylight and by night, using bicycles, and in keeping with being a mobile reserve role in the event of an invasion.' It was a very exacting, but worthwhile, exercise.

During the whole of this formative period – and throughout its lifespan – No. 4 had plenty of visitors. They were always curious to see our new training methods, which were invariably copied. A frequent visitor was our first 'boss', Admiral of the Fleet Sir Roger Keyes, who had been appointed as Director of Combined Operations by Winston Churchill. Keyes had earned a reputation during the First World War as the commander of a dramatic and successful operation on 22/3 April 1918, when a combined force of Royal Navy and Royal Marines had raided and blocked the port of Zeebrugge, thus denying its use to German U-boats. It was, in fact, a classic Commando operation, although not appreciated as such at the time.

Nevertheless, Keyes became a national hero, and when Churchill conceived his plans for an elite raiding force, his choice of man to direct the raising and development of it fell on his old friend, Sir Roger Keyes.

Suffice it to mention one visit by Sir Roger to watch training when two troops, on their bicycles, staged a 'ride-past'. This incident, coupled with the fact that our CO, Col Legard, was a cavalry officer, apparently gave rise at HQ Combined Operations to the naming of No. 4 as 'the Cavalry Commando', a nickname that was confirmed when, in an attempt to introduce some form of unit insignia, we all wore lanyards of yellow and red, the traditional colours of the cavalry.

Towards the end of September, the Commando's stay in Weymouth was drawing to a close, for as the F Troop Diary reports, 'following a four days' invasion flap and four days' leave, the whole Commando was told to pack up and prepare for a move'.

What had been achieved in those ten weeks in Weymouth? First and foremost, a new fighting unit of 500 volunteers for special operations had been formed. The officers and men had come from many different regiments and corps, they were of all ages, varied military and civilian backgrounds and experiences, but in that short time they had already been moulded into ten self-sufficient troops. They had trained hard and continuously, both by day and by night, and carried out some elementary seamanship training. They were all now physically fit, albeit they still had some way to go before they had the mental resilience that comes from pushing the body to its limits. Morale was high and all ranks were full of confidence.

However, they were lacking in several of the basic aspects of amphibious and irregular warfare, and in some cases in basic skills, such as weapon handling and firing, fieldcraft, and junior leadership in the field. A good solid start had been made, and the next spell of training, with the provision of suitable facilities, equipment and ammunition, would – as we shall see – start to redress some of the shortcomings.

CHAPTER TWO

And So to Scotland

On 13 October all ranks of No. 4, shouldering their kitbags and in FSMO with weapons, boarded a waiting troop train at Weymouth station for an unknown destination 'somewhere in Scotland'.

At 0600 hours next day, bleary-eyed after the journey, we found ourselves at a dock's siding on the river Clyde. Just a short march away was the 'unknown destination', HMS *Glengyle*. This was no ordinary transport ship, but a converted merchant ship equipped with landing craft for amphibious operations. Things were definitely looking up.

The *Glengyle* was one of three ships of the Alfred Holt Line, built for their Far East trade, and had been considered by an Inter-Services Study Group set up, belatedly, in 1938 to investigate ways and means of conducting amphibious operations should the need arise. In their conclusions the Group had recommended that, should a war break out, the *Glengyle* and her two sister ships, the *Glenroy* and the *Glenearn*, should be requisitioned and converted. This recommendation had been implemented.

The conversions included creating mess decks in the cargo holds; the limited number of cabins were retained for the ship's and Army officers' accommodation, while on the exterior, above the main deck, davits, equipment and fittings had been installed to house ten landing craft – five on each side.

We embarked and made our way down to the bowels of the ship to our allotted mess decks, where we were to live, eat and sleep while on board. The layout was sparse and cramped. The only furniture was tables and benches, above which, fastened in the bulkhead, were king-sized hooks to suspend hammocks. In theory there were sufficient spaces and hooks for every man to hang his hammock, but in reality there weren't. Some men went off and found nooks and crannies to 'kip down', and so this little problem resolved itself.

We were soon introduced to a new language, too – that of the Royal Navy, which was conveyed to us by the ship's tannoy, on which every announcement was heralded by the shrill whistle of the bosun's pipe. This was immediately followed by, 'D'yer 'ear there . . . D'yer 'ear there?' as the prelude to the actual announcement or instruction, which contained a whole lot of unfamiliar nautical terms and jargon. We gradually got used to the tannoy and its announcements; we had to. No waking up to the sounds of the reveille as in barracks, but to the tannoy blaring out, 'Wakey, wakey,

No. 4 Commando started to use 'proper' landing craft, LCAs, from HMS *Glengyle* in October 1940. This early picture clearly shows the interior, with its centre row and two flanking rows. It was in these craft that the Commando landed on the Lofoten Islands. They were also used on the Boulogne and Dieppe Raids, for the Normandy landing on D-Day (the two French troops landed from LSIs), the assault on Flushing and some of the raids on Schouwen in the winter of 1944/5. (*Courtesy of the Imperial War Museum, London*)

you've 'ad yer time', followed a few minutes later by, 'Lash up and stow'. No need for explanations.

Another odd and misleading announcement was that of: 'Cooks to the galley'. It didn't involve cooks, but was intended to summon one orderly from each mess table to the ship's galley to collect the food for his table. He was usually accompanied by another, who brought back the bucket of hot sweet tea that came with each meal.

The *Glengyle* set sail on 15 October, and Lt Munn, writing in the Diary, records: 'We sailed down the Clyde, rounded the Isle of Bute and up into Loch Fyne to anchor off Inveraray. Our opinions were obviously mixed regarding the beautiful surroundings, such large and awe-inspiring mountains filled us with equally large and awe-inspiring thoughts of being made to climb them. . . .' Those 'thoughts' were soon to become realities, but first came the novelty of being ferried to the shore in proper landing craft, not in the makeshift fleet of the recent Weymouth era.

The assault landing craft later became known to all and sundry as 'LCAs', when the nomenclature of all the craft under the control of Combined Operations was standardised. It says much for the original design of the LCAs that they remained unaltered throughout the whole of the war, and were used worldwide. Furthermore, they continued to be used for operations after the war. These flat-bottomed assault craft were excellent for the job. Lying low in the water, they presented a very small target, and offered a degree of armoured protection against small-arms fire. They could accommodate up to thirty-five troops, depending on the amount of stores being carried. Capable of eight knots, when fully loaded, they had a cruising range of about fifty miles. A most important feature was the front lowering and rising ramp, which enabled the troops, who were seated in three rows running the length of the craft, to disembark easily and quickly at the water's edge.

On arrival at Inveraray no time was lost in starting to train on the LCAs, but first, even before getting into the craft, routes had to be worked out and coordinated in getting the troops from their mess decks to the boat stations quickly and quietly without impeding each other. For No. 4, as the first Commando unit aboard the *Glengyle* for amphibious training, it was, once again, a matter of starting from scratch.

Next came the actual loading of the troops into the LCAs, after detailing each man to a certain position in one of the three rows. (Tactical loading to get the right man in the right place for the disembarkation in an operation became very important.) Once all were aboard and seated, the ship's control was informed, and the order given (on the tannoy, of course) to 'lower away'. Down went the LCAs until, with a condescending flop, they hit the water; then a gentle roar of the twin V8 engines and away they went.

All this took time to organise; even sorting out the timings and routes from mess decks to boat stations took both time and practice. Nevertheless, drills were worked out and recorded, for this was not just for No. 4, but also for those who were to follow us. In this and the subsequent landing drills we were the 'trail-blazers' – and such procedures tended to be very repetitive and irksome.

There were high hopes of a dry landing when for the first time in an LCA we were ordered by the skipper to 'Stand by to beach'. It was great to hear the flat bottom of the LCA harmlessly crunching its way over the smooth pebbled shore, as the front ramp was lowered and the order, 'Out troops', rang out. The centre row went first, followed by the two outboard rows, as quickly as possible. Right from the first landing the drill was to dash up the beach, at full speed, to a rallying point to regroup before pushing on. Conveniently, on Loch Fyne, the loch-side road provided a suitable muster point on disembarking.

It was essential to impress on every Commando soldier the paramount need to clear the beach with all speed, and never to succumb to the natural instinct and reaction of self-preservation to drop to the ground if the beach was being swept by enemy gunfire. The hope of avoiding being hit was a false one. So right from those October days at Inveraray that crucial lesson was drummed into every man in No. 4. 'Out of the LCAs and move "split-arse" up and across the beach. Never, never stop!' This became a habit in No. 4 and saved lives. In 1944, on D-Day, as No. 4 stormed ashore at Ouistreham, they were to witness the carnage inflicted on an advance infantry battalion that hadn't learnt and applied this cardinal principle of amphibious operations. They paid a heavy price for such neglect.

The terrain around Inveraray was ideal for the 'onshore' training the troop leaders had in mind. Great stretches of uninhabited hillsides and wild moorlands, interspersed with fast-flowing rivers and streams, provided testing challenges – no need for man-made obstacle courses there; Mother Nature had already done that job.

A typical day's training started with a landing between 0800 and 0900 hrs and there followed a simple scheme which involved trekking over the hills (although these 'hills' rose to nearly 1,000 ft). There were some opportunities for live firing, but not many. On one occasion a deer stalk was organised for selected potential snipers. Since there were no snipers' rifles, they had to use their SMLEs. They returned with three stags, including a magnificent twelve-pointer, bagged by the star of the shoot, Trooper Lister, a Scot and reservist from the Royal Tank Regiment. On board, the Duke of Argyll's venison had a mixed reception; some reckoned it 'tough and tasteless'. Apparently the colonel, according to the Troop Diary, received 'a rocket from the District Commander over the affair'.

Some five-night schemes were tackled during the stay on the *Glengyle*, but these were preceded by several rehearsals involving getting to the LCAs from the mess decks along dimly lit gangways, out on to an unlit deck and clambering aboard the LCAs in the pitch dark. The night schemes were limited in scope, the main object being to practise both the landing craft crews and the Commandos in assault landings and re-embarkations in the dark. Each troop managed one long night march over the trackless hills. F Troop's effort was successful in as much as no one was lost; it was also noted that 'there is much to learn in terms of night navigation and sub-section control', reinforcing the growing realisation that more and more testing night training was needed.

At the end of the period on board, No. 4 Commando could justifiably claim that it had pioneered the basic drills for Navy/Commando training on LCAs for use in amphibious operations. Such training had not only been invaluable to No. 4 and the LCA crews of the *Glengyle*, but also to those responsible for the forward planning and training in the Combined Operations Centre which was about to be established at Inveraray.

On the debit side, as the first unit on the *Glengyle*, No. 4 had been subject to some gross inefficiency in the administration on board, particularly in regard to feeding. This inefficiency on the part of the ship's company manifested itself in the disrupting of training programmes and the boat exercises. As a result there were continuous changes of orders, all on the tannoy, which worked overtime. So frequent and exasperating were they that the troops coined a new Army saying: 'Order, Counter-Order, Disorder . . .'.

At the end of this training it was time for No. 4 to move on, not back to the south of England, but to another base in Scotland, to the coastal resort town of Ayr, acclaimed by Robbie Burns to be 'a bonnie wee place for honest men and bonnie lassies'. The second part of that quotation sounded promising. But getting there proved to be a story in itself.

Sapper Allan recalls:

> On 29 October we went ashore from the *Glengyle*, supposedly to go to Oban, but there was a last-minute change of plan (an advance party which had gone ahead to find billets was unsuccessful, and went on to Ayr) and so we had to spend the night in a tented camp in Inveraray. The next morning we were roused at 0400 hrs to march the 16 miles to the railway station at Dalmally.

Normally, this would have been a nice autumnal 'stroll' in the Highlands, but the Gods weren't smiling that morning, and it didn't just rain, it 'bucketed' down – as it can in that part of Great Britain – and did so for every inch of the march. To make matters worse, on arrival at Dalmally, there was no train and very little shelter. After a couple of hours a train did steam in.

Following a long, slow journey we finally arrived at Ayr at 2200 hrs and were met by the advance party, who had managed to find some billets. However, the unlucky ones, about one hundred of them, had to pick up their kitbags and march off to spend a wet and cold November night in the grandstand on Ayr Racecourse.

The next few days were spent in finding the extra billets and settling down in the new base. Once again Headquarters were fortunate; they took over the local Town Pavilion, which met all their requirements.

But although there were reasonable facilities in and around the town for training, the stay in Ayr was short-lived. On 10 November the Commando marched as a unit from Ayr to Troon, behind the Pipe Band of the Royal Scots' Fusiliers. After dismissal they went off to the new billets in the town, which became their base until late 1942.

Troon itself was an ideal choice. It was on the coast, had a small harbour where some small boats could be moored, but no LCAs; they were not available.

The surrounding countryside was suitable for fieldcraft and tactical training, with ranges near at hand, including an area at Dundonald which was later made available for field firing and 'battle inoculation'.

The people of Troon were most hospitable and made us welcome. Many of the men made lifelong friends; Cpl John Skerry was one. He and his mate, Fred Gooch, enjoyed the hospitality of the Campbell family over a period of two years. They became part of the family, until the Dieppe Raid, when Fred was killed and, sadly, John returned alone. Notwithstanding, John has kept in touch with the 'children' of Mr and Mrs Campbell ever since – for over sixty years.

Recently 'JED' Price, another of the No. 4 veterans, who found a home in Troon, made a list of those in the Commando who married local girls. It amounted to an incredible total of twenty-eight. Many of them returned to Troon after the war, settled there to work and raise their families.

On the day that the Commando was marching from Ayr to Troon, they were all transferred 'on paper' from No. 4 Commando to No. 1 Company, 3rd Special Service Battalion. This followed a Whitehall decision, taken in late October, to reorganise the Commandos and the Independent Companies into five Special Service Battalions, consisting of two companies, with about 500 all ranks in each, making a total for the battalion of about 1,000.

The decision had been taken because Winston Churchill and Admiral Sir Roger Keyes began to favour the prospects of large-scale operations, now that suitable transport ships, such as the *Glengyle* with its attendant landing craft, were becoming available and combined RN/Commando training had started.

Some historians have suggested that Keyes advocated the idea of large-scale operations in the hope of repeating something after the style of his famous raid on Zeebrugge. More about these large-scale Commando operations later; in the meantime back to the Special Service Battalions. As a result of this reorganisation, Nos 4 and 7 Commandos were amalgamated to form 3rd SS Bn, being Nos 1 and 2 Companies respectively. Unfortunately, this meant that we lost Col Legard because the CO of No. 7, Lt Col Dudley Lister, MC, was selected to command the new battalion. Reluctantly, Legard returned to his regiment, but our previous second-in-command, Maj Mark Kerr, remained to command No. 1 Company.

The new structure was not only unwieldy, but extremely unpopular. Even the title of Special Service Battalion, when abbreviated to 'SS' Battalion, had nasty connotations of Hitler's formations with the same designation. Understandably, this reorganisation didn't last long. Within three months a subsequent reorganisation brought back the original Commando concept, name and organisation, except that the number of fighting troops was reduced from ten to six. With this decision No. 4 Commando was back in name and form.

So, as it makes little difference to the narrative, I shall continue to use the designation No. 4 Commando – as indeed was common practice at the time – in reporting the events during the period between November 1940 and February 1941, when the Commando title was officially reinstated.

Col Lister, our new CO, was a regular soldier and veteran of the First World War, during which he won the Military Cross, with his regiment, The Buffs. He was, like Col Legard, an international sportsman. His forte was boxing. He had been the Army heavyweight champion and had represented Great Britain in the prestigious Golden Gloves contest in Madison Square Gardens, New York, before the war.

Tall, well built and rugged-looking, he was an imposing figure on parade. He was a fitness fanatic, and he based his own fitness – and ours – mainly on the pre-war boxing training regime of 'road work'. So naturally, we had plenty of both speed and endurance marches which, to his credit, he led from the front.

Typically, he ended one of his CO's talks, in which he had been emphasising the necessity for the highest standards of physical fitness, with this rejoinder, 'And what's more, you can't even make decent love, either, unless you are really physically fit!'

However, he suffered from 'weak legs' when it came to cross-country marches or hill walking, when the softer underfoot conditions took their toll on him. This wasn't his only weakness, and I quote Lord Lovat, who wrote, 'Dudley Lister suffered from wife trouble (the old story) with a girl in every port. . . .' This extravagance prompted him to try to save money, so instead of living in a hotel or billet, when we were in Troon, Lister decided to rough it and live cheaply, thereby netting his subsistence allowance, by pitching a tent on the seaward side of the famous Troon golf course. Therein, with the aid of his trusty and capable batman, 'kipping' in a sleeping bag on a camp bed, feeding on meals cooked on a primus stove and reading and writing by the light of a hurricane lamp, Lister survived the winter of 1941/2. In the end, however, Lister's problems got the better of him and his command suffered, as will be related later.

Meanwhile, the reorganisation had little effect on troop training, which continued much as before in Troon, with the other Commando (No. 7) in 3rd SS Bn remaining at its previous base in Girvan.

Towards the end of November the whole of the 3rd SS Bn went on fourteen days' leave and rumours abounded that it was 'embarkation leave'. On our return to Troon from leave, the rumours gained credence, and we were all told to pack and prepare for a move. Road transport took the Commando (No. 1 Company) to Gourock, where it embarked once more on the *Glengyle*.

Back with the Royal Navy, it was off down the Clyde to anchor off the Isle of Arran. Excitement and expectations mounted as 'all the signs were that something big was about to happen, two more "Glen" ships, the *Glenroy* and the *Glenearn*, plus the troopship, *Karaja*, were alongside, anchored in Lamlash Bay. They were being loaded with stores of all kind, brought out to the ships by lighters. There were also various naval vessels in the vicinity', wrote Sapper Allan.

During the next few days the Commando took part in several exercises, including a night scheme, with landings on beaches around Broderick and Whiting Bay, and one on Holy Island, all on the east coast of the island.

The Isle of Arran, which was then and subsequently much used for amphibious training, is some twenty miles long and, on average, nine to ten miles wide. Remote and sparsely populated, with its renowned peak of Goat Fell, at 2,000 ft (628 m), and plenty of deserted and approachable beaches, it was ideal for Combined Operations and Commando training.

There was, however, a significant change in the pattern of the exercises, in that they now involved the deployment of larger groups than previously – the employment of the whole Commando as opposed to troop, or even section, operations. Furthermore, in the larger exercises signallers were drafted in to ensure control and intercommunications; this led to the raising of a brigade signals troop, and ultimately to a signals section in every Commando.

However, in spite of this obvious move towards larger-scale Commando operations to replace the original concepts of small 'bolt-and-run' raids, it was at this stage on Arran that a highly specialised small Commando raiding group, using canoes, was first formed by Capt Roger Courtney, which he later developed into the Special Boat Section (SBS) and in which at least two No. 4 men, Smithson and King, would serve in the Far East.

After two weeks of these exercises from the 'Glen' ships an announcement was made that the operation for which this large force of Commandos had been training – rumoured to be the capture of an island in the Mediterranean – had been postponed.

This rumour proved well founded. Sir Roger Keyes had persuaded Churchill and the Chiefs of Staff that the small island of Pantellaria, off Sicily, should be captured by a strong force of Commandos. This island, he argued, could be used as a valuable alternative to Malta as a staging post in the Mediterranean and would make an ideal base for disrupting the Italian lines of communication to, and in, North Africa. The codename for this operation was Workshop, and No. 4 Commando was to be included in it.

However, the operation had not been postponed indefinitely, but put 'on hold' for one month from 14 December, the very day we should have sailed, but also the day when the announcement mentioned above was made.

Other plans for Commando operations were being hatched at the same time, so it was decided for security reasons and, also, to keep the Commando forces together, that they should disembark and go into billets on the Isle of Arran. Naturally, having worked up expectations of an operation during the past few weeks, there was bitter disappointment among all ranks at this postponement.

However, all found billets in the various villages on the island and continued to keep fit and carried on training, although as it grew nearer to Christmas, one or two of the ORs were so 'browned off' with frustration that they took matters into their own hands and went AWOL for the festive season. On return to Arran most were subsequently RTU'd.

Fortunately, the islanders were kind and hospitable, and all ranks of No. 4 were lucky to find good billets in the Blackwaterfoot and Shiskine area on the western side of the island, and so spent Christmas and the New Year with locals. One veteran recalls: 'My mate and I were fortunate enough to find ourselves lodging with a schoolmaster and his wife, and three daughters . . . and although we must have disrupted their holiday, they made us welcome.'

Bill Portman, one of those who survived all the fighting with No. 4 until the end of 1945, remembers being with a very kind, but religious, family: 'we had "grace", eyes closed, hands together, before each meal'. Still, the meals were good and nourishing: porridge with salt, not sugar, but with fresh cream, for breakfast, and plenty of home-made oat cakes, 'tatty' (potato) scones and other local products. They were well fed, in spite of rationing.

During this period the men of No. 4 frequently came into contact with their counterparts in the other Commandos, especially with those of No. 7, who had solved the problem of headgear by wearing woollen cap comforters, and No. 11 (known as the Scottish Commando, and in which Sir Roger Keyes's son, Geoffrey, was a troop leader), who wore balmorals with black hackles. These two Commandos seemed to specialise in going on long marches around the island or climbing Goat Fell. There was also No. 8 Commando, known to us as the 'Blue Blood Commando', among whose officers were such well-known personalities as Randolph Churchill (Winston's son) and the novelist Evelyn Waugh, and whose CO, Col Robert Laycock, was destined to become a legendary Commando leader and, finally, the Chief of Combined Operations.

After the four weeks on Arran, No. 4 reboarded the *Glengyle* to hear Sir Roger Keyes give a rousing speech in which he said that although this 'scheme' had been cancelled he had no intention of 'allowing this bright sword to rust in the Highlands'. The Commando then disembarked and went on two weeks' leave.

While the Commandos were on leave, a decision was taken to mount a new amphibious operation in the Mediterranean to capture the island of Rhodes. So on return from leave there was a call for volunteers from No. 4 to make up the numbers of No. 7, who, together with Nos 8 and 11 Commandos, plus some small detachments, were chosen for this proposed operation. As a result, with high hopes of imminent action, several ORs volunteered.

Bill Parker, a sapper, was one who consequently joined No. 7, and within a few days he and the others from No. 4 sailed on the *Glengyle* for the Middle East, via the Cape, and ostensibly for Rhodes. However, during their final training in Egypt, the Germans invaded Greece and the Rhodes venture was quickly called off.

Meanwhile Bill took part in the No. 7 raid on Bardia in North Africa on 19/20 April 1941, then later in the forelorn action whereby Laycock's Commandos were given the unenviable task of covering the Commonwealth Forces' evacuation from Crete. Bill was one of those who had no option but to surrender to the Germans when, having covered the final withdrawal, the Commandos were left stranded on the beach after the last ship had departed. Bill and his Commando comrades spent the rest of the war as prisoners in Germany – it was a disappointing end to an adventure that had started so hopefully in Weymouth.

After Arran the rest of No. 4 returned to their base at Troon and the reorganisation of the Commando was effected with Col Lister as CO. Although they were naturally disappointed and frustrated by the outcome of events on Arran, the Commandos had been heartened by Sir Roger's positive talk, which boosted their flagging morale. They set about their training in and around Troon with renewed enthusiasm. It was not to be in vain.

CHAPTER THREE

Action at Last, in the Lofoten Islands

On 20 February our troop leader, Capt Young, told us we were going on yet another exercise, somewhere on the west coast of Scotland, and we would be away for about a fortnight. Other troops were also told of this impending exercise, so it was going to involve the whole Commando.

We were to give notice to our landladies to this effect; of course it wasn't the first time we had given our hosts such notices. Nor the last. In fact, so frequent were our notices and absences during the next couple of years in Troon that we were dubbed the 'Troon BEF', not the 'Troon British Expeditionary Force' after the British Force that went to France in the First World War and again in 1939. No, in our case 'BEF' meant 'Back Every Fortnight'.

However, once more rumours began to circulate that this would be 'a job', and these hopes were strengthened later that day when we were issued with sea kitbags and fighting knives. Finally, we were ordered to parade early next morning ready to move off in Full Marching Order (FMO) with kitbags.

What none of us knew was that Col Lister and the CO of No. 3 Commando, Col Durnford-Slater, had already been secretly briefed by a staff officer from Sir Roger Keyes's Headquarters. The two Commandos were to carry out a combined raid on the Lofoten Islands in northern Norway; the operation would have the codename Claymore.

Years later it was interesting to learn that the raid had been suggested by the Minister of Economic Warfare, Hugh Dalton (later a postwar Chancellor of the Exchequer), on 14 January 1941 in a memo to the prime minister. It was brief, to the point and read: 'I write to you about a project in Norway . . . suggesting a surprise attack . . . to land small parties to destroy herring and cod liver oil plants . . . to destroy enemy ships in harbour . . . to dispose of any small isolated German garrisons . . . and to kidnap Quislings, who are hated by the local population. . . .'

Winston Churchill liked the idea and recommended it to Sir Roger, who immediately 'took it on board'. The naval Chiefs of Staff, responsible for the safety of the transport ships, were hesitant, especially as they did not want to divert destroyers away from the vital task of convoy escorts in the Battle of the Atlantic. In the event they agreed and planning went ahead, with the COs of the two Commandos selected for the raid duly briefed and instructed to prepare for the operation.

Map of the Lofoten Islands in the Arctic Circle, with the main objectives of Nos 3 and 4 Commando.

Following the briefing for Operation Claymore both Lister and Durnford-Slater decided to keep all the details of this impending operation to themselves and merely tell their respective Commandos that they were going on yet another exercise. This was their cover plan.

Accordingly, on 21 February the whole of No. 4, less a small rear party left in Troon, departed in requisitioned transport for the port of Gourock, where a newly converted landing ship, infantry (LSI), HMS *Queen Emma*, was tied alongside and awaiting the arrival of the Commando.

Before the war this Dutch-owned ship, had been engaged on the Harwich to the Hook of Holland run, but following the invasion of the Lowlands had escaped. Taken over by the Royal Navy, it had been converted as a troop carrier for combined operations. Although it carried only six LCAs – as opposed to ten on the 'Glen' ships – it did have two larger landing craft (LCMs) which could each carry up to seventy fully equipped troops, thus making up the deficiency in numbers.

However, even at this late stage no confirmation orders had been received by the overall Force Commander, Brig J.C. Haydon, that the operation was definitely to go ahead, so fearing there might be another last-minute cancellation, he was reluctant to embark the Commandos. Happily, the confirmation instructions came through within an hour or so and we all embarked, were allocated troop decks and in the late afternoon set sail.

Next day saw us anchored in the great naval base of Scapa Flow, where for the first time Lister gave troop leaders details of his outline plan and the training programme for Operation Claymore. But first, as always, there was the routine practice of getting from mess decks to boat stations and into the two types of landing craft by day and in the dark.

On shore the priority for each troop was to rehearse its own specific task, such as establishing a bridgehead, organising a cordon around a building, working out a simple drill for searching a building, an attack on a strongpoint, action against a sniper, the setting up of a road block and, finally, the establishing of a simple anti-aircraft post with the Bren and tripod.

On board it was possible to carry out some training on deck, but this was limited, as we had previously experienced. Below deck there was an interesting series of talks and lectures on subjects relevant to the proposed raid – including one on 'escape and evasion', after which some silk maps of Norway were issued out to section and sub-section leaders. These were about the size of an ordinary handkerchief, but were for use in the event of being left behind or escaping if captured. These maps were to be concealed by unstitching the back collar of the battledress blouses, inserting the map, and then resewing the collar. An East End tailor had been installed on board for the duration of our stay in Scapa, specifically for this task.

His presence caused our intelligence officer some concern until he was assured that just before our departure from Scapa the tailor would be escorted off the *Emma* and kept, under security arrangements, at an RN base ashore. He had, apparently, been handpicked for this job by Brig Gubbins, Head of Special Operations Executive (SOE), who had also been involved in the planning stages of Operation Claymore. Gubbins not only selected and vetted the Norwegians attached to the Commandos, but was also responsible for an observer, Lt Strachan, who was attached to the Commando for the duration of the operation from M19.

We also had another little 'escape and evasion' device. This took the form of a pair of new 'fly-buttons' for our battledress trousers. These buttons, when removed from the trousers and placed one over the other, formed a little compass. They had to be sewn on by ourselves with the aid of the ubiquitous Army 'housewife' – the official name given to the handy little linen holdall that contained needles, darning and sewing, plus threads and khaki darning wool for socks, issued to all soldiers – even the Commandos – for minor repairs to clothing.

Some of the Norwegian Army personnel who had joined us on the ship at Gourock and were attached to every troop – they were to act as guides and interpreters – taught us simple and useful Norwegian phrases, such as one to warn the locals that an explosion was to be set off, and to take cover.

Recreational facilities on board were limited, as on all transport ships. There was no cinema or wireless entertainment, so most men played cards – pontoon, brag, solo whist or other games of chance. Although gambling was officially prohibited, it persisted, as did the old Army game of 'Crown and Anchor', and 'old soldier' Maund later confessed to 'making a packet on the old *Emma* . . .'. The only entertainment organised by the ship's company was housey-housey, better known today as bingo, but this was strictly supervised by the ship's master-at-arms, as was the daily tot of rum.

A couple of the men in No. 4 kept personal records/diaries of the voyage and their impressions of the raid. One was 'JED' Price, so called because the initial letters of his three Christian names happened to read JED, and the other was the intelligence corporal, Bdr Simpson, a rather eccentric character who had been a Shakespearean actor/producer before the war. He kept an account of the trip and the raid in the form of a long letter to his wife. It was subsequently published as a small book in late 1941 with the appropriate title, *Lofoten Letter*, under his stage and pen-name, Evan John.

As he explained in the preface of the book, he kept the manuscript of that long letter in the trouser pocket of his battledress, 'adding to it day by day, hour by hour, whenever I had five or more minutes' leisure. I only left it behind (for fear of death or capture) during the few hours spent on enemy-occupied ground; even then there was the opportunity to continue it on scraps of paper, subsequently incorporated with the rest.' It must be added that, as a member of the intelligence section, he was bound to have a pencil and a piece of paper!

Also in the preface he drew readers' attention to the fact that the book, being published during the war, had been subject to censorship, 'for fear of providing His Majesty's enemies with useful military information'. He adds, 'if my former comrades-in-arms [he was recommended for a commission after the raid] find the result puzzling or inaccurate I am sure they will know how to refrain from discussing the matter until after the war is over . . .'. As it happens there is little, or nothing of consequence, to disagree with in his account, and some extracts are quoted and reprinted from it.

While at Scapa the anchored fleet did have the occasional visit from German reconnaissance planes, but in each case they were kept high and flew off, deterred by heavy ack-ack fire from both shore-based and naval AA guns.

The weather during this period was very wet, very cold and very stormy. Evan John writes:

Thursday [27 February]. Early morning deck parade cancelled owing to the bad weather. There's a regular hurricane blowing and the sailors say we were within a few feet of a collision during the night. If this lasts, we shall all be very sick soon, and I should think we might easily reach our kick-off place, find it too rough to land and return home with nowt done. We've had jobs cancelled so often that I can't believe that something isn't going to happen now to stop this one coming off. . . .'

JED Price also mentions that morning too, because A Troop were due to go on an early-morning landing exercise, with reveille at 0500 hrs, but it too was cancelled, so they stayed on board and had a lecture from their troop leader until the winds died down. Then they went on deck for PT and weapon training.

Under 'Saturday, 1 March', Price wrote: 'We're off. We set sail from Scapa at midnight last night. The sea is fairly rough and many are sea-sick, but an air of excitement and anticipation is prevalent . . . and everyone has the sentiment, "Thank heavens we are doing something at last".'

Now everyone was more fully briefed and final orders were given, so that at last all knew the destination and objectives of the raid. I think it is true to say that before this time most of us had never heard of the Lofoten Islands, let alone know where they were. We were about to find out.

Interviewed on his arrival in Britain after the raid, one of the Norwegians who came back with us had this to say of his home:

I was born, brought up and have been living up to now in the Lofotens. How can I describe my birthplace to you? . . . Nearly everybody is a fisherman . . . the population consists of fishermen who cultivate the land, or if you prefer it, farmers who live on fishing.

He continued to explain the fishing season:

> Every January great masses of fishermen from the north came to
> increase the numbers to about 20,000, so that there were thousands of
> little boats. In peace time the season lasted from January to June, and
> the catch of cod was sent all over the world. Now the whole catch is
> sent to Germany.

This last sentence was, indeed, the *raison d'être* for the operation. But the
Germans were not just exporting the fish back to the Fatherland. Following
their conquest of Norway and having taken over the islands, the Nazis had
established the laboratories, factories and storage tanks to process fish oil
and export it back to Germany for a variety of uses, including the
manufacture of nitro-glycerine for high explosives.

With this in mind, the objects of Claymore were simple and clear-cut,
namely, to deny the Nazis any further supplies of the fish oil by destroying
the factories, storage tanks and the shipping used to export it to Germany.
Further objectives were to capture Germans employed on the ships, enemy
garrison troops and Norwegian quislings, to bring back volunteers for the
Free Norwegian Forces in Britain, and finally, to obtain useful military,
naval and economic intelligence information.

As regards the enemy forces and dispositions, it was thought that if the
secret of our raid were kept, there would probably not be much opposition
from any troops on the islands, but we must be prepared to fight.

The plan was that the two transport ships, *Queen Emma* (No. 4) and
Princess Beatrix (No. 3), would sail with a strong naval escort of HMS *Nelson*
and HMS *King George V*, two cruisers and five destroyers for most of the
850 miles to the Vestfjord that leads to the Lofotens. Then at this point a
submarine, acting as a navigation beacon, would lead the transport ships and
an escort of destroyers up the fjord to the LCA/LCM launching areas for the
raid.

Now that we were on our way we were all 'put in the picture' with the
final details and instructions. Nos 3 and 4 Commandos had separate
objectives. No. 3 were to land and operate on Stamsund and Henningsvaar,
while we, in No. 4, were to deal with targets on Svolvaer and Brettesnes.

Lister's Operation Orders, typed on board the *Emma*, can still be studied
at the PRO at Kew. They are concise and clear, but also flexible. They had
to be because Lister didn't know for sure the extent of any enemy
opposition or likely reaction. For that reason he kept a considerable part of
the Commando in reserve to cope with any unforeseen situation, to provide
boarding parties if required, for guarding prisoners and quislings, and also
for distributing a limited amount of food to the islanders.

Having detailed the allocation of specialist sappers, Norwegians, RN
signallers and other attached personnel to various troops, Lister had
divided the operation into seven tasks. Briefly, they were as follows:

TASK 1 · (a) Led by himself, with his small HQ and supported by Capt Hunter's G Troop, to secure a bridgehead on the main quay on Svolvaer and to seal off this area with road blocks etc
(b) Lt Webb with his section and guides etc. to take over the post office and main hotel, then also try to find and destroy a *Luftwaffe* wireless station known to be in the area.

TASK 2 · Lt Lewis and his section, assisted by Capt Linge and nineteen Norwegians, to gather information, papers, etc. from the mayor's, harbour master's and other port offices, then arrest known quislings. (Capt Lord Lovat, as Admiral Keyes's observer, to be attached to this party.)

TASK 3 · Capt Emmett with his C Troop to land near the major 'Cuba' fish factory and destroy all its production facilities, then to destroy any other facilities in the area.

TASK 4 · Lt Style and his section, plus the specialist sappers, to destroy the main storage tanks, together with any other small cod presses located in private properties in this area. Lt Style was specifically named to 'give the order for the demolitions having assured himself that all civilians in the danger area are clear'.

TASK 5 · Capt Cook and his E Troop, together with Capt Montgomerie and his A Troop, to form Lister's local and general reserve forces, and provide local ack-ack defence with their Brens mounted on tripods. This large force was to be embarked in the two LCMs.

TASK 6 · Maj Kerr (2IC), with one section of F Troop, to land on Brettesnes and establish a bridgehead with local ack-ack defence and also be prepared to assist with Task 7 if required.

TASK 7 · Capt Duveen, the rest of F Troop and specialist sappers to destroy the oil-producing facilities in three factories on Brettesnes plus any other smaller presses in the area; capture any enemy and quislings in the area.

Unfortunately the weather, as forecast, turned very nasty. We were then forced to realise that the *Emma*, especially now she had been converted, wasn't really designed for this sort of job in these seas. Ken Phillott aptly describes the problem:

> Here we were in mid-winter, crowded in a small ship . . . with a shallow draught and made top-heavy with landing craft. Anyone who knows the

North Sea, even in the summer, is aware of its roughness – but this was winter. That ship did everything but turn upside down, and I am sure that everyone was seasick – even the Captain.

It was really bad, so much so that all training sessions on deck, and even those on the mess deck, were kept to the minimum, until the day before the raid, when, as if by magic, the winds dropped and the sea calmed to just a gentle swell. Those men, especially the ones in the for'ard mess decks, bedevilled by the ever-present smell of engine fuel, who had been very poorly, gradually returned to normal and during the night as we made the last preparations calm descended on the mess decks and morale soared, and all were ready for that long-awaited first mission promised by Col Legard down in the Pavilion at Weymouth seven months earlier.

Reveille – or rather 'Wakey, Wakey, rise and shine!' – on 4 March was at 0300 hrs. JED Price wrote: 'We rolled up and stowed our hammocks, then dressed in as many clothes as we could manage. The dress of the day may be summed up in three words – two of everything.'

After some breakfast and hot drinks, the troops were called to embarkation stations and as they stepped out on to the darkened deck, wearing the minimum of equipment – but maximum clothing – with filled water-bottles and emergency rations packed into every man's haversack, just in case, they were surprised to see twinkling lights on the coastline. Obviously the locals paid scant attention to any form of blackout. They probably thought, with some justification, that, being so far north, they were out of harm's way. They certainly didn't appear to be expecting a Commando raid.

It was still dark, although a clear calm Arctic dawn seemed to be on its way; but it was intensely cold as troops clambered into their suspended LCAs. First to be lowered into the water were the parties for Svolvaer. They set off on time, but as they neared the harbour an armed trawler passed the little flotilla without taking any action. Price recorded: 'The atmosphere was so tense we had forgotten the cold. Slowly we approached the harbour with our arms at the ready; everyone was expecting a volley from the shore which was only a few yards away, but none came. . . .'

Instead, unopposed, the Commandos climbed up on to the quayside. The landing was just like another exercise. Surprise was complete. But in their heavily studded boots they weren't prepared for the slippery, ice-covered quay, and that slowed down what would have normally been a spirited dash ashore. Those assigned to Task 1 set about their various assignments without any opposition.

But soon after the landing of Lister's reserve forces from their MLCs, heavy gunfire was heard from offshore. The armed trawler that had sailed by the leading LCAs had, apparently, opened fire on one of the escorting destroyers. Their reply was quick and decisive. The trawler was sunk. Later several of the trawler's crew – all Germans – were picked up and landed, to

Scenes like this, of men of No. 3 Commando, re-embarked in one of their landing craft, leaving Stamsund, were experienced by No. 4 at Svalvoer, where the pillars of smoke rising from burning oil tanks could still be seen from the *Queen Emma* as she left the fjord in the late afternoon. (*Courtesy of the Imperial War Museum, London* – N394)

go straight into RSM Morris's POW cage; an unknown number were drowned.

Within an hour or so of the initial landing all the main buildings in Svolvaer, including the police station, the town hall, the mayor's and the harbour master's offices, had been occupied, intelligence information, documents and papers gathered and quislings arrested. In addition some arms and ammunition were found in the police station and these were taken away.

These buildings had been taken in accordance with a simple prearranged plan of 'Cordon and Search'. A Norwegian newspaper reporter who was there at the time and elected to come back with the raiders to Britain later described the scenes: 'I don't know why, but the soldiers took quite extraordinary precautionary methods. They certainly reckoned on the possibility of resistance. . . .' He was right; we weren't sure and had been trained to be prepared and to take no chances.

Everything was going according to plan, and soon the hitherto silent fjord and snow-capped mountains were echoing to the sounds of explosions and naval gunfire as factories were being blown up and enemy shipping was either being blown up by joint Commando/RN boarding and demolition parties or by direct gunfire from the destroyers.

About mid-morning information came into Lister's HQ about the whereabouts and details of the German *Luftwaffe* wireless station established on the island some miles outside Svolvaer town itself. This was a job for Lister's reserve, so a strong fighting patrol, accompanied by Lord Lovat, who was anxious to get into the action, was hastily sent off to deal with it.

The patrol commandeered some local vehicles – in typical Commando fashion, as they had done so many times on exercises against Home Guard and regular Army units in Britain – and set off in high spirits, eager for some excitement in dealing with the station. Lord Lovat in his book, *March Past*, provides the full story of this episode.

On the way to the objective they bumped, quite literally, into a group of Germans, believed to be fleeing from Maj Kerr's party, which had landed on Brettesnes. A burst of Bren fire over their heads brought a quick surrender and they were sent back under a small escort.

After reorganising the patrol, they set off once more and Lovat records:

The signal station, a converted police barracks on the forward slope of a hill, was flying a swastika flag. It looked solid and forbidding. From the locals we gathered that only Luftwaffe technicians were within. Led by a subaltern (Lt Veasey) part of the patrol worked its way to a good firing position among some bare rocks, and at a range of about 300 yards opened fire with Bren guns, firing tracers in short bursts at the doors and upper windows of the building. This manoeuvre drove the inmates into the arms of a reception committee from the rest of the patrol, who had slipped round in a detour to cover the rear exit.

Having captured the *Luftwaffe* personnel, the party set about destroying the wireless equipment inside.

Sixty years later Lt 'Monty' Banks has vivid recollections of wielding a heavy iron bar to smash the sets, much to the chagrin of the Commando signaller, equipped with only the British No. 18 set, and envious of the excellent German equipment. He was saddened to see it being so ruthlessly smashed, especially as he was having difficulty trying to raise HQ at Svolvaer, only five miles away.

Their mission completed, and with the swastika flag as a trophy, it was time to return to the quayside. There was no time to lose, given the deadline for re-embarkation. So, with their 'bag' of prisoners and more documents for the researchers and boffins at the Ministry for Economic Warfare and others back in Britain, the patrol returned to Svolvaer.

Another member of Lister's reserve, Lt Bill Boucher-Myers, later to become the second-in-command of No. 4, together with some others of

A Troop, had an exciting escapade too. Boucher-Myers was at the main post office in Svolvaer, when he was instructed to take charge of a joint Commando/RN demolition party to board and destroy three German ships lying just offshore. They set off, but as they approached, one of the ships, the largest, *Bremen*, suddenly appeared to be on fire. Apparently, having seen one of their other ships fired upon and sunk by destroyer gunfire, the crew of the *Bremen* decided to scuttle the ship themselves. Before the war the *Bremen* had been a well-known cruiseliner of some 9,000 tons, but the Nazis had converted her to a floating oil factory. With plenty of inflammable fish oil on board the crew had no difficulty in setting fire to the cargo and were now abandoning the ship. In spite of the flames, Boucher-Myers dropped off some RN ratings to deal with the engine room and open the sea-cocks, before going off to deal with the other two ships. His party was fired upon by the crew of one of them, but his Bren gunner dealt with that opposition, and the joint Commando/RN party boarded both vessels without further trouble, both crews surrendering.

Explosives were taken on board and duly detonated. However, to hasten the sinking of all three ships – and just to make sure, when all the boarding parties and prisoners were clear and on their way back to the quay – one of the destroyers, HMS *Alfrida*, fired and holed the ships from short range. All three then slowly, but surely, sank.

On his arrival back at the quay Boucher-Myers noted an almost festive, carnival atmosphere. By now the sky above was clear and blue, while the steep slopes of the fjord were glistening with sunlit snow, a lovely picture-postcard scene marred only by black smoke pillaring from the oil tanks set ablaze by Lt Style and his men.

Crowds of joyous and jubilant Norwegians had gathered at the quayside and were obviously delighted to see the German prisoners and quislings being sent off in the LCAs back to the *Emma* – and captivity. There were also little groups of young Norwegian men, all wanting to come back with us to join their compatriots in Britain and fight. All they had was a rucksack, or a small carrier of some sort, for a few personal belongings. This time the previous day they had no idea of what the next twenty-four hours would bring; now they were about to be involved in the war against the Nazis. Some never saw their beloved islands again. Today in Svolvaer a monument stands to honour eight of those brave young men who sailed back with us, but never returned.

It was then time to distribute the food, clothing and, most importantly, sweets for the children, that had been brought – in spite of rationing – from Britain for the islanders; also popular was the 'proper' coffee. There wasn't much of anything; it was more a gesture, but much appreciated. The Norwegians, plainly moved, wanted to reciprocate with presents, but all they had with them were lovely warm Fair Isle gloves and mittens, which they took off to press on our men as tokens of gratitude.

Just after 1100 hrs all the tasks in Svolvaer had been completed and Col Lister gave the orders to start the withdrawal and re-embarkation. By noon this was well under way, with each departing LCA being given a heart-warming send-off by the Norwegians.

Meanwhile, all had gone well for the smaller party, employed on Tasks 6 and 7 at Brettesnes, of which I was a member. Although we had embarked in our LCAs at the same time as the Svolvaer parties, we had to sit and wait in them until they had been launched and were on their way before we could be taken to our lowering and launching point.

It was freezing cold just sitting and waiting in the hanging LCAs, but eventually we too were lowered and on our way. We were all apprehensive, but the tension was relieved in our particular craft when our troop 'clown', L/Cpl Easton, began very softly – and appropriately – to sing the pre-war 'pop' tune, *Ferryboat Serenade*.

As we approached our landing quay, the spray coming over the ramp at the bows frequently dowsed the Bren gunner positioned there, and formed tiny icicles on the rim of his steel helmet. It was that cold. At about 0640 hrs, unopposed, we quickly and quietly clambered up on to the quay, and went about our various tasks.

I was in a little 'snatch' squad, consisting of Lt Hutton, his batman/runner ('Tich' Garnett), a Norwegian guide/interpreter and myself. Our job was to go to the known home of the factory manager and 'persuade' him to come with us to the factory, open up and generally assist the demolition party and those whose task it was to collect information and so on.

Our guide had no problem leading us to the house, where we knocked on the door and a startled man answered. When told of our 'business', he readily and willingly agreed to come with us to the factory. He was most cooperative.

Our arrival at the factory was soon followed by that of Capt Duveen and his party of sappers and searchers. Some members of his demolition team carried up to 70 lb of explosives. While they were preparing their charges we, and others, warned the nearby locals of the imminent explosions and told them to take the necessary precautions. In the event all the structural damage was limited to this main factory and the other smaller ones.

One surprise capture was that of a lieutenant of the German coastal defences, presumably visiting the area on reconnaissance. He had chosen the wrong day. He was most arrogant and truculent, and informed his captors that he would soon be freed by 'our glorious German Navy'.

As at Svolvaer, everything went well, and by about 1000 hrs all the tasks given to Maj Kerr's two groups had been carried out 'according to plan' and it was time to return to the *Emma*.

In his post-operation report Maj Kerr had this to say of our departure from Brettesnes.

Some of the 215 German prisoners and 10 Norwegian quislings brought back from the raid are seen here before, as the press caption of the day reads, 'leaving for an unknown destination'. (*Courtesy of the Imperial War Museum, London – N409*)

There was tremendous enthusiasm shown by the Islanders, who offered the utmost support. On embarking the German officer prisoner the inhabitants expressed their feelings extremely openly. As our LCAs left the quay the cheers, such as none of us will ever forget, broke out and followed us as we left the harbour. I know I speak for the rest of us when I say it was quite unforgettable, especially as their factories, which were in the vicinity of the quay, were in ruins.

Back on board the *Emma*, after the routine of unloading weapons and magazines, the defusing of grenades and the handing in of ammunition and so on, the first priority was rearranging mess-deck accommodation to cater for the sudden increase of passengers – prisoners and Norwegian volunteers. Among the latter were eight young women destined for the Norwegian Red Cross. They were duly accommodated in vacated cabins, but their presence did cause amusement when their allotted toilet was indicated with the hand-printed sign, 'BARE DAME' – 'bare' being the Norwegian word for only and 'dame', women.

In spite of the lack of actual fighting there were plenty of stories to tell about this most successful operation. One story that had already circulated throughout the mess decks was that an officer had been the only casualty suffered by the Commandos, namely the hapless Capt Cook, who had wounded himself with his own revolver. He was never allowed to forget it.

During that evening the two Commando COs and the Navy collated the results of the raid for onward transmission, via the Force Headquarters' ship, HMS *Somali*, to London. Wisely, it was decided to pool the tally of successes, so that the overall count was as follows:

Destroyed	Eleven fish-oil factories, plus laboratories and storage tanks holding 800,000 gallons
Sunk by joint RN/ Commando action	Ten German and German-used ships
Captured	215 German prisoners and 10 Norwegian quislings
Norwegian volunteers	315 loyal Norwegians brought back to Britain
Other German losses	An unknown number of German sailors lost their lives, drowned

'A highly successful operation with no casualties' was how the BBC prefaced their bulletin of the raid on the 6 o'clock news on the Thursday evening, which we were able to hear on board the *Emma*. Evan John wrote at the time: 'Listening to the BBC. Very satisfactory. True, modest and sober – and therefore more effective than highly coloured lying.'

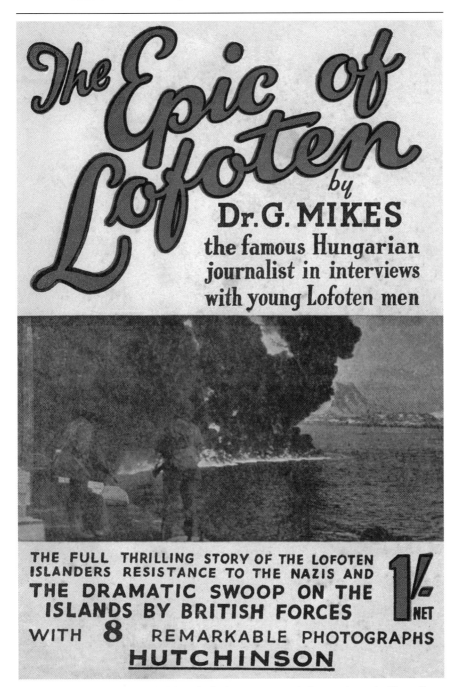

The news of the Commandos' raid on the Lofotens was a tonic for morale on the Home Front at a time when the Blitz was still taking its toll. It was followed by a series of small books and articles. The front cover of one such book, *The Epic of Lofoten*, is shown here. (*Author's Collection*)

What no one knew, or appreciated, at the time was that among the pieces of technical equipment and documents brought back from the raid was a vital link in the struggle to break the Enigma code. It was found aboard the armed trawler *Krebs*, when boarded by a small joint RN/Commando party, consisting of an RN officer, Lt Warmington, a Commando officer, Lt Harper-Gower, and a signals officer from the Force Headquarters, Maj Aslett.

Although the capture of this important piece of the jigsaw to break the code was kept secret for so many years, when the whole Enigma story was eventually told, historians and researchers acknowledged and emphasised the importance of this contribution from the Lofoten Islands Raid. It was a significant added bonus to the results already listed, although No. 4 Commando had no direct part in its discovery.

The journey back to Scapa was uneventful and the weather wasn't too bad; at least it was better than on the outward journey. One incident was recorded by JED Price:

A reconnaissance plane from home that had come out to meet us, apparently, spotted a U-boat on our starboard quarter at about 0900 hrs. Two destroyers circled around the area, dropping depth charges, which incidentally broke six plates on our mess deck. The destroyers rejoined us about an hour later, and we consequently assumed the U-boat to be sunk.

On the afternoon of 6 March the *Emma* arrived at Scapa. The wounded Germans, who had been receiving treatment from the ship's doctor and our MO, were the first to be landed, then the other prisoners. There were rousing cheers as the Norwegian volunteers filed off the ship. 'They appeared to be happy and glad to be in Britain', wrote Price.

Next day we sailed back to Gourock, where we were met by Admiral Sir Roger Keyes – and the press. The subsequent publicity given to the raid was a most welcome boost to morale at home, where the Blitz continued to take a terrible toll of life and properties, especially in London.

The disembarkation and take-off, in transport, of No. 4 from the ship and dockside was carried out in record time and it was not long before we were on our way back to Troon. The Commando rear party, which had been left behind, had warned our landladies we were returning, so everything was ready for us on arrival. The Troon BEF was back.

CHAPTER FOUR

The Lovat Philosophy – 'Train Hard, Fight Easy'

The first priority after returning to Troon was a spot of leave. For those who lived in London, or the south of England, going home wasn't trouble-free. The journey from Glasgow to London was frequently disrupted by air raids, and delays of up to twenty-four hours were quite common. In fact, all trains going to, and leaving from, the capital were liable not only to delays, but cancellations for a variety of reasons connected to the air raids and the damage caused by them.

During the first few weeks back at Troon, there was a certain amount of reorganisation within the Commando. For one reason or another several officers returned to their units, mostly at their own request, as did a number of other ranks. In F Troop all three of our officers applied to return to their parent regiments, because they were disappointed with the lack of action, in spite of the recent Lofoten Raid, which they reckoned didn't count. Two of the three had found out that the units they had left six months earlier were now off for active service in the Middle East.

There were also those who were RTU'd, as had happened after that initial amphibious training at Inveraray, because they were 'whingers' and couldn't accept a bit of rough living in a 'cooped-up' transport ship; a few who had suffered considerably from sea-sickness on the trip to and from the Lofotens and couldn't face the possibility of a repeat performance.

Not all troops had such drastic changes as F Troop; happily the three replacement officers in that troop were first class. Two, Capt Pat Porteous and Lt Knyvet Carr, both 'gunner' officers, became decorated stalwarts of No. 4 Commando – more of their exploits later. F Troop was further changed, in that in a reorganisation it now became D Troop. For a short while the old F Troop Diary, mentioned earlier, reappeared and was written up, in retrospect, as the new 'D Troop Diary'.

The command structure of the Commando remained unchanged – Col Lister, CO; Maj Kerr, 2IC; Capt Dunning-White, adjutant; Maj Vaughan, admin. officer, and 'Jumbo' Morris, RSM.

From April all training was focused, although we didn't know the reason, on a projected operation, codename Puma. And here I need to explain the background, which is revealing.

After the success of the Lofoten Islands Raid, there was a lull in UK-based operations, while Admiral Keyes built up another amphibious striking force to replace the one that had taken Layforce to the Middle East. However, there were signs that Franco's Spain was preparing to enter the war on the side of the Axis partners. As a precaution, plans were made to seize the Canary Islands to prevent the Germans from using the ports there as bases for their U-boats.

A considerable land force, consisting of two Royal Marine Brigades (not yet converted to Commandos), an Army Infantry Brigade, five Army Commandos (including No. 4), plus supporting armour, artillery and services, was earmarked and started training for this operation.

In the ranks of No. 4, we were unaware of this background as we started to train for an operation which involved a six to seven-mile speed march, carrying all troop weapons, plus as much reserve ammunition as we could manage.

Various means were sought to carry these extra loads, without success, so in the end we resulted to 'pack mules' – human ones. These men, volunteers, in every troop, carried the reserve ammo in extra basic pouches. The heaviest load was that of 1,000 rounds of .45 ammunition for the Tommy guns.

Another feature of this particular training was the emphasis and practising of taking up all-round defensive positions and digging-in. It was an emphasis we didn't favour or cherish, especially as the digging-in was attempted with the almost useless entrenching tool, and, furthermore, all the freshly dug trenches had to be filled in afterwards.

In addition to the land training, which was carried out in and around Troon, the Commando had two sessions of amphibious training at Inveraray and on Loch Fyne. During the second session, training for No. 4 was interrupted on 27 June, a typically wet Highland day, for an inspection by the prime minister, Winston Churchill, who, accompanied by Sir Roger Keyes, had previously been watching our landings from LCAs.

The Commando lined up on either side of the drive up to the Duke of Argyll's splendid castle at Inveraray. Winston went between our two ranks. The awful 'Scotch mist' weather prevented the great man from speaking to any of the men, but we were all enthralled to see 'Winnie' in the flesh. There he was, with shoulders hunched, cigar in mouth, blue naval-type peaked cap on head, and as he marched between our ranks, staring into our eyes with those almost-twinkling blue eyes of his, he seemed to strike a bond with us. It was a memorable occasion.

Returning to Troon, there were odd welcome diversions from operational training. With an international sportsman like Col Lister, it was only natural that competitive sports, such as football, rugby and, of course, boxing, should have a high rating on the training programmes too. The unit football team was an excellent one. In the D Troop Diary, which was now being written up by L/Cpl Garnett, a first-class footballer who but for the war would have played professionally, records that the Commando team had yet to be beaten. Even Col Durnford-Slater, in his book, *Commando*, proudly extolling the achievements of his No. 3's sportsmen, had begrudgingly to acknowledge the supremacy of No. 4's footballers.

In mid-summer there were command changes. Maj Kerr left to return to his unit and, rather surprisingly, Maj Vaughan took over as second-in-command. Vaughan, or 'Charlie', as he was fondly known to all, had joined the Army as a Coldstream Guardsman before the First World War, and had fought with his battalion in the first months of that war. As an 'Old Contemptible', he had been in the Retreat from Mons, and was one of those riflemen whose accuracy and high rate of fire had inflicted such casualties that the Germans swore they were facing machine-gunners.

Vaughan survived the war to have a splendid record during the inter-war years, gaining promotion – and an MBE – to Regimental Sergeant Major in the Brigade of Guards. He was subsequently commissioned as a quartermaster in The Buffs, in the same battalion as Dudley Lister. Always one, even as an old warrior, to fancy the challenge of active service, he had volunteered for the Commandos as an administrative officer and was appointed to that post in No. 7 Commando, which was commanded by Lister. He subsequently moved with the latter when he took over command of No. 4, via No. 3 Special Service Battalion.

Vaughan's unquestionable ability as an organiser and supervisor of basic training, plus his 'firm but fair' philosophy of military discipline, was just what was needed in No. 4 at this period.

To balance Vaughan's apparent 'old school of Army discipline' approach, Lister was fortunate in having Capt Lord Lovat serving as a supernumerary officer attached to Capt John Hunter's B Troop. Lovat had applied for an official posting to a Commando after his experiences as an attached observer for COHQ on the Lofoten Raid.

Now, with the departure of Maj Kerr, who had previously supervised all training, Lister appointed Lord Lovat as 'training officer', and he brought with him all his experiences as an instructor in fieldcraft and irregular warfare at the Special Training Centre at Lochailort.

'Shimi' Lovat was just twenty-eight years old when war was declared; he had succeeded to the title of the 'Master of Lovat' and head of the clan Fraser in 1933, when his father died. The latter, a celebrated sportsman, had in the Boer War raised and commanded the Lovat Scouts, a yeomanry regiment of his own clansmen.

Between leaving school and going to Oxford Shimi Lovat had spent a period working on a coffee and cattle ranch in South America. At Oxford he was a member of the University Cavalry Squadron, and after coming down he joined the Scots Guards as a regular soldier, and served for some six years, with a tour of duty in Egypt. Back in England, he found routine duties in London rather dull and left the Army in 1937. He went back to the family estate in Inverness-shire, but on the outbreak of war two years later joined the Lovat Scouts, with whom he served until taking up the appointment as an instructor at Lochailort, then to COHQ and finally to No. 4 Commando.

It was thus a most unusual combination, Vaughan and Lovat, with their vastly different social backgrounds: one an ex-Guardsman sergeant-major and a Cockney by birth, the other a Highland chieftain, an ex-public schoolboy, Oxford graduate and ex-Guards officer. But it was a very successful combination and worked well. In Lovat's memoirs he pays a handsome tribute to the old warrior, Charles Vaughan.

Concurrent with the special training for Operation Puma, Vaughan ran a series of unit cadres for both senior and junior NCOs, while among Lovat's innovations was the weekly 'Strength Through Joy Marches', held every Saturday morning, according to Lovat, 'pleasant little non-stop walks of twelve miles in light "skeleton order" with personal weapons along the Ayrshire roads, 'just enough exercise to work up a thirst to start the week-end'.

On 5 August HMS *Royal Scotsman*, a landing ship infantry (LSI), sailed into Troon harbour and the Commando, with all its weapons and stores, embarked for an exercise as part of the preparations for Operation Puma.

We headed for the Orkneys, where we carried out a series of exercises on the island of Hoy and concluded with a 'crash landing' on the dockside at Kirkwall. As its name suggests, in a crash landing, instead of landing in the usual manner from LCAs on a beach, the ship itself goes right alongside and the troops disembark direct on to the quay under cover of darkness. Dummy runs were made in daylight and then, on the night of 13 August, came the real thing.

As the ship edged alongside the quay, we on the mess decks and gangways below, waiting and ready 'to go', heard and felt a shuddering 'crr . . . unch' as the ship gradually lurched into the quay. We didn't need any word of command to set off. We all knew it was time to go. Staff officers with watches timed our disembarkation and, although we weren't particularly pleased with it, the hierarchy was well satisfied. The War Diary records a report from General Alexander's staff, which reads:

> Thanks to the magnificent seamanship of the Master of the A10 [HMS *Royal Scotsman*] the difficult night crash was carried out perfectly. All troops disembarked quickly and quietly, and leaders and men knew where to go and cleared the quay at the highest possible speed. All personnel were clear of the A10 in 12 minutes and all ammunition/ stores in 23 minutes.

The report concluded that the general 'was impressed with the speed, silence and general sinister efficiency of the Commando troops'.

Next day we set sail, heading west and then south past the Outer Hebrides once more. The weather was lovely and we were able to get out on deck for various training sessions, plus a very successful inter-troop boxing competition.

The *Royal Scotsman* brought the Commando back to Troon and off on leave, with rumours abounding that it was 'embarkation leave'. It was but a rumour. In his book, *The Commandos*, Charles Messenger provides details of the bigger picture in respect of Operation Puma, which now had become Operation Pilgrim. He records that after various discussions and delays by the Chiefs of Staff, the operation had been put 'on hold'. Also it had been 'decreed by the Prime Minister that part of the force was to be despatched. The unhealthy West African climate and lack of accommodation precluded the complete force being sent. It was reckoned, however, that the main body could deploy and mount Pilgrim if given a month's notice.'

A token force of some ten amphibious landing ships with advance parties from all the units represented in the Force (officially known as 'Force 110') were, therefore, sent to West Africa, including a detachment from No. 4. This, then, is how a 'special troop' from the Commando embarked on the *Royal Scotsman*, once more, on 13 September at Gourock. Commanded by Capt David Style, this troop totalled twenty-six all ranks and comprised a small HQ and two sections. Each of the latter was commanded by a sergeant. One of these, Sgt John Groom, was an original volunteer from the Royal Engineers, and he kept a diary of the subsequent exploits of this *ad hoc* troop over the next five months. It makes interesting reading.

In 1988, while preparing another book, John kindly sent me a copy of his diary. The following account is based on those entries.

After four days at the port loading stores and equipment, the *Royal Scotsman* set sail from the Clyde, and some seven days later on 25 September it arrived, in company with the other ships, in Gibraltar.

With the ships anchored in deep water, just off the dockside, and using rope scrambling nets, the Commandos enjoyed several sessions of swimming – the water was still warm in September. To keep their legs in trim they spent their only day ashore on a route march, but as Groom noted, 'it was not far as "Gib" has its limitations for this sort of thing'.

After just two days the convoy set sail and headed south towards the Tropics. As the temperatures rose, battledress was discarded and packed away, and tropical gear ('KD' – khaki drill) became 'the rig of the day', but sunbathing was forbidden between noon and 1800 hrs. Groom also records: 'Started taking quinine daily from today.' But the Commandos still had no idea of where they were heading.

On 4 October, however, Style told his troop that they would be landing in Freetown, Sierra Leone, to establish a base camp and training facilities for the Commando, which would follow, but he was unable to elaborate further; wrily, Groom added, 'at least we should have a warm winter'.

Next day they sailed into the harbour of Freetown, where, at anchor, 'the ship was soon surrounded by vendors in their boats . . . and it started to rain like hell!'

On disembarking they headed for a tented camp some five miles out of the port, which was earmarked as their base. It was near a village with a pertinent name for this part of Africa: 'Wilberforce'.

As soon as the troop had settled down they started on the major tasks of improving the basic facilities of the camp to receive the rest of the Commando, searching out suitable training areas and also, most importantly, a firing range.

Within a few days an improvised, but adequate, range was ready for use and, fortunate to have plenty of ammunition, they were able to spend several days using it for themselves, most successfully: 'at the end of our firing, not one man out of the twenty-six can be called a rotten shot . . .'. This was a relevant comment in that one of that number, L/Cpl 'Dickie' Mann, would later be awarded a Military Medal for his deadly sniping on the Dieppe Raid.

In addition to shooting on the ranges, they naturally had other training, including route marches, and, having to 'keep house' in the camp – as opposed to billets back in Troon – they had plenty of domestic camp chores. They also had to maintain their stores on board the *Royal Scotsman*, which was still in harbour along with the other assault landing ships of 110 Force.

With temperatures that averaged in the nineties, their route marches were tackled progressively, but by the end of October Style considered his troop

Good weather and a calm sea enabled No. 4 Commando to stage an inter-troop boxing contest on board HMS *Royal Scotsman* while returning from the exercises and 'crash landing' rehearsal for Operation Puma in August 1941. All the spectators are wearing their 'Mae Wests'. (*Author's Collection*)

sufficiently acclimatised to carry out a four days' exercise that was to start off with a twenty-mile march wearing full equipment and carrying full scales of ammunition.

Apparently the major problem on this scheme was mosquitoes in the bivouac areas at night. These little pests took their toll too. Several men were hospitalised as a result, but quickly recovered. Lessons were learnt – the hard way.

During November Style's troop had to transfer all the Commandos' stores from the *Royal Scotsman* to the *Queen Emma*. They remained on board to carry out a series of landings on nearby Banana Island.

On 10 December there was a sudden outbreak of excitement when the troop was told that they were remaining on board and sailing immediately to Ascension Island, 1,200 miles south of Freetown, because it had been reported by an RAF reconnaissance flying boat that an 'armed raider had been spotted near the Island and an enemy landing could not be ruled out'.

They left Freetown in high spirits and in eager anticipation that this might mean some action at last. However, after three days of sailing south, the excitement fizzled out when they were told that the reported presence of 'an armed raider' had been a false alarm, and so the little convoy turned about and sailed back.

Groom, in his diary, poses the all-important question: 'Did the flying boat that reported the armed raider actually see it?' and adds: 'We shall never know.'

Strangely enough, Messenger, with the benefit of hindsight and research to help him, records the following incident, which ties in with Groom's account to some degree:

On 2 December HMS *Devonshire* intercepted a German raider, which scuttled herself. There were then reports that her crew had been taken off by U-boats and were heading off for Ascension Island, which had a very weak garrison. *Queen Emma* and *Princes Beatrix* were ordered there, but, although the Ascension Island garrison reported firing on a U-boat, the operation came to naught.

Back in Freetown, Style's troop returned to Wilberforce Camp and carried on as much as before with still no news of 'if and when' the rest of the Commando were coming out to join them.

Christmas and the New Year came and went, and still no news. For the next few weeks the troop carried out a mixture of various duties, helped the local authority to build a road through 'the Bush', took part in exercises with the local company of the West African Frontier Force (WAFF) and sailed down the coast on the *Queen Emma* as extra ack-ack gunners to Takoradi and on to Lagos in Nigeria, before returning to Freetown on 9 February. The following day they were told that Operation Pilgrim had been cancelled and they were returning to the UK. Fifteen days later, on 25 February, they docked at Gourock and arrived back to 'a very wet and cold Troon', having been away for 159 days.

While they had been away the Commando had continued training for its role in Operation Pilgrim. There had been other exercises and training ventures too. In addition, officers and NCOs had attended a wide range of courses; Sgt Bend of C Troop had even been to Iceland for a short course on Arctic warfare, and returned as an expert in the art of building an igloo!

Also there had been the first whole-troop expedition to carry out mountaineering and rock climbing, one of Lovat's innovations. Previously only selected officers and NCOs had attended such courses of instruction on the Isle of Skye and in Glencoe, but now with a handful of them qualified to instruct and to lead on climbs, the time had come to put a whole troop through this more specialised form of training.

C Troop led the way on these expeditions, which Lovat later called 'On Commando' exercises. Capt Dawson was now in command of the troop, after David Style, at his own request, had relinquished command and reverted to a post as section officer. Dawson had been brought up in Switzerland and loved the mountains. In fact, seeing that he was later to command No. 4, which was to include two troops of French Commandos, it is an opportune place to outline his pre-war background.

Dawson's father had been a police officer in India, but for some reason left the sub-continent and brought his family back to Europe, settling in Switzerland, where the young Robert Dawson went to school and later graduated from Lausanne University. He then went to Canada with the intention of following a mining career, but returned for postgraduate studies in Lausanne. Nevertheless, he had acquired a taste for – plus some experience in – mountaineering and climbing. His education in Switzerland had also enabled him to become fluent in both English and French. With the outbreak of the war he came to England and enlisted, then was commissioned in the Loyal Regiment, whence he had volunteered for the Commandos.

September saw C Troop established in civilian billets in the slate-mining village of Bethesda in Snowdonia, North Wales, an ideal location for climbing. Four of the senior NCOs in the troop, Sgts Langlands, McCarthy, Lindley and Bend, had already qualified as climbing instructors and were eager to put their newly acquired skills and 'know-how' to the test. Having established ourselves in the village with billets and requisitioned empty shops for Troop HQ and stores (including ammunition and explosives for field firing exercises), all were ready to start training.

We set off for Tryfan, a recognised climbers' mountain, which towers above Lake Ogwin in the Nan Francon Pass about five miles from Bethesda. There on the rocks at the foot of Tryfan, unencumbered with equipment or weapons, we were introduced to the basics of rock climbing – bouldering and scrambling – and the techniques of climbing with ropes in teams of three. It wasn't until we had mastered these fundamentals that we started on the more difficult climbs on this mountain and the Idwal Slabs, and subsequently progressed to climbing with equipment and weapons.

Initially, with only four qualified instructors, who could only cope with two trainees at a time, actual instruction on the rock faces was limited, so a rota system was introduced and those not on actual rock climbing spent their days mountaineering/fell walking, tackling such local challenges as the Crib Goch Ridgewalk, Carnedds Dafydd and Llewellyn, and ascents to the summit of Snowdon. A limited amount of field firing was also carried out.

As always, our presence in the area prompted a request from the local Home Guard to carry out an exercise against them. On this visit to North Wales, we were asked to test out their defences on the coastal road that runs south from Conway, through Penmaenmawr, towards Bangor. We surprised the defenders by making our approach via the mountain route; it was a move that made them revise their defence plans.

At this time there was attached to C Troop a very bright and capable young subaltern, Lt Brian Hilton-Jones, who later left when he was chosen to raise the special X Troop of No. 10 Commando. This was a troop of Free Germans; it was one of the strangest, if not the strangest, sub-unit to serve in the British Army, and those wishing to find out more about the troop are recommended to read Ian Dear's book, *Ten Commando*. The justification for mentioning them here is that Hilton-Jones based much of the training of his X Troop on that received in C Troop, and, in particular, the time spent in Bethesda and Snowdonia in the autumn of 1941. It was, therefore, gratifying that some of Hilton-Jones's splendid men should ultimately serve with No. 4 in Normandy in 1944. After three excellent weeks of training in North Wales, C Troop returned to Troon, and thereafter was regarded as the 'climbing troop'.

Meanwhile, back in Troon, training was less exciting, although morale in the Commando was raised when No. 4's footballers won the Inter-Commandos' Soccer Competition.

Another event of importance was the last visit of Admiral Sir Roger Keyes, who came to say farewell to his Commandos. He had been forced to stand down as Director of Combined Operations for a variety of reasons – mainly clashes of personalities with members of the Chiefs of Staff Committee over proposed operations and priorities of shipping and equipment.

In his letter to Winston Churchill, in which Keyes accepted the decision that he had to go, he wrote; 'Please don't feel pain on my account, I have none. I only grieve to have let down my splendid Commandos.'

In the official account and history of Combined Operations, Sir Bernard Fergusson outlines the reasons behind his departure, and adds: 'His tenure of fifteen months had been stormy, but beyond doubt he had accomplished a great deal.' He concludes: 'His departure was mostly mourned by the Commandos, whose purpose and character were alike and so close to his own.' We were sorry to see him go.

Following Lovat's introduction of sending troops off 'On Commando', Capt Dawson took his troop to Snowdonia for mountaineering and rock climbing. Above, the leader of a team of three is tackling the Idwal Slabs; opposite left, abseiling on Mt Tryfan, and opposite right L/Cpl Shearing crossing over to the Bell View Terrace, some 1,500 ft up on Mt Tryfan. Shearing was later wounded during the raid on Hardelot (Boulogne) in April 1942. (*C Troop Collection*)

Apparently, again quoting Fergusson, Churchill's brief to Keyes's successor, the 41-year-old Lord Louis Mountbatten, was on these lines:

> I want you to succeed Roger Keyes in charge of Combined Operations. Up to now there have been hardly any Commando Raids. I want you to start a programme of raids . . . so as to keep the enemy coastline on the alert from the North Cape to the Bay of Biscay. BUT YOUR MAIN OBJECT MUST BE THE RE-INVASION OF FRANCE. You must create the machine which will make it possible for us to beat Hitler on land. . . .

A couple of months after taking over, Mountbatten did launch the first of his new programme of raids, but this operation was allotted to No. 3 Commando, and their objective was Vaagso in Norway. No. 4 was not involved in it, although D Troop was sent to Invergordon, ostensibly to supply extra men for the raid if needed. But they weren't. Nevertheless, during the next few months there were several indications of Mountbatten's 'new broom' influence, and this was reflected in morale and the training programmes of No. 4.

In February 1942, three troops, A, B and C, under the command of Lord Lovat, left Troon for the Outer Hebrides, where a series of exercises against the local Home Guard, some ambitious field firing practices, including mock attacks on 'strongpoints' with live ammunition and a variety of landings from LCAs on to sea beaches, lochside shores and small jetties, using bamboo ladders, were carried out in a hectic spell of training lasting just some ten days.

The exercises against the Home Guard were all dawn attacks, and they provided much mutual excitement. Not only were the Home Guard very keen and active, but their official numbers were supplemented by enthusiastic local youngsters wielding hand-made weapons modelled on the old pike!

The three troops returned to Troon on 1 March, but not for long. They had hardly time for a wash and brush up; then they were off again, this time in the opposite direction. A special train took them, plus a full scale of weapons and ammunition, down to Dartmouth in Devon. The wet and windy Hebrides one week and sunny Devon the next – and there was glorious sunshine in Devon that March.

Waiting at Dartmouth was HMS *Prince Albert*, on which A, B and C Troops embarked, under the command of Lovat, once again. At this time Capt 'Bill' Boucher-Myers had A, Capt Gordon Webb B, and Robert Dawson was in command of C Troop.

All three troops started training for an operation, codename Bludgeon, the object of which was to land on the coast (of Holland, although at this stage none but Lovat knew the location), move rapidly a short distance inland, and surround, attack and destroy a large house which was being occupied and used by senior German officers.

With this in mind the operation fell into four distinct operational phases: one, establish a beachhead on landing; two, approach and set up a cordon around the objective; three, assault and destruction of the objective; and four, withdrawal and re-embarkation. For the assault, B Troop were issued with small portable flame-throwers to set the objective ablaze before withdrawing.

After several days' training in the area, we set sail from Dartmouth and, hugging the south coast, finally anchored in the mouth of the Thames, and waited for the signal to set off across the North Sea. But once again the operation was cancelled. The reason given was increased enemy E-boat activity in the 'offshore' area where Operation Bludgeon was due to take place. So it was back to Troon, to chants of 'Here comes the Troon BEF again'.

However, just before Lovat's party had left for the aborted Operation Bludgeon, another small party left Troon too. The War Diary records: 'Lt H. Pennington and 12 other ranks proceeded on "Harbour Demolition Course".' They were all sappers and experts in demolitions, but what they didn't know at the time was that this so-called 'Harbour Demolition Course' was a cover plan for the preparation of Mountbatten's second big Commando raid, that on St-Nazaire by No. 2 Commando, with detachments from other Commandos.

The raid was a daring action of high strategy and, as such, played an important, if not vital, part in the Battle of the Atlantic. It was undoubtedly one of the greatest and boldest raids of the war, as is suggested by the fact that no fewer than five Victoria Crosses were awarded to participants in the raid.

The main result of the raid was that the great dry dock at St-Nazaire, the largest in the world, was put out of action for the whole of the war by the single Commando raid on 28 March 1942. Unfortunately, it is not practical to enlarge on the raid here, only to relate the story of those thirteen members of No. 4 who were 'lent' to No. 2 for the operation, because that Commando had insufficient expert demolitionists from within their ranks for the exceptionally large number of demolition tasks envisaged.

Bill Portman, one of the group, recalled:

We went off to train at the small port of Burntisland on the Clyde, then at Cardiff docks and finally at Southampton's giant King George V Dry Dock. We learnt everything there was to learn about demolitions in a port, especially one such as St Nazaire with its complicated dock caissons and other equipment.

At the conclusion of this intensive training only six of the thirteen from No. 4 went on the raid. Sadly, Lt Pennington, L/Cpl Borgman and Spr Coulson did not return; they were all killed, by enemy coastal fire, on board their motor launch on the run-in to the dockside.

Portman and the other six, however, returned to Troon, but within days they were sent off again, together with Cpl John Skerry, a non-sapper, but one of those in the Commando who had qualified as a demolition man on a special course at Lochailort.

This time the group was attached to a joint Nos 1 and 6 Commandos force that was to carry out a raid on Bayonne. They embarked in HMS *Queen Emma* and *Princess Beatrix*, fresh back from West Africa. They were disguised as Spanish merchantmen, but were accompanied by five destroyers. The object was to land at the mouth of the River Adour, by Bayonne, attack military and other selected commercial targets and also destroy merchant shipping.

After cruising off the Spanish coast, a landing was attempted on 5 April, but their approach was blocked by a sand bar, and the operation, codename Myrmidon, was aborted and the two landing ships and the Commandos returned to their bases in Britain.

By this time, mainly due to the increased publicity being afforded to the exploits of the Commandos, there was a constant stream of requests from British and Allied formations and units for teams and individuals to come and instruct their units in 'Commando Training'. For example, an entry in the War Diary in late March reads: 'Lieuts Lockett, Earle and Nimmo, plus 13 ORs to Far East to instruct in Commando Warfare.' Not only did this group instruct and help Wingate's Chindits prepare for their expeditions behind the Japanese lines in Burma, but they also went into action with one of Wingate's columns.

A formidable duo, Charles Vaughan and Lord Lovat. This photograph was taken after they had left No. 4, on promotion, Vaughan to colonel as commandant of the Commando Basic Training Centre (CBTC) at Achnacarry, Scotland, and Lovat to brigadier to raise and command 'No. 1 Special Service Brigade', better known and later retitled as 'No. 1 Commando Brigade'. (*Author's Collection*)

Two of them, in particular, distinguished themselves in the jungle operations. Lt Locket, from D Troop, a kilted Seaforth Highlander – and a persistent 'snuff-shunter' – won a well-deserved MC and promotion to major. One of the ORs, Sgt 'Jock' Blain, a fine and capable regular NCO from the Dorset Regiment, also did well. Blain, one of the original volunteers, was among those who became frustrated and 'browned off' on Arran over Christmas 1940, but, showing much initiative and cunning, managed to bluff his way over on the ferry to the mainland. Then, after a couple of days of festive revelry, he 'borrowed' a boat back to Arran. He accepted Lister's punishment, rather than a court-martial, was reduced to the ranks but allowed to stay with No. 4. In truth, he was too good to lose and soon had his three stripes back.

Out in Burma, Blain became Mike Calvert's column sergeant-major, and his bravery, leadership and marksmanship won him the Distinguished Conduct Medal (DCM). He was subsequently commissioned and ultimately promoted to major. No. 4's loss of officers and men of this calibre was, of course, to Wingate's benefit.

The War Diary entries of the next few days also note:

Capt Cook and Lt McDonald and 17 ORs detached to train Canadian Army units in Commando Warfare for 15 days. . . . Two officers and two NCOs from the Royal Netherlands Army attached (to D Troop) to observe and undergo Commando Training.

These above-quoted examples were not isolated; there were over the years many such detachments, and the Commando was frequently called upon to give demonstrations on a wide range of training activities, from set-piece attacks with live ammunition to cliff-climbing and street-fighting methods and techniques. Thus it is, perhaps, true to say that the benefits and value of the Commandos went beyond the limits of their operations, by setting new and innovative standards in military training, and also inspiring a new spirit of offensive and aggressive training that was lacking in 1940. These influences and factors should not be overlooked in assessing the significance of the Commandos in the Second World War.

The next few months saw major changes 'at the top' of the Commando. Lister left, and moved 'sideways' to raise and command a new Commando of volunteers from the occupied countries who had, by various ways and means, joined their respective countries' forces in Britain. The new Commando was designated No. 10 (Inter-Allied) Commando and included French, Dutch, Belgian, Norwegian and even those Germans mentioned earlier.

As a temporary measure, Vaughan took over as commanding officer, and Lord Lovat became second-in-command. Then, after a short period, Vaughan left to command the Commando Depot at Achnacarry and to convert it into the renowned Commando Basic Training Centre (CBTC), where from 1942 all volunteers for the Commandos had to pass the rigorous course there before getting their green beret and joining an operational Commando.

Vaughan took with him a couple of No. 4's warrant officers, TSM Woodcock, who became Vaughan's RSM at Achnacarry, and RQMS Jack Joy, who was commissioned and installed as Vaughan's adjutant, so that the new CBTC was headed by a formidable trio of ex-No. 4 Commandos.

Achnacarry is very much a part of the Commando story; none who endured and passed the course ever forgot it. Further information about 'Achnacarry, the world's finest battle-training centre', can be gleaned from the books *It Had To Be Tough*, *Commando Castle*, and the brochure 'Commando Trail'.

Waiting in the wings, as it were, to take over as CO of No. 4 when Vaughan left was Lord Lovat, and he brought in as his second-in-command a dynamic wartime officer from the Irish Guards, Maj Derek Mills-Roberts, about whom much will be told later.

Sandwiched between these changes a small operation, Abercrombie, was carried out by two troops of No. 4, plus detachments from a Canadian regiment and the Royal Engineers, all under the command of Lord Lovat. The intention of this operation was 'to make a reconnaissance of the beaches and sand dunes to the north and south of Hardelot [in France, just west of the Channel port of Boulogne], to capture prisoners and inflict the maximum damage in the vicinity'.

B and C Troops were chosen for this mission and duly departed from Troon on 6 April with all weapons, ammunition and so on for Southampton, where we boarded HMS *Prince Albert*, once again, as our base for the land training. This was mainly carried out on heathland in the nearby New Forest and on the beaches of Lepe on the shore of the Solent. As a security precaution we were transported to these training areas in closed troop carriers.

Although we were to land from LCAs, there was to be a different system for this proposed raid. Instead of boarding the LCAs and then heading for the enemy beaches from the parent ship, we were to travel across the Channel in motor gun boats (MGBs), which were to tow the LCAs across and, when within striking distance from the coast, we would transfer from the MGBs to our LCAs for the run-in. After the raid we would return all the way in the LCAs. We would not be using the *Prince Albert* at all, only her LCAs. This was certainly a bit different.

The plan for the raid was simple enough. C Troop was to land first, breach any wire obstacles on the dunes and establish a beachhead. B Troop would then pass and proceed through the sand dunes, moving in small independent groups to their various tasks.

On 18 April we left Southampton on the *Prince Albert*, which took us to Dover, where we and the LCAs were off-loaded. We were accommodated in dungeon-like quarters in the depths of the Redoubt in the Old Fort, and the LCAs were moored alongside the MGBs in the harbour.

We set off on the night of 19 April. No. 4 were aboard the MGBs, each of which towed two LCAs. However, after a couple of hours' sailing one LCA

The Commandos soon realised the value of being able to use captured enemy weapons. Officers and NCOs attended special courses on 'Foreign Weapons' – such as the German machine gun seen here. No. 4 Commando subsequently exploited this knowledge in the Normandy campaign and at Flushing. (*Courtesy of the Imperial War Museum, London* – B5604)

started to ship water and in no time sank. The little convoy was halted and a search was made for the LCA crew and the two men from C Troop, manning a Bren in the bows. Fortunately, the sailors were rescued, but no trace could be found of our two chaps. The search and the raid were called off and we returned to Dover, saddened by the loss of our two comrades from C Troop.

A replacement LCA was made available and another attempt was made on the night of 21 April. This time the crossing was successful, the transfers from MGBs to LCAs in the dark off the French coast went well and we, in our group, landed undetected, but the smaller Canadian party, who had a different landing beach and a separate mission, failed to find their beach, didn't land and so returned home.

At our selected landing point, flat sandy beaches extended for some 400 yards and as we waded ashore there was a phosphorescent glow around our legs, which was most uncanny and we all thought it would warn the enemy. However, we got to the wire defences undetected and started to cut a way through for B Troop. Hardly had they reached us when all hell broke loose; the enemy machine-guns, covering the beaches, opened up. Not only was there tracer fire, but also illuminated flares and coloured light signals. The searchlight tried to light up the beach, but it couldn't depress sufficiently to succeed. However, it did manage to illuminate one of the LCAs lying off-shore. It was quite a spectacle. Fortunately, all the enemy machine-guns were on fixed lines and the fire whistled harmlessly overhead.

B Troop went through on their various missions, reconnaissances were carried out and an attempt made to attack the searchlight, but it was found to be protected by two perimeter belts of wire, about 250 and 450 yards respectively from the searchlight post. The raiders had insufficient time to deal with this unexpected defensive layout, so abandoned the attempt.

Lord Lovat briefing his officers for Operation Abercrombie – the raid on Hardelot (Boulogne), April 1942. On the right looking down is Capt David Style, his fighting knife fastened to his left thigh; also in the picture is Lovat's control signaller with the No. 18 set on his back – an awkward burden on a wet wade ashore. (*Author's Collection*)

A section of C Troop, No. 4 Commando, taken within the ramparts of Dover Castle on the afternoon of the first – aborted – crossing for the Hardelot (Boulogne) Raid, April 1942. (*Author's Collection*)

Unfortunately, one of the groups missed an opportunity to capture a prisoner when they opened fire prematurely on an enemy patrol, which then made off in the darkness.

Although there was a strong force of enemy in the area for coast defence duties, the Germans did not react to the landing. In his report Lovat, commenting on this, wrote: 'The interesting feature of this operation was the very small opposition encountered throughout. It seems probable that the enemy was confused from the onset by the naval engagement which took place some 15 minutes after the landing.'

At the end of the limited time allowed for operation on shore, all returned to the beach on time, and without loss, to re-embark in the LCAs, although one man in the beachhead, L/Cpl Shearing, of the Commando boxing team, was wounded by a stray enemy bullet which, inexplicably, hit him in the leg, just before re-embarkation. He was the only casualty.

We re-embarked with no problems except for the fact that we had to wade out to the LCAs and got thoroughly wet, then set off back to England. The journey was uneventful, but we were very wet and very cold on that slow trip, in the cramped LCAs, back to Dover, where we docked in the afternoon. That night some of us celebrated in a pub, being allowed out in public for the first time since leaving Troon. We were able to see for

A group of D Troop, late 1941. On the ground in the centre can be seen the unpopular Boys' anti-tank rifle, most are armed with the reliable SMLE rifle. (*Milton Smithson*)

In the summer of 1942 No. 4 Commando were warned of possible operations in the Middle East and accordingly issued with KD (khaki drill) clothing. C Troop is seen here with Capt Dawson, who is standing on the extreme left. (*Author's Collection*)

ourselves how much damage Dover – in 'Bomb Alley' – was suffering from the Germans' long-range guns that shelled the port almost daily from the Calais area.

The reports on the operation compiled by Lovat and the specialist RE officer, who was attached, provided a great deal of useful information about the state of the beach defences in the area, but on the whole the results did not justify the effort put into the operation.

Considerable publicity was given to the raid in the home press. Not all of it was accurate; for example, some headlines read, 'Canadians land in France', while the *News of the World* had a headline, 'Commando Lands in Carpet Slippers', referring to Lt 'Jock' Ennis, of B Troop, who reportedly had somehow lost his boots just before leaving for the raid and consequently put on his only footwear at hand, his carpet slippers. Most unlikely. But as far as the Commando was concerned the story stuck, and from that day onwards his sobriquet was, understandably, 'Carpet Slippers'.

Undoubtedly the most blatant untruth is a report in John Parker's book, *Commandos – The Inside Story of Britain's Most Elite Fighting Force*, stating that on the first attempt 'about thirty men died' when the ill-fated LCA sank. This is strongly repudiated; it is grossly untrue. The tragic losses were restricted to the two men of C Troop, of which I was TSM at that time.

With Operation Abercrombie behind them, the Commando settled down to training, now under the direction of Lord Lovat and his new second-in-command, Mills-Roberts, whose distinctive style and manner soon earned him the nickname of 'Mills-Bomb'.

During the next few weeks the two most significant features of the training were the intensive sessions of classification of all ranks in the firing of their personal and troop weapons on the open ranges. Lovat, himself a keen shot, insisted on the highest standards, and many hours were spent on the ranges during the long summer nights when, under the wartime 'double-summer-hours' of daylight, it didn't get dark until almost midnight in Scotland. The other was an ambitious landing exercise on the Isle of Arran, which ended in tragedy. The scribe of the D Troop Diary tells the story – he was there.

A, B, C and D Troops embarked on LCTs at Troon to make a landing on the nearby Isle of Arran and attack positions which were being defended by E and F Troops. We were wearing full fighting order with all our weapons and ammo. At last the order came to disembark. We were about 200 yards from the shore, it was bright moonlight, we stepped into deep water, up to our waists, then the water suddenly got deeper – very deep. The LCT had struck a sandbank, but the LCT skipper thought we were on the beach and we would have shallow water. It wasn't so, beyond the narrow sand bank it was so deep we had to swim for it, with all our weapons, equipment and ammo. Once ashore a quick check revealed two men were missing.

It was assumed these men would follow on, and the exercise went ahead. It was only after the completion of the exercise that it was realised that the two were still missing. Searches were made for them, but to no avail. The Commando returned to Troon. Two days later the bodies of the two men, Privates Orchin and Hellyer, were recovered from the beach at Broderick Bay on the island. Realistic Commando training had its risks. The two Commandos were buried with full military honours in Troon. It was a sad blow for all in D Troop, especially as Orchin had recently married. In spite of this tragic accident, the Commando was now at the height of its efficiency and ready for the next challenge – the Dieppe Raid.

CHAPTER FIVE

The Dieppe Raid
– 19 August 1942

Arguably no single land battle in the Second World War has provoked more controversy than the Dieppe Raid on 19 August 1942.

In the course of just a few hours on that sunlit summer day the casualties suffered by the British, Canadian and other Allied forces were horrendous. Some 10,000 men, Navy, Army and Air Force, mounted a five-hour raid on the German-occupied French port of Dieppe. Tactically the raid failed. Of the nearly 5,000 Canadian soldiers, the main landing force, some 65 per cent were casualties, with nearly 1,000 killed and 2,000 marched off as prisoners. The naval losses in ships, craft and men were also severe, while the Allied air losses were equally heavy – 108 planes shot down with 60 pilots lost.

For sixty years historians have sought answers to such questions as 'Were the Germans alerted?', 'Why was the operation really mounted?', 'Who drew up the overall plan and who authorised the operation?', 'Was it a politically motivated operation as opposed to a military one?' and 'What were the real objectives of this disastrous raid?'

A plethora of books and TV documentaries have, for over half a century, attempted to answer these and other related questions. And still the debate continues, for each new study seems to provoke more arguments and further discussion. But this is not the place, or the time, to enter this contentious arena. The object here is to record the role and participation of No. 4 in the operation, the largest amphibious raid in modern history. For make no mistake, from the onset the operation was planned to be nothing more than 'a reconnaissance raid in force'.

Although it is not intended to discuss the full background to the raid, it is helpful to sketch in some details, starting in the spring of 1942, when bowing to political pressure from the Americans and the Russians, the Chiefs of Staff drew up a plan, under the codename Rutter, for a large-scale raid, with limited objectives, on Dieppe. The operation was to take place on 4 July and the Canadians were to provide the main landing force. However, with everything prepared for the operation – all aboard the landing ships and craft – the operation was cancelled on 2 July. There were two major factors that led to this cancellation: first, the onset of bad weather, and second, an attack by German fighters on some of the assembled shipping. However, continued political pressure resulted in revival of the plan. Modified, it reappeared as Operation Jubilee and went ahead under the control of Admiral Lord Louis Mountbatten, Chief of Combined Operations.

The Canadian government were most anxious that their troops, who had been 'sitting around' in the south of England since 1940, should gain battle experience, and it was agreed that the 2nd Canadian Infantry Division would – as in the cancelled Rutter – provide the main assault force.

In that original plan two battalions of the Parachute Regiment were to attack and destroy two enemy coastal batteries dominating the landing beaches at Dieppe, but in the revised plan these tasks were allocated to Nos 3 and 4 Commandos, and also the newly formed 'A' RM Commando (later known as No. 40 RM Commando) was given objectives and tasks in the area of the harbour.

Massive air support was to be provided by sixty-five fighter and fighter-bomber squadrons of the RAF and a further nine squadrons from the Royal Canadian Air Force. In addition to providing the sea transport for the landing forces, the Royal Navy was to make available eight supporting destroyers of the 'Hunt' class armed with torpedoes and 4-inch guns plus gun-boats for close support.

The plan of attack was a simple one, aimed at occupying the town of Dieppe for some few hours, and manning a protective perimeter inland. A number of objectives and tasks were assigned to the units and specialist detachments. These included knocking out gun positions, attacking the airfield, collecting equipment from a radar station, bringing back prisoners and 'invasion barges', collecting intelligence information, and demolition tasks.

An essential factor in the success of the main frontal assault on Dieppe and the flanking resorts of Puys, to the east, and Pourville, to the west, was the destruction of the coastal batteries, 'Goebbels', at Berneval, in the east, by No. 3 Commando, and 'Hess', at Varengeville, in the west, by No. 4.

So much, then, for the background to the raid; now for the account of No. 4 Commando's part in that fateful operation. It is quite a story, but if there is controversy and debate about the overall Jubilee operation, one thing is indisputable: the action of No. 4 was the only land success of the whole operation.

So successful was their operation, codename Cauldron, to destroy Hess battery that the War Office hailed it as 'a classic example of the use of well trained infantry . . . and thoroughness in planning, training and execution', and in February 1943 issued a special training publication for study by infantry officers and NCOs 'in order that all may benefit from the story of a stimulating achievement'. Surely, this was high praise for the action of any single unit.

Indeed, it is such a great story that a book, with the title *The Commandos at Dieppe – Rehearsal for D-Day*, written by Will Fowler, was published in 2002 to coincide with the sixtieth anniversary of the raid and is

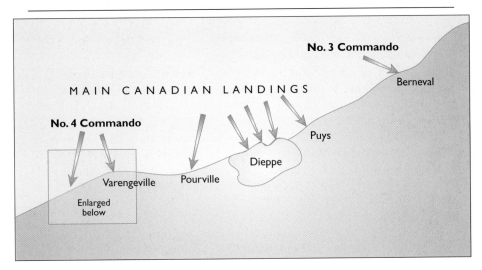

The Dieppe Raid, 1942. Operation Jubilee – Overall plan.

Operation Cauldron – No. 4 Commando.

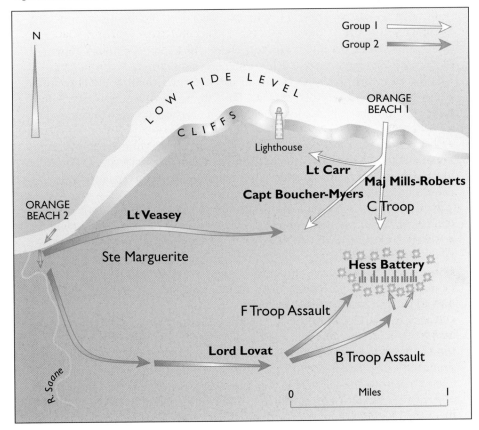

devoted entirely to the part played by No. 4 Commando on that August morning.

The book deals at great length and in great detail with the preparation and action of the Commando – 'a job well done' – which was duly recognised as such by the number of decorations for valour, including one Victoria Cross, and the Battle Honour, 'Dieppe', emblazoned on the Commando Battle Honours Flag that hangs proudly in Westminster Abbey.

In contrast to Will Fowler's book, the aim here is to present the story of Operation Cauldron in just one chapter – no mean task. However, it should be borne in mind that, successful as it was, Cauldron was but a single operation efficiently executed on a single morning, and even if one includes the preparation and training, barely extended to three weeks in No. 4's life from 1940 to 1945.

The story of the Commando's involvement in Cauldron started, appropriately, during a field firing exercise being conducted by the commanding officer, Lord Lovat, at the ruined castle of Dundonald in Ayrshire at the end of July 1942, when Brig Laycock, commanding the Special Service (Commando) Brigade, came personally to inform Lovat that his Commando and No. 3 had been selected for 'a very big job'; he didn't say where or when. He did add that it would involve some cliff climbing and it was so urgent that he (Lovat) and Durnford-Slater (CO of No. 3) must catch the night train to London for a full briefing at Combined Operations Headquarters (COHQ) the following morning.

Lovat takes up the story: 'I caught the night train with John Durnford-Slater to start planning in London. The Commando were to leave within forty-eight hours, destined for Weymouth. There was no time to spare. The job was on.'

In London, next morning, Lovat continues, 'I gave John breakfast at the Guards' Club, a meal punctuated with the wail of air-raid sirens. The war had come a stage nearer and we got a reminder from the Military Police to carry our gas masks walking across to Whitehall.'

At COHQ the two COs were briefed by the new Chief of Staff, General Charles Haydon, who had been in overall command of the Lofoten Raid. In a heated discussion with 'the planners' that followed the general's briefing, Lovat and Durnford-Slater won two very important concessions. First, they would land before daylight, and second – most importantly – each Commando would be independent, planning, preparing and fighting in its own way with no outside interference.

Returning to Troon, Lovat, in conjunction with his second-in-command, Maj Mills-Roberts, and the intelligence officer, Lt Tony Smith, made a thorough appreciation of the problems posed by the projected operation and produced an outline plan. At first sight the problems appeared formidable. 'Hess' battery – the codename for the enemy coastal battery that was the objective for No. 4 – was sited some 1,100 yards inland from the cliffs and consisted of six 150-mm guns set on concrete emplacements, defended by a

Landing craft approaching Orange Beach One below the cliffs to re-embark Lovat and his men after their successful assault on Hess Battery. (*Courtesy of the Imperial War Museum, London –* HU1833)

double-apron barbed wire fence, which appeared to be covered by several machine-gun posts, while the whole battery was overlooked by a flak (anti-aircraft) tower with a gun that could also bring automatic fire down to bear on any ground assault.

There were two possible landing beaches, at Vasterival and Quiberville. The former offered a direct approach, albeit overlooked by daunting and sheer chalk cliffs. Fortunately, there were two scalable steep gullies in the chalk face that had steps down which the pre-war holiday-makers had descended to a 'paradise' of rock pools for the youngsters and a rich harvest of shell-fish for their parents. Obviously, as an anti-invasion precaution, the Germans had removed the steps and filled the gullies with coils of barbed wire and, possibly, mines. This beach was designated Orange One.

About one and a half miles further along the coast to the west, at the eastern end of the seaside village of Quiberville, was another possible landing beach. Here the cliffs gave way to the mouth of the small River Saane, and thus offered a better option; but it was known to be covered by two machine-gun pillboxes, and barbed wire fences had been erected along the beach. In addition, from this beach – codename Orange Two – the distance to Hess battery was at least one and a half miles.

The enemy formation responsible for the coastal defence in this region was, at the time, believed to be the German 110 Infantry Division, with its 813 Battery manning the guns at Varengeville. The strength of this battery was estimated to be between 120 and 175 all ranks. Intelligence sources also reported that at least one infantry company, possibly two, were known to be stationed in the vicinity on coastal defence and anti-invasion duties.

Lovat's basic plan was to split his force into two groups and carry out a simple 'fire and movement' operation on a Commando basis, but limiting the size of his entire fighting force to just four troops (A, B, C and F) plus the Commando specialists, namely signallers, 'medics' and the intelligence section, and some other attached personnel from outside the Commando.

Each of the four fighting troops, however, was made up to full strength, any 'lame ducks' or 'non-runners' being replaced by selected men from D and E troops. As a result the force, including four US Rangers, three French Commandos from No. 10, two signallers from the Canadian Division (to provide a link between the Canadians landing at nearby Pourville and No. 4), an officer and two signallers from 'Phantom Squadron' (to provide links between No. 4, the overall commander of Operation Jubilee and COHQ back in Britain), made a total of 255 all ranks. This total was about the same as the estimated number of enemy in Hess battery and its immediate area. So much for the broad outline; now for more details of the two groups.

Group 1, under Maj Mills-Roberts, consisted of C Troop, a fighting patrol from A Troop, the 3-inch mortar detachment and some of the attached personnel mentioned above. This group would land on Orange One, climb the cliff by one or other of the gullies, make a direct approach to a wood in front of Hess battery and engage it with accurate small-arms fire, thus carrying out its role as the 'fire' element of the plan.

Meanwhile, Group 2, led by Lord Lovat, and consisting of B and F Troops plus the rest of A Troop, would land on Orange Two. Then, after dealing with the beach defences and detaching the A Troop section to act as a protective force between Groups 1 and 2, it would move with all possible speed along the eastern side of the River Saane to a position at the rear of Hess battery, whence it would assault and destroy the guns and the garrison.

After destroying the battery, Group 2 would withdraw through Group 1 down to the gully and to the beach, Orange One, where all the LCAs would be ready to re-embark the whole force.

On 29 July, armed with this basic plan, Lovat left Troon with his advance party for the Weymouth/Portland area which was to be his base for the preparations and training of No. 4 for Operation Cauldron.

Back at Troon, the Commando got ready for yet another 'exercise' and duly warned their landladies that they would be away for about a fortnight on a scheme. So on 1 August the main body left by a special troop train and headed south. On arrival at Portland they embarked on HMS *Prince Albert*, a pre-war Belgian cross-Channel ferry, which had been converted to an LSI carrying seven LCAs and a new support craft (LCS).

Before the Commando's arrival Lovat finalised his Operation Orders. These can be studied at the Public Record Office at Kew, and provide a model of clear, comprehensive yet concise orders. The rest of his advance party prepared to receive the main body and initiate the training arranged.

A full training programme was hurriedly prepared and was ready for troop leaders when they arrived, so they were able to start as soon as they did so on 2 August. Also on that same day four US Rangers and the three 'Phantom' signallers joined the Commando force and were immediately attached to the two troops and HQ with whom they would be for the operation. The four US Rangers had come direct from Achnacarry, where they had been training, so they were fit and 'raring to go'. They would be the first US troops to set foot in Europe and fight the Germans. One cannot over-emphasise the thoroughness of this training; nor can anyone dispute the fact that the training of the next fifteen days provided the key to success on 19 August at Varengeville.

In my previous book, *It Had To Be Tough*, I described that training in some detail. Here the emphasis is on the course of the battle, so the training is summarised. Two main points about the training are, first, that there was collective training for everyone going on the raid regardless of his rank or role in the operation, and second, that there was detailed training to meet the specific requirements of the two groups, whose roles were different. Group 1 had the 'fire' role and Group 2 the 'movement' role, which included the assault on the battery and the destruction of its guns.

The first priority for the collective training was to get everyone to a very high standard of 'battle fitness'. This started straightaway and continued daily with a one-mile run in battle order with weapons – before breakfast.

Next in collective training came LCA loading and landings, with initial practices and then rehearsals: first as drills in daylight, and then in darkness/first light. LCA drills and landings started on 4 August, and next day an exercise was carried out using two beaches (representing Orange One and Orange Two) at Arish Mell Gap and Warbarrow Tout, near Lulworth.

The initial landings were followed up with coordinated landings, based on the actual battle plan for Cauldron. The first attempt was unsuccessful and very disappointing, but greatly improved when repeated at first light on each of the following two mornings. A total of eight such landings was carried out, culminating with full dress rehearsals, before Lovat and Mullineux were satisfied – and they weren't easily satisfied.

In Group 1, as the 'fire' element, their next obvious priority was 'skill at arms' – the handling and firing of all their troop weapons to be able to produce accurate and well-controlled fire at opportunity targets in the battery at ranges between 200 and 300 yards. In this crucial requirement their concentrated 'stint' on the ranges in Ayrshire just a couple of weeks earlier was most opportune.

Just for this operation the firepower of C Troop was boosted by the allocation of two more Brens, and again the recent range practices, during which everyone had fired the Bren, helped Dawson make choices for the Nos 1 and 2 on these extra Brens. Lovat also decided that C Troop would take four EY rifles fitted with cup dischargers to boost the troop's own mortar fire.

That brings us to this handy little weapon, the 2-inch mortar, in which I had a vested interest, but more about that later. Suffice it here to add that our mortar men, Privates Dale and Horne, aided by a generous allowance of ammunition, were able, during the field firing 'shoots', to get some nine bombs out of ten in a square of about 10 yards by 10 at the optimum range of 250 yards.

Finally, on this aspect of weapons in Group 1, mention should be made of the 3-inch mortar detachment under Lt 'Carpet Slippers' Ennis. The crew of this mortar had to concentrate not only on the firing of this heavy and cumbersome weapon, plus the carrying of the bombs, but also on devising – and practising – ways and means of getting the weapon and ammunition, plus OP equipment, ashore over a pebbled beach, up a cliff face and into action.

Common to both groups was the use of Bangalore torpedoes, required to blow gaps and clear a passage in the gullies, and also for Group 2 to deal with barbed wire obstacles on the beach and the defensive perimeter of the battery. Men had to be selected and trained for these specific tasks.

The nominated leading section of C Troop in Group 1 had to be prepared to climb/scramble up the gully; this was the reason for selecting Dawson's troop for Group 1. C Troop had specialised in rock climbing and mountaineering and was recognised as the Commando climbing troop. Most of this training had, however, been on solid rock faces such as those in Snowdonia, and apart from some climbing on the granite sea cliffs in the Tenby area, the men hadn't tackled any coastal cliffs like those around the port of Dieppe. But on the Dorset coast around Lulworth there were chalk cliffs, so C Troop took advantage of this bonus too. Being responsible for covering the withdrawal of the whole force, C Troop worked out and rehearsed a phased withdrawal using plenty of smoke from the mortars and canisters.

Group 2's priorities were obviously different. To start with, their standard of battle fitness needed to be higher, for they had that one and a half to two mile dash over uneven countryside to outflank Hess battery. So in addition to the 'early-morning jaunts' they had runs carrying all their weapons, token explosives and Bangalore torpedoes.

The A Troop section attached to Group 2 (under Lt 'Fairy' Veasey), having been allotted the task of overcoming the pillboxes on the beach, and using scaling ladders and 'rabbit' netting to overcome barbed wire obstacles, practised their role with live ammunition and grenades.

Both B and F Troops, under Capts Webb and Pettiward, the main assaulting and demolition troops, had to practise simple little section and sub-section tactics to deal with any opposition en route to the battery. This involved plenty of short-range firing at snap and opportunity targets, which were improvised on the ranges of Lulworth.

Under Lt 'Jock' McKay (one of the original volunteers as a sergeant in the old Weymouth days, now commissioned), the six NCOs chosen to demolish the six German guns visited a local coastal battery to familiarise themselves with the layout of a battery and the vital parts of 'an artillery piece' with a view to destroying it. Based on this and other information applicable to the enemy weapons they were able to prepare 'made-to-measure' charges for the operation.

Life aboard the *Prince Albert* during the boat and landing training was hectic, but well organised. By now, of course, all were well accustomed to life on board and, fortunately, the *Prince Albert* was an efficiently run and happy ship. So from the moment we stepped on board, when Lt Mullineux reported in his log that 'No 4 Commando, about 250 strong, have joined the ship and they seem to be a nice crowd of toughs', cooperation and relations between the 'matelots' and the 'brown jobs' were harmonious and cordial. It made such a difference and augured well for the operation. Morale was high and confidence grew daily.

Fortunately, the weather helped too, because during the whole of the training period it was glorious; practically every evening a hard day's training ended with a welcome swim in the sea.

On 11 August the troops, having completed the amphibious side of the training to the satisfaction of Lovat and Mullineux, disembarked and moved into billets, while the *Prince Albert* docked in Portland. There, as part of a cover plan, a dummy funnel was erected and the ship flew the 'Red Duster', the red ensign of the Merchant Navy.

From the billets training continued, unabated, in the area. It was during this period that three French Commandos from No. 10 joined the unit. Their main task was liaison with the local French people and the gathering of intelligence information on the German forces and dispositions in the area.

Throughout the whole of this period security in the Commando was very tight; extra precautions were imposed, and Lt Smith, the intelligence officer, even arranged for a detachment of an outside field security unit to be stationed in Weymouth as an extra security-monitoring measure.

Very early on the morning of 18 August the Commando paraded in 'fighting order', with all troop weapons, for yet another '48-hour exercise', the landladies having been paid for the week's accommodation the night before.

Waiting for the troops was a convoy of troop-carrying vehicles. JED Price, now one of Ennis's mortar men, records a long day spent in a circular/detour journey from Weymouth to Southampton – about sixty miles – that took hours.

At long last we stopped and received the order to dismount. We were in Southampton Docks, and alongside was our ship, the *Prince Albert*.

We were aboard in no time, and within an hour were hard at work. There was ammo to be issued, weapons to be cleaned, LCAs to be loaded, and a hundred and one odd jobs to be done.

About seven o'clock in the evening we paraded on deck to hear a talk by Lord Louis Mountbatten who calmly informed us, 'As you shouldn't know, but have no doubt guessed by now, there's a party on tonight!'

He told us it was to be the biggest raid yet. We had an extremely important part to play. We were to destroy a battery of guns over-looking Dieppe. These guns were to be destroyed at all costs, and if they were not it would be impossible to carry out the main attack. He wished us luck and then departed. Well that was that! Now let's get on with it.

Now for the first time we knew where we were going. In spite of later reports, none of us knew the actual location of the raid until then. Following Mountbatten's departure Lovat held his final 'O' group and for the first time revealed the precise location of the battery to his troop leaders. Troop leaders then held their own briefings and everyone was 'put in the picture' and also got the chance to study the model and aerial photos.

In spite of the pressure, as TSM of C Troop, to ensure that all the preparations were being completed, I did manage to go up on deck in the last rays of a setting sun, on that perfect summer evening, to gaze inshore in the direction of Shirley, a district in my home town of Southampton, where my widowed mother lived just a couple of miles away, but was oblivious to my nearby presence, or the purpose of that presence. I stood there for a few minutes with my thoughts, then went down below to rejoin the troop and, with Capt Dawson and Lt Style, check all our final preparations. By now this was hardly necessary, but nothing could be left to chance.

Preparations went on until late into the night, by which time we had set sail and had already cleared the Isle of Wight to start meeting up with the rest of the RN force assembling for the raid. It was a clear night and the sea was dead calm. Just the night for a trip across the Channel.

It was almost midnight before some got their heads down for some 'kip'; others had settled down by 2200 hrs, but neither group had much sleep for reveille was at 0145 hrs. Although a good hearty breakfast was available, a few preferred a full mug of hot, sweet tea – and a fag. Then it was 'get ready' – watches were synchronised and the password 'Monkey' and the countersign 'Nuts' were given to all. With the tannoy announcement, 'Troops to boat stations', we were off. The die had been cast. In single file along those familiar passageways and up the darkened stairs we went, almost automatically, as we had done so many times during the past couple of weeks. Out into the pitch-black night and along the deck to clamber into our allotted places in the landing craft. Some of the heavier gear, weapons and Bangalores, had already been stored alongside the places of those detailed to carry them. We didn't wait long before the command to lower away was given, then with a subdued splash our LCA hit the water, a 'rev' on the engines and we were on our way. . . .

All went well as our flotilla headed towards the final run-in to the French coast until about 0340 hrs when, at some distance from our port bow, there was a spectacular display of starshell and tracer fire. This could mean only one thing: the run-in on our left flank had encountered opposition.

No. 3 Commando, destined for Goebbels battery, in their mixed flotilla of LCPs ('Eurekas') and a light RN escort, had bumped into an armed escort of enemy ships. Helpless and unable to retaliate, No. 3's flotilla was crippled, scattered and unable to continue with the original plan. Nevertheless, two small parties, one under the leadership of Maj Young, did manage to land on their planned beach and courageously advanced to engage the Goebbels battery for some time with effective small-arms fire. It was a commendable achievement. Young and his party were able to withdraw succesfully but the others weren't.

Unaware of the consequences of this naval action, No. 4's flotilla had an uneventful run-in with no enemy inteference or navigational problems, the latter, wrote Mullineux in his post-operation report, 'Thanks largely to the fact that the Porte D'Ailly light showed for about five minutes in every quarter of an hour, and the harbour lights of Dieppe kept gaily burning.'

Undetected and unopposed the LCAs of Mills-Roberts's Group 1 approach their landing point, Orange Beach One – right place and right time – just before first light. The gullies in the cliff are just visible. (*Drawing by Cpl Brian Mullen*)

In contrast to the unopposed landing on Orange Beach One, the Canadian tanks landing on the heavily pebbled beach at Dieppe became sitting targets for the German anti-tank weapons positioned along the sea front of the town. (*Courtesy of the Imperial War Museum, London –* HU1905)

As a result Group 1 landed on Orange One at the right time, just before daylight, as planned, dry-shod and unopposed. The beach was quickly cleared and Sgt Langlands's section, under Lt Style, started to scramble up the left-hand gully, but after a short while reported that it was impossible to go further because it was so full of barbed wire. So they turned their attention to the other gully and found this a better proposition. But it still required a Bangalore to blow a gap. In the event one was not sufficient, so a second was detonated. Fortunately, the noise of the detonations was muffled by some RAF aircraft flying overhead. No time was lost scrambling up the gully, the leading men clearing a passage and keeping a wary eye for mines.

Once at the top, Langlands's section started to establish their little defensive perimeter, while Mills-Roberts and the rest of C Troop pressed on towards the battery, making enquiries and searches at some of the houses. In this the French Commandos were very helpful, and thrilled to be back in France.

In the context of English/French language, my two mortar men, Dale and Horne, thought it was most obliging of the Germans to put up warning signs bearing a skull and crossbones below which were the words 'ACHTUNG – MINEN' followed by 'DANGER – MINES', not realising that the last two words, spelt the same, were pronounced differently in French, but, of course, meant the same.

The advance up the narrow road to the battery was going nicely and according to plan. Group 1 had to be in position to bring coordinated and concentrated fire on the battery by 0615 hrs, 15 minutes before Lovat's main assault. But then at 0545 hrs the battery suddenly fired a six-gun salvo.

The ground shook and the shells whistled overhead – out to sea. A minute or two later Mills-Roberts's signaller gave him a message from Lt Smith, the IO, who was on Orange One, to the effect that the main convoy was in sight and apparently in range of the battery.

Mills-Roberts reacted immediately. He decided to speed up the advance and engage the battery as soon as possible – ahead of the timetable. Accompanied by Lt Ennis, their signallers and the 3-inch mortar OP/linesmen, Mills-Roberts rushed forward to the wood in front of Hess battery, having sent his batman/runner L/Cpl Smith back to instruct Style to stop the searches and bring the fire sections of C Troop, including my 2-inch mortar team, forward immediately. Within minutes C Troop were taking up positions in the area of the wood and also in the old deserted holiday home, 'La Volière'.

Sgt McCarthy and his three Bren gun teams, the No. 1s of which, Cpl Wallis, L/Cpls Humphries and Hampton, were all marksmen, were selecting their firing positions, with McCarthy detailing their specific targets which they could now see in front of them. Likewise Sgt Lindley, who was in charge of the three snipers, was also getting them forward into position.

Meanwhile, however, the battery fired another three rounds, again out to sea and over our heads, but still unaware of our nearby presence.

At a single given signal the Brens and the riflemen opened fire. There were plenty of targets in the unsuspecting battery. Sgt Lindley was with the pre-war Reading butcher, now C Troop's star sniper, L/Cpl Dickie Mann, when he calmly took aim and claimed the first victim of his 'own private war' with the enemy in Hess battery, at a distance of about 130 yards.

At the same time, working his way to a position to the west of the wood, but towards the battery, whence he could get a clear view, Gnr McDonough, with his Boys A/Tk rifle, and accompanied by his No. 2, Gnr 'Barney' Davies, opened up on the flak tower. Firing the armour-piercing .55 rounds, McDonough scored several direct hits, which silenced it for a while, but it did open up again before being later silenced for good by Group 2.

By now I had already arrived at the wood with the 2-inch mortar duo, late because we had not received the 'hurry-up' message. We immediately got ready for action. Horne unloaded the HE bombs and we were all set. We had no pre-arranged fire plan, so I decided to aim for the centre of the battery, which was well in range. It was a fortuitous decision. The first shot fell just short, the second slightly to the left, but the corrected third landed right in the centre. Luckily – it was pure luck – we had scored a 'bull's eye'. The results were spectacular and decisive. That third bomb had exploded among the bagged cordite charges laid out by the side of one of the guns – a careless and fatal mistake.

A.B. Austen, a war correspondent who had landed with us and was in the beachhead on Orange One, later wrote: 'There was an explosion – louder and longer than anything we had heard that morning. It made us crouch immediately. It seemed to be the mother of all explosions.'

More importantly, Hess battery did not fire again. But the battery garrison resolutely fought on, as Lord Lovat and his Group 2 were rapidly moving to positions behind the guns. This group had had a smooth and quiet run-in towards beach Orange Two, obligingly guided by the lighthouse. And they, too, landed on the right beach at the right time, but not unopposed.

Their first party, led by Veasey, was fired upon as they swarmed over the wire, with the aid of the rabbit netting. They had casualties, including L/Cpl Heckman, who had been married only a few weeks earlier. The LCS, which was in support of this group, retaliated with covering fire and this enabled Veasey's men, with the aid of the tubular ladder, to scale the bank and knock out the two machine-guns.

Meanwhile, the rest of Group 2 were landing a little further to the west of this beach. Lt Gilchrist, who had recently joined the Commando from Achnacarry and was in Webb's troop, takes up the story as his section were touching down on the beach. 'A stream of tracer bullets suddenly leapt out at us . . . a mortar bomb thumped as our LCA grated on the shingle . . . Webb cursed and clutched his shoulder, hit by a mortar fragment', but they swept on up the beach. None faltered; they all knew that to hesitate, or go to ground, was fatal.

On to the wire, led by selected men in B Troop who wore leather jerkins and carried the rabbit netting, their aim was to flatten the wire by

Having put Hess Battery out of action the Commando withdrew to Orange Beach for the re-embarkation, seen here being effected under cover of smoke. Enemy in the area of the lighthouse, towards the right on the cliff top, continued to fire on the flotilla until it was out to sea, but it was ineffective. (*Drawing by Cpl Brian Mullen*)

wrenching, rolling and lying on it, to enable their follow-up mates – 'like loose forwards following a rugger ball' – to rush over the wire.

Gilchrist, having crossed the wire in the wake of Sgt 'Fergie' Watkins's recce party, suffered a sickening fate – his trousers started to fall down! But, clutching his trousers in one hand and his Tommy gun in the other, he raced inland until he got the chance to hitch them up – and carry on.

'Les' Lilley well remembers the reception they got on landing: 'as the "muck" was coming down on us . . . it seemed to be coming from the direction of the lighthouse, probably on fixed lines, making the beach a "lively place"'. But what he remembers most vividly was the coolness of Lovat, who was but a few feet away from him on landing: 'His coolness seemed to be imperturbable . . . he was so calm . . . there he was in corduroy slacks with his rifle, stripped down to the essentials . . . he clearly had the air of absolute confidence. . . .' Others also record similar tales of Lovat's coolness and inspiring leadership.

Over the wire the Commando group paused to regroup by the road. They had suffered eight casualties on that beach. As the group continued its advance, the enemy's fire was diverted by three RAF Bostons, which luckily happened to pass overhead. These planes could have been the same ones that had muffled the sound of C Troop's Bangalores in the gully on Orange One.

Having cleared the beach and led by B Troop, with Lovat's little HQ of adjutant, signallers, runners and 'minders' between B Troop and Pettiward's F Troop, the group pressed on at a steady trot along the east bank of the river, as planned. But it was hard going, through long grass and over boggy ground – 'just like running through rice pudding', recalls one of B Troop.

All that hard training and those early-morning runs with full loads were paying off, Lovat later wrote:

> One of the remarkable things was the speed we got around, considering that we might have run into trouble – and didn't. Although we went through German infantry located on both sides, we weren't even shot at once after we left the beach. We ran the whole damned way, just stopping occasionally to regroup, but nobody got out of breath and we didn't have to wait for any laggards. These chaps were trained like athletes and to run the course, and my word, they did!

But, as we shall see later, that luck didn't hold.

Meanwhile, after dealing with the machine-guns overlooking the beach, Veasey's section went along the Quiberville/Ste Marguerite road to cut the telephone wires connecting the enemy locations in this area to the battery HQ.

Selected as the man to cut the telephone wires, little Tpr Finney, under heavy enemy sniper fire, climbed up and on to the broad shoulders of the six-foot-plus US Ranger, Cpl Brady – how they escaped unscathed was truly miraculous – and successfully cut the wires. Finney was later awarded the Military Medal, but Brady confessed to being more concerned by the possibility of Finney's boots ripping off his ears.

Later this section worked their way towards Orange One and Group 1's location to clear any enemy in this area who might be planning a counter-attack and also to link up with the rest of their troop, which, under Capt Bill Boucher-Myers, were to take up a position around the important cross-roads in Ste Marguerite.

Moving up to this crossroads, Boucher-Myers's party managed to sight, surprise and ambush an enemy patrol, but not without some casualties, among whom was 'Charlie' Williams, the TSM. It was in this action that the two US Rangers, Koons and Szima, became the first American soldiers to kill an enemy soldier in Europe, in this war.

Williams, although badly wounded, was one of those fortunate ones to be taken back safely to the beach and evacuated. Several others, also badly wounded, had to be left, where they were unselfishly looked after by Jim, one of two Pascale brothers, both Commando 'medics', who, knowing full well he would be captured and made a POW, remained with his wounded comrades to tend them. His brother, Ted, escorted some of the other wounded back to Orange One. Tragically, Ted, who was with No. 4 on D-Day, was killed on the beaches, and Jim only learnt of the death of his brother when he was released from POW camp in 1945.

Another sub-section of A Troop, under the command of Lt Carr, had been given the task of cutting the land telephone line between the enemy OP on the lighthouse and the battery, which they succeeded in doing in two places, so that it could not be quickly spliced. On completing this task they joined up with the rest of their troop in the area of the crossroads.

On reaching the point which Lovat had chosen for his two assault troops to split in order to attack the battery, from two different directions, B Troop were able to take a covered approach along the edge of a wood, but F Troop had a more difficult approach with far less cover.

As B Troop skirted the wood, they could see the flak tower which McDonough had engaged with the A/Tk rifle, but now from their different angle they spotted a couple of Germans moving about on it, obviously out of sight to McDonough, and with their gun probably still operational the Germans now posed a threat to the assault troops. So Webb called up a couple of his riflemen and 'Chalkie' Blunden, with his Boys A/Tk rifle, to deal with it.

Watching, Gilchrist recalls having the satisfaction of seeing a German soldier topple over the edge and fall to the ground, 'like an Indian in a western movie'. A few minutes later B Troop came across and surprised a machine-gun post, manned by two Germans, which they destroyed without loss, and continued to their start line for the assault, where they reported back to Lovat, at 0615 hrs, that they were in position and ready to charge the battery.

After leaving B Troop to make their way to their final forming-up position, F Troop came across a small group of the enemy, apparently preparing to mount a counter-attack on Group 1. Caught in the act and surprised, the enemy were routed, offering no resistance as Tommy gunners and Bren gunner, firing from the hip, charged into them.

But then, as F Troop carried on, their luck changed. Moving between some buildings in a small orchard, they, in turn, were surprised as they came under heavy fire from short range.

'Ossie' Hughes, who was carrying a Bangalore torpedo, recalls: 'Capt Pettiward and Lt McDonald [both highly regarded and popular troop officers] were killed outright . . . TSM Bill Stockdale was leading us through a hedge when a stick grenade landed on his foot, badly wounding him, but he kept firing from a sitting position.'

At this stage it was fortunate that Capt Pat Porteous and his 'reserve-link-up' team were at hand, ready for him to take over in such a situation. However, Porteous and his men had also come under fire, and suffered casualties. He had been been shot at very close range; the bullet had passed through his hand and into his lower arm. Undaunted, he closed with his assailant, succeeded in disarming him and killed him with his own bayonet, thereby saving the life of one of his sergeants, on whom the German had turned. Furthermore, the other sergeant in Porteous's little group, 'Honk' Horne, and another of his men, Pte George Cook, were also badly wounded – so badly that they were left behind, 'presumed dead' – but they did survive, thanks to some excellent care by the French/German hospital staff and subsequently fully recovered – in captivity.

Unperturbed and disregarding his own wounds, Porteous rushed over to F Troop, now without an officer or TSM, rallied them and, leading them from the front, dashed over open ground to their start line. They, too, were on time, and ready for the final assault.

Lovat's two troops were now both in their positions and as they fixed bayonets, a pre-arranged RAF strike came in to strafe the battery. From their position, too, Group 1 intensified its fire, which by now was augmented by the 3-inch mortar.

Right on time at 0630 hrs, up went Lovat's Verey-light signal: the assault was going in. Everyone in Group 1 knew what it meant, and stopped firing into the battery position, while B and F Troops started their spirited bayonet charge on to Hess battery. It was a dramatic moment.

B Troop, led by the wounded Webb, made for the area of the battery buildings to seek out the enemy and destroy them, while F Troop, plus the six demolition men, were to make straight for the guns. Porteous was still in the lead (he was one of the first to reach the guns), but was wounded again, this time in the thigh. However, he kept going, urging his men to continue on to the last gun. Shot once more, he passed out, but not before F Troop had accounted for all the gun crews, and the demolitionists were beginning to start their own special tasks.

The return of No. 4 Commando after the raid on the quayside at Newhaven, the soldiers in steel helmets are on dock security duties. Most of those in the foreground are from C Troop. On the extreme right, hatless, is L/Bdr 'Dusty' Maund, batman, 'minder' and runner for Robert Dawson from 1940 to 1945. (*Courtesy of the Imperial War Museum, London* – H22590)

Porteous's gallantry and inspirational leadership in rallying F Troop, after the loss of their two officers and TSM, then leading them, under enemy fire, to the start line and subsequently in the bayonet charge to rout the crews of the guns – in spite of being twice wounded – earned him the award of the Victoria Cross.

Those responsible for demolishing the guns began their final preparations, which were simplified with the made-up charges prepared back in Weymouth. As Sgt Bill Portman explained, 'all we had to do was to open the breach, make sure there was a shell in it to take the blast of the explosives and that would do a really good job'. Always one prepared for the worst, Portman had also brought a ready-made limpet charge, which he now placed on the side of the barrel of the gun.

The charges, in specially made metal containers of the same size as the breach, contained the malleable explosive '808', and were fitted with just one-minute fuses. 'They all fitted like a glove – just like a glove', McKay commented in his post-operations report.

Cpl John Skerry, the only non-RE demolition man of this team, had just lost his battle comrade, Pte McGann, fatally wounded, as they fought their way through to the guns. But Skerry had a job to do; his gun was the furthest away. Off he ran, alone, to No. 6 gun. Once there he inserted and prepared his charge, then dashed to cover. His gun was the last to be put out of action: No. 4 Commando's mission had been accomplished – Hess battery had been destroyed.

But there were jobs still to be tackled, including searching the battery offices for any intelligence information. Joe Burnett was one of B Troop involved in the searching; he recalls:

I tossed a grenade into the guard room, when it went off, I dashed in, there was an alarm clock on a table – still going – I picked it up and stuck it into my blouse pocket. Going home later in the LCA as I was snoozing the alarm went off . . . everyone got a shock . . . and thought it was a bomb.

There was a short period of reorganising, during which time the medical officer, Capt Walker, and three of his 'medics' were called forward from the beachhead with stretchers, but in the meantime, doors were ripped off their hinges to carry Pat Porteous and a couple of the other badly wounded back to the beach.

Lovat gave orders that the dead of No. 4, who had fallen in the assault, be brought together and a Union Jack was draped over them; the German dead were left where they had fallen.

It was time to withdraw. This went according to Dawson's well-rehearsed plan – in spite of continued enemy sniping and mortar fire. The assault troops of Lovat's group were relieved to pass through C Troop. Les Lilley wrote:

There was C Troop and people we knew . . . some were wearing camouflage face veils because they were prime targets for German snipers, but the sight of our chaps gave us confidence and we thought at last we were all right. We knew they would massacre anyone who tried to get us. . . .

Once Lovat's group, carrying their seriously wounded on the stretchers, and aided by three German prisoners, had passed through, C Troop left the wood, leaving one of their dead, L/Cpl Garthwaite, behind. He had been killed by a mortar bomb fragment while attending to a wounded comrade.

On the quayside Lord Lovat discusses the action with Capt Bill Boucher-Myers, flanked left by one of the Phantom signallers, and, right, fair-haired Len Ruskin, TSM Chatteraway, centre, and Sgt Freddy Ham; these three were in the B Troop assault on the guns. (*Courtesy of the Imperial War Museum, London* – H22584)

C Troop started to thin out, down the road past the Hotel Terrasse (still there – and prospering – they have quite a collection of memorabilia of the attack on the battery in the hotel) and on to where Langlands had his cliff-top perimeter. Taking great care with the stretcher cases, they all scrambled down the gully and on to Orange One, where offshore, ready to come in, was Mullineux's flotilla of LCAs.

Throughout this final withdrawal phase, continuous, but largely inaccurate, enemy mortar fire was brought down on the flanks of the road to the beach and on the beach itself. Fortunately there were no further casualties during this stage; perhaps the inaccurate fire may be credited to Ennis's counter mortar fire, which continued right up to the last possible moment.

In accordance with the planned withdrawal, smoke generators were set off to screen the final re-embarkation, which started at about 0730 hrs. Among

Safely back at Newhaven, Capt Webb (OC B Troop), who was wounded by a mortar shrapnel on landing on Orange Beach 2, talks to Lt Coulson, then one of his section officers but later promoted to lead F Troop for D-Day. Lord Lovat can be seen hatless, pointing. (*Courtesy of the Imperial War Museum, London* – H22581)

the first to be loaded into LCAs were the badly wounded, who were subsequently transferred to a destroyer for further treatment and a quicker return to England.

By 0815 hrs the re-embarkation was completed, the last to withdraw being Capt Dawson and Langlands's section. Ironically, as the last LCAs pulled away from the beach they came under fire, from a light flak gun, machine-gun and other small-arms fire from the lighthouse, which up to this time had not been active. This fire, although it continued until the flotilla was about one and a half miles out to sea, was ineffective.

No. 4 was on its way back to England; the sea was calm and the sun shone, but overhead there was plenty of aerial activity as RAF and German fighters fought their duels, while to the east onshore smoke and the sound of explosions provided evidence of bitter fighting there, although at this stage

One of the German prisoners, Marsinak, captured in Hess Battery and then used as a stretcher-bearer on the withdrawal, is escorted ashore in the company of three Bren gunners from C Troop. (*Courtesy of the Imperial War Museum, London* – H22597)

none of us knew how disastrous the landings on the beaches of Dieppe and the flanking beaches at Pourville and Puys had been.

All we knew, and quite frankly all we cared about, was that Operation Cauldron had been a success and we were on our way back home.

Mullineux's naval report provides an apt summary of our trip back:

There were no further events of importance on the return passage. There was no doubt that the sight of anything up to sixty friendly fighters in the sky filled us with great confidence, but an even happier sight was the white cliffs of England . . . at 1745 hrs our flotilla of landing craft entered and made secure in Newhaven harbour.

Perhaps the concluding remarks of Mullineux's report, coming from an officer of 'the Senior Service', provides a fitting note on which to end the story of Operation Cauldron: 'I am convinced that the success of the operation carried out by No. 4 Commando was due, in very large measure, to sound and intensive preliminary training for the job in hand and to the determined leadership by their officers. . . .' My only comment would be to add 'and to the courageous and resolute manner all ranks carried out their allotted tasks'. No. 4 Commando's action on 19 August 1942 at Varengeville had surely earned them a place in the history books of the Second World War, rightfully under the heading of 'classic operations of battle'.

CHAPTER SIX

Post-Dieppe and the End of the Lovat Era

The whole Commando, less those badly wounded who had been transferred to a destroyer off the coast of France for a speedier return to England, landed at Newhaven.

There to meet the Commando was Brig Bob Laycock, commander of all Commando units at the time. He looked grim-faced as he discussed the operation with Lovat. He knew more than we did.

We didn't stay long on the quayside, although official press photographers and reporters took photos and held one or two selected interviews. Some of those photographs of the return have become well-known historic war pictures; indeed, a few are included in this book.

Lord Lovat, Mills-Roberts and the adjutant went off to London to report to Mountbatten and his staff at HQ Combined Operations.

The rest of us were transported to a tented transit camp for a welcome meal and a night's rest before we started to sort ourselves out next morning. It was then we learnt of the fate of some of our missing comrades. We stood in silence as we remembered them. Our losses were twenty-three killed and missing. Of these, although we didn't know at the time, six were severely wounded, but were to be well treated and nursed back to health by German/French medical staff, and then interned as POWs.

During the day of the raid there had been brief reports on the radio of Allied landings on the coast of France, but few details. Next day, however, it was different. There were widespread radio and press reports, but the appalling losses suffered by the Canadians were not mentioned. Of course, one has to remember that under wartime censorship and the need for favourable home-front propaganda the news had to be slanted in favour of the Allies. However, reading some of the reports one would have had the impression that the landing force consisted mainly of 'Commandos'.

Typical of the press reports for 20 August is that of the *Daily Mirror*. The banner headline read: 'BIG HUN LOSSES IN 9-HR DIEPPE BATTLE'. This was followed by: 'After the nine-hour battle yesterday, in the biggest Commando landing yet made on occupied territory, Canadian, American, British and French troops were last night returning to England.'

In the next paragraph, mention is made of the destruction of the six-gun battery with ammunition dump, and the destruction of a radar station and

The post-Dieppe Raid parade, Troon, 5 September 1942, when Brig Bob Laycock read out a congratulatory message from George VI and all ranks of No. 4 wore the green berets for the first time, although the officers wore their regimental headdress as the officer-type green berets had not yet arrived! (*Author's Collection*)

flak battery. The impression is given that all the landing forces re-embarked safely: 'The Allied forces re-embarked only six minutes late on scheduled time . . .', and so it went on. Consequently none of us in the Commando knew, and neither did the general public, of the huge losses of men, tanks, ships and aircraft until much later.

Fortunately, in spite of these shortcomings, fundamental home truths and bitter lessons were learnt, and applied to the future planning of the invasion of Normandy in 1944. First and foremost among these lessons was the impracticability of capturing a defended port, so on Operation Overlord the Allies took their own, namely, the portable Mulberry Harbour.

Meanwhile, after we had sorted ourselves out in the transit camp, we were given ration cards and some pay and sent off on a short leave, with rail warrants from our leave addresses to return to Troon. There we got back to a heroes' welcome; by now the good news of the Dieppe Raid was clearly centred on Lovat's Commandos' successful destruction of a six-gun battery and its ammunition dump.

The first priority was to reorganise the troops, as there were gaps in some, where there had been casualties. F Troop was most severely affected, with the loss of two officers and the TSM. Lt Veasey took over command. He was quite a character, a mountain of a man, with a king-size moustache. Tough and fit, he excelled at the strenuous sports of rugby and boxing. However, his boxing career was cut short earlier in Troon, when, fighting in the Commando trials to choose a unit team, he had knocked out Bdr Hinde of D Troop. Counted out, Hinde left the ring and later went back to his billet, but during the night he had a massive brain haemorrhage and died. We were all shattered when, on muster parade next morning, we were told of this tragic death. None was more upset than Veasey – he never went into the ring again to box. Bdr Hinde was rightly remembered in the Commando's own Roll of Honour.

Lovat decided, while this reorganisation was being effected, that the Commando should have a spell of 'spit and polish', plus some foot drill, in preparation for a special parade and march-past for Brig Laycock when he visited on 5 September. This parade was to be remembered by all who took part in it for another reason – it was the first parade when we wore green berets.

Ever since the Commandos had been formed there had been a desire to have standard headdress. One or two Commandos had solved the problem by wearing the tam-o'-shanter, but this was not acceptable for those with a majority of non-Scots. Now, some two years after the formation of the Commandos, they eventually had their own distinctive headdress – the coveted green beret – which has subsequently become the symbol of elite forces worldwide.

The parade on 5 September was held on the playground of a local school in Troon, instead of the local football ground, which was usually used for Commando parades, but at the time the latter was far too wet and muddy for such a ceremonial occasion. Morale in the unit was high, and the turnout

Forty years on . . . veterans at reunion, Ste Marguerite, 19 August 1982. Left to right: Jim Pascale, James Dunning, head of John Skerry, Eric Cross MBE, Bill Boucher-Myers DSO, Robert Dawson DSO, Pat Porteous VC, George Cook, Pete Burrows, Donald Gilchrist and Maurice Chauvet. (*Pete Burrows*)

and drill were excellent. Even the RSM was satisfied, although reluctant to say so until afterwards.

Laycock congratulated all ranks on their success at Varengeville and then read out a special message from the king, George VI, in which he sent his congratulations. It must have been one of the rare occasions when a single unit received such a special message from the monarch.

Finally, to sum up our part in the Dieppe Raid, I can do no better than offer two reports, one German, the other British. The British report is that of a well-respected war journalist, A.B. Austen, who accompanied No. 4 on the operation. Both extracts are taken from Fowler's well-researched book, the only one devoted entirely to Operation Cauldron. He quotes the German LXXXI Army Corps' action report on the events of 19 August, which was written two days later. It starts by commenting that in the raid the selection of the landing beaches was vital, and more important than the 'mass of men and material', for the latter should 'not be considered so important as choosing an unexpected locality and the fighting value of the first troops who will first touch land'. It then comments, in a most complimentary way: 'this is proved by the fact that the action of No. 4 Commando of 200 men [*sic*] succeeded, while the action at Dieppe with ten times as many men landed, supported by tanks, and was a complete failure. . . .' The quote ends: 'The combat efficiency of the Commandos was very high. They are well trained and fought with real spirit. It is reported that they showed great skill in climbing steep coastal cliffs.' Coming from an enemy source, in war, it is a nice tribute.

Austen's summary focuses more on assessing the character of Lovat, yet acknowledging the importance of planning:

> As with most fine soldiers, I think there was a little of the poet or artist in him. He had the marauding chief's satisfaction at having destroyed his enemies, but his main pleasure was having completed a perfect, rounded, neatly finished and timed little operation, a tactical model of amphibious warfare.

In a subsequent enemy proclamation after the raid the Germans offered a reward for the capture of the Commando leader, Lord Lovat, dead or alive!

With the raid and parade behind us, it was 'back to business' – the business of more training. However, Lovat, who was well aware of the dangers of complacency following the success and publicity, was determined that this continuity training should be demanding yet innovative, stimulating and challenging. So as a 'starter' he sent the troops away 'On Commando' to locations of the troop leaders' choice. They had to make all the necessary arrangements, as normal, for the movement and administration of their troops.

We, in C Troop, were split into two parties. One, the bulk of the troop, went to Settle in North Yorkshire, where the nearby Dales provided plenty

On the occasion of the fiftieth anniversary of the Dieppe Raid the local community of Ste Marguerite renamed the village square Place du 4e. Commando – No. 4 Commando Square. (*Author's Collection*)

of varied and rugged training areas and facilities. Our little group, of just eight, opted for the Lake District, where under the guidance of our mentor climber and mountaineer, Sgt Langlands, we spent an energetic fortnight rock climbing and fell walking. We had taken airborne folding bikes with us as we had no other transport, and they were easy to handle on the train to Windermere, via Glasgow.

Other troops went off to locations that included Buxton in the Peak District and bases near Harrogate and Scarborough in Yorkshire. As always, we made our own arrangements for billets – and very successful they were too. In most of the venues the troops managed to organise a Friday night hop in the local hall before departing.

Spirits were high on returning to Troon. With Dieppe now behind us and all feeling refreshed by the 'On Commando' breaks, we settled down to training once more. However, as a result of the reshuffles and various other factors we spent the next few weeks on what one might call 'revision of basic skills' and also Commando-run cadre courses for junior NCOs to replace those lost on the raid, others who had been promoted to senior ranks and the few who left to take commissions.

At the end of September No. 4 received a very special intake of newly trained Commandos fresh from Achnacarry – the 'Police intake'. The story behind this intake is a fascinating and unique one. Earlier in the year it had been suggested to the commissioner of the Metropolitan Police by Brig (later Gen) Haydon that there might be many fit young policemen who would like to serve in the Commandos. The commissioner, seemingly, agreed because there followed a nationwide notice calling for volunteers. There was a splendid response and after some interviews close on 500 volunteers were enlisted.

In successive intakes during the summer and early autumn volunteers arrived at Achnacarry straight from 'civvy street' in their ordinary clothes. One, 'Sonny' Bissell, seven times national wrestling champion and physical training and self-defence instructor to the 'Met' arrived, recalls Col Charles Vaughan, the commandant, 'in a blue suit, complete with his bowler hat and a small case'.

From the onset of their gruelling course, which 'started from scratch', few having been in the Army before, they were keen and enthusiastic. Vaughan later wrote:

> there were only a few huts and tents in which to accommodate them, we also had to equip them with uniforms and the accoutrements of a soldier . . . and the conditions at Achnacarry, I can assure you, would have horrified the War Office recruiting agents or any Commandant of an ordinary infantry training centre . . . but, believe me, nothing deterred those chaps. They entered into the spirit of the situation and in two months I had the pleasure of presenting to those who passed (understandably not all did) their green berets, the hall-mark of a

trained Commando . . . they were the finest material that I ever had to deal with in all my soldiering. . . .

This was a rare but fitting tribute from the old warrior, Vaughan.

Rowland ('Rollie') Oliver was one of that first intake who joined No. 4, and the first from Achnacarry to get green berets. He recalls their first parade at Troon, just before going off on leave after Achnacarry, when they all had a rifle inspection, and some of them had dirty rifles, unclean barrels and so on, 'not up to the standard we expect in No. 4', they were told – and they lost a day's leave. It was a salutory introduction to an operational Commando.

The intake had been posted to all the Commandos, and to make things fair, they had been posted according to the first letter of their surname; that is, No. 1 got those from A to D, and so on. In C Troop, all our chaps' names started with 'M' – McCubbin, Mahan, Manley, Martin . . . a fine bunch who gave unstinted service to the unit.

In the autumn we left Troon once more and the whole Commando was based in and around Shaftesbury, Dorset, but it wasn't a good training area and within a matter of a few weeks No. 4 moved again. Christmas and the New Year of 1943 saw the Commando well established in the Winchester area – 'a pleasant station, with friendly people, the right size for quarters, set in a happy valley with suitable training areas', summarised Lovat on this new location.

It was here, during the next few months, that No. 4, in Lovat's opinion, 'reached its peak in morale, efficiency and numbers'. It had been, for a while, with the reinforcements, slightly over strength, but although this could have been an embarrassment, it was soon evened out because of officers, warrant officers and NCOs being promoted and leaving the unit. The most important example of this was the departure, on promotion, of Derek – 'Mills-Bomb' – Mills-Roberts to North Africa, where he took over command of No. 6 Commando.

As there were not quite enough suitable billets in the city of Winchester, C Troop was detached and billeted in the nearby village of Alresford, famed pre-war for its watercress and in postwar years for its restored steam-railway enterprise, still known to thousands as the 'Watercress Line'. We actually used the station yard for all our muster and drill parades. However, because of the short distance involved we were often able to join up with the rest of the Commando for exercises, lectures and other training sessions.

It was while we were on detachment, however, that Capt Dawson took the troop down to Southampton, where in blitz-damaged Woolston, near the old Supermarine Aircraft Factory (where R.J. Mitchell designed and developed the original Spitfires), we underwent intensive training in street fighting and house clearing. For this specialised form of close-quarter fighting the ever-inventive Dawson soon created techniques and 'drills', as he had already done for the deployment of 'fire and movement'.

Improvised 'pop-up' targets were set up in the rooms of the bombed houses for live firing, not only for the standard short-range weapons such as Tommy guns and Colts, automatic, but also for rifles and Brens, firing from the hip, while explosive charges were used for 'mouseholing'. We were able to get rid of the much-disliked 'sticky' anti-tank grenades for this job too.

Methods of climbing up walls and over garden fences were developed using the ubiquitous toggle rope. Although many of us had undergone this sort of training previously, several of the newcomers to the troop hadn't. And in any case we were able to revise and, with Dawson's new ideas and drills, improve.

These bombed houses were ideal for the purpose, and it was ironic to think that Hitler's *Luftwaffe* was responsible for providing the means for us to develop tactics and techniques for street fighting that would later enable No. 4 to defeat his troops in the suburbs of Ouistreham on D-Day and in the town of Flushing in November 1944. Some might say this was 'poetic justice'.

It was also during the Winchester era that Lovat introduced another training 'ruse', rather like his 'Strength Through Joy Marches' in the Troon days. This time it was cross-country runs on Friday afternoons, all culminating at Commando Headquarters, or to be more precise at the Commando pay table. Anyone who failed to complete the course in the given time was deemed to be too late for pay that day! Defaulters had to wait until next day.

As Winchester was a military town in peacetime, with barracks, nearby ranges and the like, we were well provided for training, especially as in addition to these normal facilities, some of the surrounding downland was requisitioned for field firing. Nevertheless we did lack boating facilities, in spite of being so near the Solent. However, this shortcoming was overcome by sending troops off 'On Commando' to locations where they could carry out amphibious training. This was particularly relevant for Capt Porteous's D Troop. Now fully recovered and wearing the ribbon of a holder of the Victoria Cross, which he received from King George VI at Buckingham Palace in the autumn, Pat was keen that his troop, designated as the 'Boating troop', should get on with their special training for small-boat raids. He wasn't the only enthusiastic troop leader; others wanted to get on with specialised training too.

Before recalling the specialised training that the Commando undertook in various locations from their base in Winchester, it would be appropriate to mention some of the new officers who had joined in the closing months of 1942 and the early months of 1943, for they certainly made their mark in No. 4, both in training and on the field of battle.

First, there was Lt 'Hutch' Burt, known as 'Hutch' simply because it was short for his unlikely first name of Hutchinson. He was a fiery Scot, a regular other rank of the Brigade of Guards, who graduated from a drill sergeant in the Scots Guards to a commission in the Norfolk Regiment, before joining No. 4. He was infamous for his 'flowery' language, as

Capt Pat Porteous, VC, pictured here during the filming of Exercise Brandyball in Cornwall, June 1943. (*John Leal*)

becomes an ex-drill sergeant, but he was a great and fearless soldier, who was to lead E Troop on D-Day.

Lt Alastair Thorburn, a young regular officer from the King's Own Scottish Borderers, joined the Commando at Winchester and went on to command A Troop for the invasion of Normandy. For the rest of that campaign he continued to command the troop, although its title was changed, in the campaign on Walcheren in November 1944 and afterwards. He gained the endearing nickname of 'Bambi' from his troop when mountain training in the Cairngorms.

Lt Murdoch McDougal, 'Big Mac', a nickname that had no connection with the postwar advent of the American fast-food outlet, but referred to his huge size. A rival to the ex-policeman, McCubbin, of C Troop, Murdoch was also 6 ft 5 in tall, with feet to scale! He was an academic, had been a German scholar, and joined No. 4 from the Intelligence Corps, but he didn't want to be the intelligence officer, and was delighted to serve as a section officer in F Troop, which he continued to do throughout the Normandy and Walcheren campaigns. He stayed with No. 4 until their final days in Germany. After the war he wrote the book, *Swiftly They Struck*, which graphically relates the deeds of the men in his beloved F Troop.

Finally, an officer, of whom Lovat wrote, 'strictly not a soldier'. He was referring to Lt David Haig-Thomas, an extraordinary character, Cambridge rowing Blue, Olympic oarsman, naturalist, explorer and family man. He became one of the most popular and respected officers in the Commando,

One of the training legacies of the Lovat era was the high standard of marksmanship in the unit; this was maintained. Here a group of marksmen is seen at Penhale in Cornwall on a snipers' course, April 1943, run by Lt McDougal and Sgt Fraser; one can see the telescopic rifles used. (*Courtesy of Rowland Oliver, seated front row on left*)

in spite of his unsoldier-like bearing and habits. Unfortunately, David was killed in Normandy, after dropping by parachute with the Airborne Division as the Commando liaison officer.

But there was also one outstanding other rank who joined the Commando in early 1943, namely Cpl Peter King. His passage to the Commando provides one of the strangest and – if it were not true – most unbelievable stories of the war. To start with he had enlisted in the Army Dental Corps as a non-technician shortly before the outbreak of hostilities. He quickly established himself as a first-class instructor in weapon training and drill.

Consequently he became a fixture at the Dental Corps Depot as a drill sergeant, at which he excelled, but after a couple of years in that role he longed for action in a fighting unit. He applied for a transfer, but was refused. Angry and frustrated, he decided to mount his own two-man clandestine raid on the French coast. So, aided and abetted by a like-minded comrade, Cuthbertson, he carried out the planned raid, setting off from the West Country in a stolen motor boat. They landed and spent three days in France conducting their own private war against the enemy, including an attempt to cut a railway line with a grenade. Then they made off in another stolen boat, this time a French one. But their luck ran out: they spent twelve days adrift in the Channel, before being picked up by a launch of the Air Sea Rescue Service – only to be treated as spies.

Both men were court-martialled. King was reduced to the ranks, but he got his wish, in that he was posted to Achnacarry to train for the Commandos. When Lovat heard of this story, he asked Vaughan to post King to No. 4 on completion of his course. This Vaughan did.

It is an incredible story, fully told in a book, *The Amateur Commandos* by Raymond Foxall, and, surprisingly, as I was writing this book a new film was premièred, entitled, *Two Men*, also based on the story.

King quickly settled down in No. 4, rapidly rose through the ranks to TSM of C Troop, and distinguished himself in action in Normandy and Flushing, where he was not only 'commissioned in the field', but also won a well-deserved Military Cross – an outstanding and courageous soldier.

One of the successful 'On Commando' exercises carried out from the base at Winchester was when both D and E Troops went to the coast of North Devon for training with No. 62 Commando, this title being the cover name of the Small Scale Raiding Force, which operated under the control of

An especially organised assault section of C Troop for the boating and climbing Exercise Brandyball in Cornwall, 1943. All were armed with Tommy guns. Back row, second from left, with binoculars, is Lt David Haig-Thomas (Cambridge graduate, Olympic oarsman, naturalist and explorer). (*Author's Collection*)

Special Operations Executive (SOE), being known in that organisation as 'Station 62'.

On the Devon coast the two troops underwent small-boat training on the much-favoured 18 ft Dories. These sturdy little craft, powered by an Austin 7 hp motor engine, could carry from eight to ten men, depending on loads and so on, including the coxswain (skipper), usually a senior NCO, and the kedge-anchor man. These two needed to train as a team, so their selection was most important.

This spell of amphibious training ended with E Troop preparing and presenting an assault landing demonstration for the local coastal defence units at Newquay, which according to the War Diary was 'most successful . . . and greatly impressed the local troops'.

While E Troop were thus engaged, part of D Troop, headed by Pat Porteous, was detached to the main base of 62 Commando at Wraxham Manor near Dorchester. From there Porteous's little party of just eleven all ranks started more specialised training.

Larry Phillips who had joined the Commando in the January of that year takes up the story: 'From this base we met up with our dories in Portland harbour and our specialist instruction and training took place from there.' He continues:

> Berthed in the harbour was the Royal Navy's Motor Torpedo Boat (MTB) No. 344; this was a specially adapted and stripped down MTB, converted to carry one dory in the stern, which was lowered from and over the stern with the aid of a winch and rollers. . . . The crew reckoned that MTB 344 was the fastest craft in the Royal Navy . . . and from clearing the boom at Portland, it could cover the ninety-odd miles to the Channel Islands in two hours, with a full crew and landing party on board.

Unbeknown to Phillips at the time they were preparing for a little operation, codename Fathom, but it was cancelled. However, before they left Wraxall Manor to return to Winchester, the local District Commander requested that Porteous's detachment should carry out an 'attack' on one of his local searchlight batteries to test its defences. Such requests were common and of benefit to all involved.

Phillips recalls that the searchlight battery was located alongside the main railway line. They were to make a night attack, posing as German para-troopers. On the night all went well: they easily captured the sentries, making them prisoners, and then woke up the rest by shouting out in German. He concludes, 'They were a very frightened lot until we told them who we were.'

It was then the turn of A Troop to have a spell 'On Commando', and they opted for Falmouth for a extensive session of firing their rifles and Brens, with an emphasis on sniping. The latter was a pet subject of Lovat's. He was a good shot and a keen stalker, qualifications he had acquired and developed on the family estates in the Highlands from an early age, under the critical eyes of the family's ghillies. In fact, soon after he had taken over command he had managed to get one of his favourite ghillies, Fraser, posted to No. 4 from the Lovat Scouts to help with the training of the snipers. So Fraser was there at Falmouth, as was Lt McDougal, also a qualified sniper, to help with the instruction and coaching.

Not to be left out of these trips away to the West Country, Webb's B Troop went off to Minehead for some boating/landing exercises, while Dawson took C Troop down to Tenby, in South Wales, for an intensive session of cliff climbing, their first since Dieppe. And, lastly, F Troop, now settling down under the command of Lt Veasey, also went 'On Commando' to the Cheltenham area.

While D and E Troops were back in Winchester after their training exploits in Devon and Dorset, Lovat organised a couple of ambitious joint exercises for four other troops 'On Commando'. Under the exercise codename Scarecrow 1, the first one involved A Troop making a forced march from Falmouth, some sixty-odd miles, to the Launceston area, where they were to make a joint dawn attack on a mock objective, in conjunction with B Troop, who were to make their approach march from Minehead, across Exmoor, a distance of some eighty miles.

Likewise C and F Troops finished their stint 'On Commando' with a joint exercise, Scarecrow 2, with their objective in Aberdare. They started from Tenby and Cheltenham respectively for their approach marches, each of about ninety miles, to rendezvous and launch a joint dawn attack against detachments of the regular Army and Home Guard forces. After a successful attack the two Commando troops had to make a 'forced-march' withdrawal, non-stop, to two separate finishing points: C Troop, down the Neath Valley to Neath itself, and F Troop to Abergavenny. Exercise Scarecrow 2 ended at these two towns, apparently much to the relief of the men involved. However, Lovat was most pleased with their performances, for the War Diary records that the commanding officer congratulated all the troops on Scarecrow 1 and 2 for 'impressive performances'.

At the conclusion of these exercises the whole Commando spent a couple of quieter weeks in Winchester on 'make do and mend' – an Army euphemism for sorting things out, some 'spit and polish' and other domestic chores – and sport.

The end of March saw the whole Commando entrained, again for the West Country; this time Dartmouth was the destination. There for the next three days they carried out landing exercises and schemes against local units. These were most successful, especially for one NCO in A Troop, who got a special 'mention' in the War Diary. It read:

> Although the enemy opposition was poor, the Commando did well,
> especially Bdr Lament of A Troop. Besides an outstandingly good

performance in leading his section in an attack at West Prawle, he escaped after capture and reached Commando Headquarters at Ivybridge with much valuable information of the enemy's dispositions.

The report went on: 'As a result, Lament was promoted to Sergeant for outstanding leadership, daring and initiative.' This incident clearly demonstrates the manner in which Lovat encouraged, fostered and rewarded good performances during training. He rightly argued and believed that whatever one achieved in training would be repeated in action – and this included learning from mistakes. He certainly believed in the old Army adage: 'Train hard, fight easy'.

During the next few weeks in and around the base at Winchester No. 4 took the opportunity to compete in football, rugby and boxing matches and contests against other Commandos, local units and also the US Army. The Commando soccer team, under the able 'management' of Lt Donald Gilchrist, did very well. It won a local inter-services competition and was unbeaten for a long time afterwards.

Not to be outdone, the boxing team did well too. It took on a representative team from the US Army for a challenge cup in a contest held in the Winchester Guildhall, where to the delight of Lovat, the rest of the entire Commando and their friends, they beat the 'Yanks' handsomely and 'won the cup outright'.

About the same time all the officers and the full-rank NCOs of A, B and F Troops had the novel experience of driving tanks on a three-day attachment to an armoured regiment stationed in the area. Although nothing new to the likes of Sgts Bend, Woodward, Frank Major and George Jones, who had all served in the 'Tanks' before joining the Commandos, it was novel for the rest. They also got some idea of how these armoured vehicles could cooperate with infantry in battle. Little did they realise how much this would mean to them in the following year on D-Day.

In late April there was an important change of command due to a significant development in the Commandos. The number of Commandos was planned to increase, with the decision to have not just two Royal Marine Commandos but, ultimately, nine. This meant that with the seven Army Commandos there would be a total of sixteen Commandos, and they would be organised into four Special Service (Commando) Brigades. Lord Lovat was to raise and command No. 1 SS Bde. By the end of 1943 this brigade was earmarked for the invasion of Normandy.

Maj Robert Dawson, who had been acting as Lovat's second-in-command, following the departure of Mills-Roberts for North Africa, was promoted to command No. 4. In a little under three years Dawson had risen from a subaltern commanding a section to lieutenant colonel, commanding officer – no mean feat. Among other things, Dawson's rapid promotion clearly illustrates that promotion in the Commandos was based on ability – and capabilities – rather than seniority. He had displayed over that period personal qualities, professional knowledge, resourcefulness and ingenuity to mark him out as a potentially outstanding Commando leader.

Just before this Capt Ronald Menday had been posted to No. 4 and taken over A Troop, then promoted to second-in-command. So with the departure of the adjutant and the intelligence officer, who went with Lovat to his new appointment and new replacements in their posts too, the Commando was, as one might say, 'under new management'. It was the end of the Lovat era.

CHAPTER SEVEN

Training, Training, and Preparations for D-Day

The change of command coincided with another move of the unit, this time from Winchester to Falmouth in Cornwall. Winchester had proved an excellent base in many ways, and for some it had special memories too, but not all were happy ones, as Cpl 'Maxie' Maxwell, of HQ Troop, recalls. He shared a billet with Sgt Joe Powell, in a small terraced house which belonged to the Rabbi for Southampton. 'I think that fact saved us', he writes pointedly, remembering a sudden enemy air raid on the city early one morning. 'Their bombs destroyed six houses next to our billet, and brought down a ceiling in our house . . . we dashed out into the road, only to find one man dead by our front door, and others lying in the street, or buried under the rubble. . . .' Maxwell and Powell set about giving first aid and then helped with the rescue of those under the rubble. It was a grim reminder that the Commandos were not the only ones involved in the war.

The Commando quickly established itself in Falmouth, where – as customary – the local people were friendly, helpful and supportive. Many friendships between the Commandos and their landladies' families were made; some continued after the war. Veteran Dennis Clement was a member of E Troop at the time and billeted in the Globe Hotel on Customs' Quay. He writes: 'I had an elderly landlady and we got on well, and I went back to Falmouth for holidays with her for many years after the War until she passed away.' After the stay in Falmouth Dennis sustained a bad injury during training and so he became a despatch rider in the Commando, 'because I didn't want to be RTU'd'. It was a job he carried out with such courage and distinction in the Normandy and Walcheren campaigns that he was awarded the Croix de Guerre towards the end of the war.

There was little change to the training policy for the Commando after Dawson took over. Lovat had established a sound and challenging one. With this in mind, Dawson's first programme after settling down in Falmouth was to get all ranks in the Commando to reclassify on their personal and troop weapons, and to give the crews of the Commando's new heavy weapons, the Vickers Medium Machine Guns (MMGs) and the 3-in mortars, firing practices.

Although No. 4 did boast one 3-in mortar before the Dieppe Raid and had taken it into action, there had been no proper establishment in the

Commandos for these heavy weapons. However, they had been officially issued to all Commandos following the decision to extend the roles of the Commandos beyond the scope of the original concepts of 'butcher and bolt' raids to prolonged action after an invasion, followed by the holding of ground and occupation of defensive positions 'in the line' alongside orthodox infantry units. Nos 1 and 6 Commandos had been so employed in North Africa and it had become painfully obvious that the normal armoury of the Commandos was woefully inadequate to carry out such roles. As a result a heavy weapons troop had been formed in every Commando.

In No. 4 this newly formed troop was commanded by Capt 'Muscles' Carr, who, as a gunner officer, had knowledge of the principles of supporting fire and also of the range-finding techniques involved with both the MMGs and the 3-in mortars. Furthermore, he had been an MTO (Motor Transport Officer), so was well qualified for the job, as the new troop was to have a fleet of fourteen jeeps to carry the weapons, ammunition and equipment.

The troop was self-contained and consisted of Troop HQ and two sections, the MMG section and the 3-in mortar section. Both were commanded by subalterns and each had two detachments, with one heavy weapon in each, together with all the ancillary equipment and ammunition. Each section had its own signaller, and the adequate number of jeeps to transport the weapons and men gave it a high degree of mobility. However, it must be emphasised that in landings, both in training and in action, the heavy weapons and ammunition had to be manhandled ashore – as the 3-in mortar had been at Varengeville – because the jeeps could only be landed in the follow-up waves of landing craft.

A word or two about the characteristics of these weapons would not be amiss at this stage. The Vickers MMGs and the 3-inch mortars were well-established British infantry weapons. The Vickers had originally been introduced to the Army in 1912, and widely used, with success, in the First World War. Indeed, so successful were the MMGs that a whole corps, the Machine Gun Corps, had been formed. Compared with the Bren, the MMG was complicated and needed a fair amount of specialist training; nevertheless, it was a formidable and reliable weapon in the hands of well-trained crews. Because it had a recoil action system and was belt-fed, it was capable of firing some 500 rounds per minute. Using .303 ball ammunition – the same as for the rifles and the Brens – there were no problems of resupply.

However, with all its bits and pieces, which included a condenser can as part of the water-cooling system, and a tripod, the MMG weighed some 90 lb (42 kg). It could be fired direct, over open sights, or by using compass bearings and working out the angles of elevation; it had, in theory, an optimum range of about 3,000 yards.

The 3-in mortar, like all mortars, was a rather crude – but lethal – weapon. With its basic ability to deliver bombs in high-trajectory flight, it was most effective in both attack and defence roles, to counter enemy shelling and ideal for engaging the enemy in woods or in positions on reverse slopes.

However, it was also a very heavy weapon, but could be broken down into three-man loads, consisting of the barrel, baseplate, bipod and sights. Unfortunately for the Commandos involved in amphibious operations, another snag was that the bombs, both HE and smoke, were bulky and heavy – about 10 lb each.

In Falmouth the firing on the ranges went well and was followed up by sending the best rifle shots from each troop off on a week's sniping course, under the supervision of Lt McDougal and Sgt Fraser, down at Penhale in Cornwall, where they had unrestricted chances to fire in, and from, the sand dunes under realistic conditions. Little did they know then how similar those conditions – in the dunes – would be to the ones they were to encounter at Ouistreham in about twelve months' time. The report on the course reads, 'They enjoyed good shooting and had a most instructional week.'

Determined to extend his men and add extra realism to their training, Dawson set A Troop to build a tough assault course and C Troop to build a 'mock-up' to practise street-fighting and house-clearing drills. Their efforts pleased the Colonel, who commended them 'for the hard work and enthusiasm with which they tackled the job . . . it is a good example of getting a difficult job done'.

But there were distractions, not least a chance to show the local people that they could be smart and well drilled 'on parade' for, under the 'beady eye' of RSM Morris, the Commando rehearsed for a parade and march-past as part of the town's 'Arms for Victory Week'. This was one of several national government schemes to encourage wartime savings. Others included 'Warship Week', 'Wings for Victory' and 'Salute the Soldier Week'. They were considerable money-spinners and helped to fund the war. They also provided some light relief from the worries and trials of the war. One contemporary writer recorded: 'in all these efforts the towns and villages all play their part – and they are a lot of fun too'.

On 31 May a 'Special Party' under the command of Capt Style (now wearing the distinctive purple and white medal ribbon of the Military Cross he had been awarded for his part in the Dieppe Raid) and consisting of three troops and a detachment of the heavy weapons troop, left Falmouth for St Ives in Cornwall for what turned out to be the most hazardous and challenging training exercise ever attempted by any Commando – codename Brandyball. It was officially labelled as a 'special boat and climbing exercise'.

The object of the exercise was to carry out a mock seaborne raid on an objective, a few hundred yards inland, that was 'protected' by 300-ft precipitous cliffs that rose vertically from the sea-washed rocks below.

Initially the exercise was to be carried out using dories, but in the event, the original plan was curtailed. The dories were replaced by the little canvas

Goatley boats and instead of three troops, only two were used, C and D (the obvious choices, D being the boating troop and C the climbing one) plus one mortar and one MMG detachment.

The basic plan was for the assaulting Commandos to land on the rocks at the foot of the cliffs from their Goatleys, and once ashore, for the first wave to climb the cliffs and establish a little bridgehead on the top, thereby enabling the remaining troops to follow up, pass through the bridgehead to attack and destroy the enemy target, which was an old disused tin mine. Ropes and hauling equipment were to be taken up by the leading climbers to help both the mortar and MMG men with their heavy weapons and ammunition.

The whole exercise was the brainchild of Col Dawson, who was keen to demonstrate the potential of Commandos to exploit their boating and climbing skills to gain tactical surprise on a landing point which was considered impossible to use. Dawson's proposed exercise was supported by his superiors at Commando Group Headquarters, who were equally keen to show the skills and capabilities of highly trained and adventurous troops for such daring missions.

It was therefore planned that the exercise would not only be watched by an audience of senior Allied 'top brass', but was also to be filmed. It was to take place on cliffs called the 'Brandys', near Zennor. On arrival at St Ives, training began immediately, as for a proper operation. A tank landing craft was made available to carry the Commandos and their Goatleys to the launch area off the Brandys. During the next four days intensive boat-handling, rocky-landing and cliff-climbing training was the priority in the area of St Ives. The numbers in the Goatleys varied, depending on the amount of equipment being carried, but averaged ten to twelve, including the coxswain and the kedgeman. Generally the men were only lightly equipped, wearing what was known in the unit as 'raiding order'.

Larry Phillips, of D Troop, recalls: 'The "Skipper", Capt Porteous, decided we should use the dory technique and method for the approach, kedge anchor and bowline, and we, in D Troop, helped C Troop in this method.'

Acually Phillips reckoned that the launching of the Goatleys from the LCTs 'wasn't too difficult. The LCT dropped its ramp, the Goatley was pushed down to the water line and was loaded from the bow, and as the Goatley entered the water the crew jumped aboard from each side, and started to paddle, and then with a final push all were aboard and away.'

The actual demonstration was fixed for 7 June, with a final rehearsal on 6 June – they had no idea that a year ahead, exactly to the day, they would be storming the sandy beaches and dunes of Ouistreham, rather than tackling any daunting cliffs!

Unfortunately, on the final rehearsal all did not go well. Phillips recounts what happened. 'The weather was not good, the rise and fall [swell] of the sea near the foot of the cliffs was very bad.' His boat paddled in, 'dropped the kedge anchor, felt for it to grip, then continued to paddle in. One C Troop boat on our port side also approached, but their kedge anchor didn't hold, and the waves capsized the boat at the base of the cliffs.' All were tipped into the swirling sea around the landing rock ledge. Some managed to scramble on to it, but others were swept into the maelstrom between the rocks. Seeing their plight, many men made brave rescue attempts. Prominent among these were two sergeants – Eric ('Nobby') Clark and Sid Meddings; both deserved medals for their efforts that day. Sadly, Larry Phillips ends this part of his account with just six telling words: 'two of our lads were lost'.

The dramatic moments of C Troop's capsized boat and the men floundering in the swirling water were captured on film which is now in the archives of the Imperial War Museum, so that posterity can see how hazardous and dangerous the exercise was.

Following this tragic accident, the exercise was called off. Phillips records: 'Capt Porteous ordered our boat to pull back and return to the LCT, once aboard, we all returned to St Ives.'

Back in port, Col Dawson had to decide whether to go ahead on the following day. In effect his men made the decision, because he offered them the option, without any fear of reprisal or RTU, to drop out of a re-run. Not a single man wavered. So, as Phillips concludes, 'The following day, Col Dawson issued orders to try again and as the weather was much better and the sea had moderated, successful landings were made and the exercise was a great success.'

All the VIPs were able to witness a first-class and impressive demonstration. Understandably, some of them, who didn't like heights, were reluctant to go to the edge of the cliff top to watch the actual landings and climb. Exercise Brandyball was described by one spectator as 'one of the most startling examples of Special Forces training ever'.

The film, taken by official Army and RAF film units, was never edited; nor was there any 'talk-over', which is a great pity. Nevertheless, the unedited collection of film sequences covers the loading of the Goatleys aboard the LCT at St Ives, the sea passage to the Brandys, the dramatic run-in of the Goatleys, the capsized boat and the struggling crew in the water, the rocky landings, climbing up the cliff, the haulage of the MMG and the 3-in mortar, the tactical movement of the troops to the objective, and the final assault and demolition of the objective. As such it is a valued historic record of a hazardous training exercise for all time.

There was no respite in training for those who had been on Brandyball, for on rejoining the rest of the Commando in Falmouth the whole unit departed for Scotland once more. This time they were heading for the Cairngorm Mountains, whose granite peaks thrust upwards through Inverness-shire and into Aberdeenshire and Banffshire. With six peaks over 4,000 ft and at least a dozen more that top 3,000 ft, it was ideal country for No. 4's next session of training – mountain warfare.

The special troop train dropped the Commando and the stores at the little station of Ballater, whence transport took them to Braemar, the base of the Commando Snow and Mountain Warfare Training Camp (CSMWTC), whose staff and instructors were to 'host' No. 4 for the next few weeks.

Those who had been on Brandyball certainly couldn't say they had time to get bored, with the granite cliffs of Cornwall and the swirling swell of the Atlantic one week, and the snow-capped mountains and granite peaks of the Cairngorms the next.

On the face of it, going up to this area for climbing and mountaineering was not something altogether new; after all, they had done rock climbing in North Wales, the Lake and Peak Districts, as well as cliff climbing in South Wales and Cornwall, but such climbing had been geared to raids, to 'quick in-and-out' operations. The object of this attachment to CSMWTC was quite different. It was to train and familiarise No. 4 to 'live and fight in the mountains, not for a raid, but for a sustained period in a campaign, or assist partisans, in a mountainous country'.

Indeed, CSMWTC had been established following some successful operations by members of No. 12 and Free Norwegian Commandos in the latter's homeland, to train specialist Commandos to carry out more sustained operations in Norway. No. 4 Commando wondered if they were being trained for such a role.

On arrival in Braemar the Commando HQ was established (cosily) at the Fife Arms Hotel, but for the rest it was to be two-man Arctic tents and 'compo' rations out in the mountains.

On day one, 'We were all kitted out with mountain clothes, windcheaters etc and what we called "German Afrika Corps peaked caps"', wrote L/Cpl Glynn Prosser. They then had an introductory talk from the Commandant of CSMWTC, Sqn Ldr Frank Smythe, a celebrated pre-war international mountaineer and climber, who had taken part in expeditions to reach the summit of Everest.

His talk was followed by one from his deputy, Maj John Hunt, a regular Army officer of the King's Royal Rifle Corps, who had served in India, during which time he had undertaken several expeditions in the Karakoram and Himalayan Mountains. After the war he was to organise and lead the very first successful ascent of the world's highest mountain, Everest, and to become Lord Hunt. The subject of his talk was 'the role of Commandos in mountain warfare'.

Thus prepared, all the troops, accompanied by their instructors, left the base at Braemar for their individual troop bases, whence they would carry out their basic training in the art of moving and living in the mountains. And although it was now mid-June, there was still snow on the mountains and the temperatures at the higher altitudes were still low, especially at night.

There was much to learn. One of the major subjects to master was route finding and route maintenance, especially when weather conditions deteriorated, as they could in a matter of minutes, from clear skies and visibility to dense mountain mist with little or no visibility. Then, not only was direction finding and maintenance difficult, but so was keeping control of sub-sections on the move over the mountainous terrain.

Apropos movement in the mountains, Prosser recalls that Smythe, who used to come and accompany the Commandos, 'taught us by word and example how to "lope" along the mountain terrain, with steady, slow and long strides – and it was generally agreed that our normal marching would suffer as a result'. But it didn't.

There seems no doubt that Sqn Ldr Frank Smythe, whom John Hunt described as 'a gentle most unwarlike character, whose main contribution to the work of CSMWTC was to impart his deep poetic love of the mountains to the tough high-spirited wearers of the Green Beret', did succeed, earning the respect and admiration of all in No. 4.

Consequently it was left to John Hunt, in his own words, 'to put the Commandos through a rigorous programme of all the permutations of actions, in all weathers and seasons, in the testing vastness of the Cairngorms'.

The weather during their period in the mountains was reported as 'unsettled, mixed with rain and wind', sufficient to test them as they trekked through the mountains during a hectic and gruelling first week, a week in which, as McDougal wrote, 'each day started with a climb of at least 1,000 ft'.

The journeys into the mountains had some unexpected lighter moments, as Prosser recalls: 'We met a group of civilian hikers. One of them said whereas they were paying for their holiday, walking in the mountains, we were being paid and supported by the Army.' He doesn't say whether he put the other side of the situation to those hikers, namely, whereas after their days in the mountains they retired to a nice comfortable bedroom with all 'mod cons', plus cooked meals, he and his mates had to return to a two-man tent, often being lashed by rain and wind, to crawl inside and try to prepare their food of compo rations on a little tommy cooker, and then set about the cleaning of their weapons or go out on 'stag' (guard) duties, for although it was only training it was carried out on an operational basis.

At the end of that first week troops returned to the Commando base for a day off and 'to make do and mend'. The second week was devoted to 'fighting' – as opposed to 'living and moving' – in the mountains. This involved all troops, less A Troop, concentrating on formations, tactics and field firing. A Troop took part in an exercise with troops from the 52 Lowland Division which had been specialising in mountain warfare since 1941, but ironically enough, first went into action in the water-logged dykes of Holland, alongside No. 4 Commando, at Walcheren in November 1944. Furthermore, A Troop leader, Capt Thorburn, had joined No. 4 Commando from a battalion of this Division and was destined to meet up with his old comrades in the fighting on Walcheren.

On the last day of training an inter-troop shoot was held, firing rifles and Brens. In a most successful contest, much to the delight of Capt

'Hutch' Burt and his sergeant-major, Les Haynes, E Troop came out as winners.

No account of No. 4's sojourn in the Cairngorms, whether written or verbal, is complete without mention of the 'Salmon Story'. Everyone who served in the Commando at the time remembers it – not without a knowing smile.

Situated in the Cairngorms, where the Commando did this stint of training, is Royal Deeside, with Balmoral and the royal fishing preserves, abounding with salmon. L/Cpl Gerry Swailes's recollections are short and to the point:

> Some of the lads went on a gun-cotton [a useful high explosive, produced in one-pound slabs, easy to carry and conceal] fishing expedition in a salmon pool. They collected several ground sheets full of fish! The CO took it very well, as I well remember, no charges. . . . The pool was in the Balmoral Estate. . . . The whole unit had a good fish supper. . . .

Donald Gilchrist was adjutant, and in his book, *Don't Cry For Me*, he made light of the situation with a colourful account of the incident. He had just finalised the arrangements for the unit's move from Braemar, when on returning to his hotel he was completely unprepared for the sight that awaited him.

> Inside the hotel I drew up shocked, stunned. . . . The terrazzo floor of the hall was covered with fish, red-brown, gold-flecked, gleaming fish – salmon.
>
> My mind boggled. Fish came from a river. There had been no heavy rain recently so they could not have swum here by themselves and died. The nearest river was the Royal Dee. Royal Salmon? Circumstantial evidence!
>
> Who would have the cunning, the daring, to commit such an outrage?

In a light-hearted, almost farcical vein, he described his dilemma, namely, how should he deal with the poachers of royal salmon?

Fortunately, the ever-ready and reliable RSM Morris came to the rescue and with the speedy assistance of a lip-sealed squad of Commandos the evidence disappeared as magically as it had appeared in the first place. The story provides a nice little tail-piece to No. 4's stay in the Cairngorms, except to add John Hunt's assessment of the Commandos' potential to fight in any mountainous terrain. In his book, *Life is Meeting*, he wrote: 'The Commandos would have been a match for the crack German Gebirgs-truppen and the Italian Alpini – the special mountain-trained troops of the Axis forces.' He regretted that they were not used in the Italian campaign as mountain troops.

On leaving the Cairngorms, No. 4, rather surprisingly, returned for a short spell to their old 'hunting grounds' in Troon, but then it was back once more to the south of England, this time to 'Sussex-by-the-Sea'.

So August 1943 saw the unit, in civilian billets, in adjacent locations, with HQ plus A and B Troops in Seaford, C and D Troops in Newhaven and E and F Troops in Lewes 'as far away from HQ as possible', wrote McDougal, more in good humour than rancour.

However, he went on to record:

It was here that the whole unit fell into a period of depression. The troops were 'browned off'; they were fitter than they had ever been, confident and ready for action. It had been a whole year since Dieppe, and a few men were even applying for posting back to their parent units, many of which had been sent overseas in the meanwhile. These men pointed out that they had joined the Commandos for action and as McVeigh bitterly put it, 'I have seen more action coming out of a pub on a Saturday night than I get in this lot. . . .'

The frustration of the troops and their reaction to being subjected to tough, purposeful and exacting training and then nothing, only false hopes, was understandable. In a similar peacetime context one could compare it to the disappointment and frustration of an athlete training for the Olympic Games for a year or so, or even longer, then being told, 'Sorry, they're off. We don't know when or where they will be held. Meanwhile, keep training.'

However, Dawson was not the CO to allow this mood to continue. He fell back on the apparent panacea that had worked before, in the aftermath of the Lofoten Raid, when Lord Lovat had taken over – split up the unit and send them off 'On Commando'. Selecting their own location, organising the move, training and the administration of their troops for a short period would keep them fully occupied, and 'recharge the batteries'.

Among the locations chosen was the Norfolk Broads, where the troops handled a wide variety of craft, ranging from powered boats such as dories to smaller craft such as the rubber inflatable dinghies and canoes. This area became a popular choice.

The Commando even put on a demonstration of small-boat handling for Gen Sturges, now in overall command of all Special Service (Commando) Brigades, who was accompanied on the visit by Brig Lord Lovat. Thus it was on this visit that Lovat took Dawson into his confidence, and under the terms of strictest security, told him that his new brigade, consisting of Nos 3, 4 and 6 Army Commandos and the recently formed 45 Royal Marine Commando, was to be involved in the Second Front, but where, when and how he didn't know – or couldn't say. At this stage Dawson could not pass on this information. He had to keep it to himself, but at least it gave him, personally, hope and the promise of action.

As regards the training on the Broads, the boating was undoubted fun and provided a pleasant and novel interlude away from field training.

Competitions, combining boating, map reading and the use of the compass for navigation, were organised on troop and section levels.

However, to keep alive the climbing side of training, a small group of potential climb leaders and climbing instructors was sent to Llanwryst in North Wales in late September for a course held by the CSMWTC, which had recently moved from the Cairngorms to Snowdonia.

This party included two of the Weymouth originals, now sergeants, John Skerry and Ernie Brooks, who had the unique experience of being personally taught and taken on climbs on the Idwal Slabs and Tryfan by John Hunt, who, incidentally, used the same climbing area after the war to train his Everest team. Skerry and Brooks never forgot those climbs and treasure their snaps taken at that time.

Early October saw the whole Commando encamped in tents in the Brandon area, Lincolnshire, for a session on 'forest warfare', a subject which had not previously been given much specialised attention.

In this type of warfare, as in the jungle, say in Burma, where No. 4's comrades in No. 3 SS Bde were soon to be involved, navigation using the compass was of paramount importance and needed plenty of practice – this forest was ideal for the purpose. In addition the Commando was able to train in other aspects of jungle warfare, such as the setting of ambushes and the siting of defensive positions in such close country. It was an interesting change of environment.

However, mostly remembered from this training are the night exercises through the dense forests, marching in the dark on compass bearings. Members of F Troop, in particular, had good cause to remember one such night march in the forest. For this march the troop had attached to it, just for the night, a most extraordinary character, Admiral Sir Walter Cowan, who had previously, at the age of seventy-three, and long since retired from the Royal Navy, somehow managed to get himself attached to Laycock's Commandos in the Middle East and went with them on an operation in the Western Desert. There, he was captured by the Italians while engaging a tank with his revolver! He spent some time, subsequently, in a POW camp in Italy, but the Italians decided to repatriate 'this gentle old man'. Now he had turned up in Brandon with No. 4, as an observer and 'to brush up his forest warfare techniques'.

For this night march the admiral was attached to a section in F Troop. Frank Farnborough remembers the admiral's arrival:

We were going on a night scheme through the dense conifer woods of the area, when, out of the blue, an old man joined us. He turned out to be Sir Walter Cowan, an Admiral, a tough old boy, a Commando unit on his own, he was quite a character and insisted on coming with our Section, so our officer, Lt McDougal, told one of the men, Fraser, from the Welsh Guards, to keep an eye on the Admiral. When the exercise finished, we gathered together in the camp, but no Admiral . . . Fraser was just saying he had lost the Admiral, when bursting through the trees, he came, shouting 'Who's lost the ruddy Admiral? Give me some of that ruddy cocoa!'

None ever forgot the 'Old Admiral', least of all Guardsman Fraser.

After Brandon, it was back to Sussex, and morale was lifted once again when Dawson told a Commando assembly that it was going to be a 'winter season of small raids'. Pat Porteous's D Troop was to be in the forefront of these operations, as they had already been nominated as the 'boating troop', but the other troops hoped 'to get into the act'. Indeed, three troops, under the command of Maj Menday, the second-in-command, went off to the Solent area for intensive training for a large-scale raid from landing crafts infantry (LCIs), a new type of landing craft, carrying about eighty fully equipped troops, 'in acute discomfort'. LCIs had two ramps forward on either side of the bows, which were let down and acted as steps. In doing so, 'they invariably jut out above deck level so that the leading man cracks his shins on the jutting ends of the ramp and either hurtles down the thing on his hands and knees or falls headlong into the drink, closely watched by the sniggering sailor whose incompetence has been the cause of the mishap', caustically commented McDougal, who had good cause to write in this vein. Needless to add, LCIs were not popular with the Commandos.

It was now the winter of 1943 and already plans were well advanced on Operation Overlord, the invasion of Normandy, for which No. 4 was destined to play an important role.

As part of the overall preparations for the invasion a series of cross-Channel Commando raids was planned for December. There were two types. The first type was small-scale reconnaissance raids, possibly bringing back a prisoner, to be carried out by a single or two groups, landing from dories, having been launched from naval MTBs. The coastal area for this type of raid extended from Le Havre in the west to Ostend in the east. The Commandos involved in these small raids, which had the codename Hardtack, included D Troop (Capt Porteous) from No. 4 and also French Commandos from No. 10, who would later come under the command of No. 4 for the Normandy campaign and also for subsequent operations in Holland.

The other type of Commando raid planned was a much larger operation, involving two, or even three, whole troops, and having for its objective a coastal strongpoint. A party of three troops from No. 4, under the command of Maj Menday (second-in-command) went to a Combined Operations Centre located at Warsash, on the river Hamble, just off Southampton Water, to train for one such operation, which went under the codename Manacle.

Menday's party trained hard, carrying out landings from the LCIs by both day and night and even rehearsed in detail for an operation, but, like so many before, it was cancelled and the party returned to their billets in Sussex.

Their hopes were raised when soon after they were alerted for another Manacle operation and this time they did set off from Dover to destroy a strongpoint in the Quand Plage area (halfway between Boulogne and Dieppe), but en route the raid was aborted because of bad weather and a heavy sea.

However, D Troop were luckier and were employed on the Hardtack operations. A member of D Troop, who went on one of these small-scale raids, and who was mentioned earlier when D Troop started this specialised training, Larry Phillips, recalls his experiences:

> Late in 1943 D Troop went down to the Southampton Water and used the old Empire Flying Boat Station, near Calshot. This time several dory crews were in training. . . . From this training a landing was made near Boulogne over the Christmas period, two dory crews were selected. The crews were billeted in Dover Castle, and the operation took place from there.

Phillips didn't go on this raid, but Portman, who was by now TSM of D Troop, did go and he takes up the story.

> The raid (codename Hardtack 5) took place two days after Christmas. We went from Dover in MTBs with two dories. The first was under the command of Capt Porteous. (The other was under Lt Hunter-Gray.) We were launched from the MTBs and made towards the coast in our dories, using the Austin engines, until we were about half-a-mile from the shore, when we quietly paddled in. We landed and got ashore OK, but one of our men, Cpl Richards, set off an 'S' mine, and was wounded. We made for the road, and lay in wait to ambush the Germans, thinking they would come for us. But nothing happened. However, we did take back samples of the beach defence wire, a beach mine, details about the depth of the minefield and other useful information. We withdrew, got out to the MTB and then sailed safely back to Dover.

Meanwhile, the other dory crew patrol, under Lt Hunter-Gray, located the strongpoint planned for one of the Manacle raids, but found it was unoccupied, with no traces of occupation, so also returned to re-embark and sail back to Dover.

Phillips continues his story, 'Soon after this operation (Hardtack 5, as related by Portman) the No. 1 dory crew was called together and sent under command of Lt Carlos-Clarke to Great Yarmouth to sort out some billets and start training. Soon Capt Porteous and Lt Hunter-Gray arrived and dory work began.' When the training was completed:

> We set out for our mission on the Dutch coast, but due to a very heavy fog, we were unable to effect a landing so the 'Skipper' [Capt Porteous]

decided to return to the MTB. Unfortunately, we failed to do this and as there was complete wireless silence, we were 'up the creek'. For a long time we could hear Church bells and even motor traffic from the Dutch coast, but the intense fog persisted all that following day. Very lucky for us and our MTB escorts! Eventually the 'Skipper' decided to break radio silence and we did manage to contact Lt Cdr Bradford, commander of the escort MTB. He gave us navigational instructions and also said that he would fire his gun so that we would have some idea if they were near. But all this failed, so off we set for England. With a limited amount of petrol we soon ran out – so it was out with the paddles.

After paddling and drifting for two days and nights, the following morning we spotted an Air Sea Rescue buoy. We were soon alongside and found water and rations, also a Verey Pistol and cartridges. The 'Skipper' immediately fired off the distress signal. This was spotted by Air Sea Rescue boats who were soon down to our location and picked us up.

They reported to the 'Skipper' that their search instructions were for ten men in a boat. They thought they were searching for a USAAF Flying Fortress crew and were very surprised to find ten Commandos. They told us we were ten miles off Lowestoft and ten miles south of Great Yarmouth. They soon had us back in Great Yarmouth. . . .

So ended No. 4 Commando's experiences of the Hardtack and Manacle operations, and it was, in Phillips's own words, 'a return to normal Commando training' back in their base in Sussex.

By now it was mid-January 1944 and all attention and efforts were clearly focused on the long-awaited 'Second Front'. At the highest levels the American Gen Eisenhower had been appointed Supreme Allied Commander for Operation Overlord, and Gen Montgomery, following his successes in the Western Desert and in Italy, had been appointed operational commander of the ground forces committed to the invasion of Normandy, until a 'foothold' had been established on the soil of France to enable the breakout into north-west Europe to go ahead.

One of the problems that must have faced Dawson in his command of No. 4 Commando at this stage, bearing in mind the already battle-fitness of his unit, was how to keep them at this level without becoming 'stale'. However, with his ever-inventive and imaginative mind he pursued an enterprising programme of training which, at the same time, contained much that was relevant to his assigned role for Operation Overlord, as outlined earlier to him by Lord Lovat.

Accordingly, in February, Capt David Style's C Troop, hitherto known as the 'climbing troop', aspired to even greater heights when they were despatched to RAF Ringway to undergo training to qualify as parachutists. In his original concept for the Commandos, Churchill had envisaged a strong force of Airborne Commandos. This hadn't materialised, albeit the first paratroopers in the British Army were the members of the original No. 2 (Para) Commando.

At Ringway C Troop went through the normal Airborne Forces' course for all parachutists, namely ground training, learning how to land and go into the standard 'para-roll', indoor training on the swings to acquire the techniques of controlling the 'chute's descent and to correct any twists in the lift-webs of the 'chute, then the drill in the aircraft. This completed, they faced their first jump, not from an aircraft, but from a balloon. After two introductory jumps from the balloon, there followed jumps from RAF planes, five of these, before the final jump, which was again from the balloon, but this time in the darkness at night. Having completed all eight jumps, C Troop were distinguishable in No. 4 by the coveted 'para wings' worn on the top of the right sleeve, under the 'No. 4 Commando' of their battledress blouses.

Two of the troop, and only two, would be jumping into action on D-Day with 6 Airborne Division, Lt Haig-Thomas and his batman/runner, Pte Ryder. The rest of C Troop were to land with the Commando from the sea. Nevertheless, they had all enjoyed the experience of the exciting and exacting parachute training at Ringway.

Meanwhile, A, B and D Troops prepared for a demonstration of a cliff assault using an amphibious DUKW (pronounced 'Duck') on which had been mounted a London Fire Brigade extending ladder, together with a cunning home-made device known in the unit as a 'Dawson', which when embedded on the top of a cliff, with the aid of in-built rollers, enabled a rope to be paid out over the cliff-edge and face to haul up or lower men and equipment. The inventive Cpl Brian Mullen had been instrumental in the design and making of the 'Dawson'.

Gilchrist wrote; 'as usual we practised and practised until Dawson was pleased, then he ordered a full scale rehearsal . . . [when] some 400 men of No. 4 Commando, reached the top in under 30 minutes. We had done some stunts before, but this beat anything in Billy Smart's circus.'

On 21 February the whole Commando, along with the rest of Lovat's Commando Brigade, paraded in Portslade, near Brighton, for an inspection by Gen Montgomery. This went very well and 'Monty' was much impressed – and told them so. The general's Chief of Staff wrote to Lord Lovat and in his congratulatory message said Montgomery had considered the turnout and soldierly bearing of the Commandos as 'the best he had seen since returning to England'.

Glyn Prosser recalls the amusement that followed 'Monty's talk, when he was so impressed. He said, as a compliment, that they were 'proper chaps', a high compliment from the austere and demanding general. Thereafter, the men of No. 4, when passing each other in the street, would invariably greet each other with 'Hi, there, "proper chap".'

On a more serious note, that inspection by Montgomery heralded some eight weeks of intensive and realistic preparations for their role in Operation Overlord, which is accordingly recorded in the War Diary.

At the end of the month the whole Commando moved into billets in Bexhill for collective training. The immediate aim was to 'reach the highest standards of physical fitness', with daily speed marches – carrying full loads – and also the practice of tactical battle drills 'to cope with snipers, machine gun positions and pill boxes' – situations envisaged in the forthcoming invasion.

Although the whole Commando was together in Bexhill, most of the training was carried out on a troop basis and so varied in some of the finer details, from troop to troop, especially in the heavy weapons troop which also competed in brigade competitions for the firing of their 3-in mortars and MMGs; the mortars won the brigade shoot, while the machine-gunners came third.

Although the heavy weapons troop normally transported their weapons, ammunition and equipment in jeeps, in the operational plans they would be required to manhandle their weapons ashore, so they had some really tough training. Knyvet Carr writes: 'My special memories of the training for D-Day were the strength and stamina that was displayed by all the men in carrying the mortars, MMGs, plus our heavy Bergen rucksacks on speed marches.' To spread the load of the ammunition, 'every man in Troop carried at least two 10 lb mortar bombs, including myself' concluded Carr.

The next priority was the practice of assault landings from LCAs and rapid attacks on objectives inland, following these landings. In mid-March the Commando embarked on HMS *Astrid*, which was to become a popular ship among all ranks of No. 4, and sailed to anchor off the Dorset coast, then carried out a series of landings in the Warbarrow Bay/Chapman's Pool area, quite near to where Lovat had trained No. 4 for the Dieppe Raid. The final amphibious landing was 'opposed' by live firing, on fixed lines, and other explosives, reminiscent of the famous 'Opposed Landings' at Achnacarry.

From these exercises, the *Astrid*, with the Commando still on board, sailed along the south coast and up the North Sea to the Moray Firth for further amphibious training. For several days the Commando carried out landings by both day and night on unfamiliar beaches, which were, incidentally, quite near the battlefield of Culloden (1746), just to the east of Inverness.

These landings were followed by three days of field firing in the area. This was most successful, and the Diary records:

Field firing at Tarbot, Troop Leaders had the opportunity to practise every form of attack with fire, having under command a detachment of 3-in mortars and MMGs . . . this area contains much farmland, hedges, and small features and was the best area we have had for training for several years. Great value was obtained from these exercises and every weapon was fired to a maximum. . . .

It had been an excellent choice – an ideal area for No. 4 to prepare for its operational role in Normandy.

This spell of amphibious training ended with the Commando carrying out an exercise attack on a manned coastal battery at Burghhead and an exercise in conjunction with troops of 3 Infantry Division, whom they would encounter again on the beaches on D-Day.

The sixteen days of training from HMS *Astrid* ended on 31 March when the Commando disembarked at Inverness and returned by train to Bexhill, where after a couple of days' 'tidying up', they went on ten days' leave.

It's fascinating to note, amid all the hectic operational training at Moray Firth, an entry in the War Diary for 27 March: 'Small detachment under Capt Burt to London for the "Salute the Soldier" Parade and March' – evidence of the importance of these national 'flag-waving' and morale-boosting – also fund-raising – events.

On return from leave the next really important event was the posting of two French troops of Commandos from No. 10 to join No. 4 and their placing under command of Col Dawson for the impending invasion. As outlined earlier, Dawson was bilingual, and this, coupled with his understanding of the French, their backgrounds, culture and national pride, together with his outstanding military ability and leadership, was to earn him much respect and loyalty from these Allied Commando comrades.

The two French troops were originally commanded by Kieffer and Trepel, but the latter disappeared on one of the Hardtack raids, and his place was taken by Lofi. On joining No. 4, Dawson made Kieffer his 'senior Officer of French Troops' and Guy Vourch took over Kieffer's troop.

The background to the forming of these two troops is a story in itself, which has been widely told elsewhere and is also a feature of the excellent No. 4 Commando Musée in Ouistreham, but more about that in the final chapter. Suffice it here to quote Dawson's comments on this new addition to his Commando:

> They were tough, self-reliant soldiers, quick in action and very brave indeed. Even before D Day a measure of mutual respect had developed . . . but after the initial phase [of the invasion] the Commando became so firmly welded together at every level that it seemed entirely natural that we should fight and live side-by-side till the end of the War, as indeed we did.

During the remainder of the month of April training was geared to maintaining the high standard of speed/endurance marches in and around Bexhill. This included – often to the amusement and sometimes to the consternation of the local residents – the sight of the Commandos making their way in battle order and formations along the streets, carrying out mock attacks and going through back gardens and over the garden walls in some realistic training for the anticipated fighting in a built-up area on D-Day.

There was change in the Commando armoury when all the riflemen exchanged their SMLE rifles for the newer Lee-Enfield No. 4 rifles with their much shorter bayonet. This necessitated spending several days on the ranges to enable all these riflemen not only to zero their new weapons, but also to get plenty of practice shoots with them. The ranges were also used for the other troop weapons, and especially for the newly acquired Vickers 'K' guns.

Also at this time there was a very impressive demonstration of German weapons and German patrol tactics staged by No. 6 Commando who had been, earlier in the year, fighting in North Africa. They even used some captured German uniforms for their 'demo', which gave it an authentic atmosphere.

The end of the month was given over to some inter-Commando sports' contests; No. 4 also held its own 'Eccentric sports' meeting' followed by an all-ranks Commando dance – morale was high as everyone in the unit sensed the exciting and momentous occasion of the imminent invasion.

In his book, *March Past*, Lord Lovat succinctly summarises the 'intention' of his brigade's role for D-Day and the 'method' he had planned to fulfil his mission. The following is quoted from that summary.

> *The intention.* The 6th Airborne Division and 1st Commando Brigade would be responsible for holding the left flank of the Allied bridgehead of the invasion of Normandy.
>
> *The method.* The Commando Brigade, consisting of Nos 3, 4, and 6 Army Commandos and No. 45 Royal Marine Commando, to land on the extreme flank of the Allied Forces on Queen Beach (Sword) and cut inland to join forces with two Brigades dropped inland by night by glider and parachute. No. 4 Commando to destroy a battery and the garrison in Ouistreham and then later rejoin the Brigade. The rest of the Brigade, landing thirty minutes after No. 4, to fight through enemy defences to reach and reinforce Brigades of the 6th Airborne Division, meeting astride bridges spanning the River Orne and the Caen Canal. Glider Regiments of the Air Landing Brigade would arrive later the same evening descending in country cleared of the enemy.

Lovat concluded: 'We had been assigned a formidable task', but, always the perfectionist, having made his plans Lovat suggested a dress rehearsal with identical landing craft and crews carrying the same personnel they would put ashore on D-Day. The selected beach (cleared of mines, but with the wire left standing and backed by similar terrain) lay between Angmering and Littlehampton, near Arundel, on the Sussex coast. His suggestion was accepted and under the codename Exercise Fabius, No. 4 embarked on the *Princess Astrid* and *Maid of Orleans* and, with the rest of the brigade, successfully carried out this dress rehearsal. Lovat records that 'All the top brass came down from London' and at the conclusion of the exercise, 'the planners were impressed'. Exercise Fabius was to be the final large-scale training exercise for No. 4 before setting off for the port of embarkation.

On 22 May a small party of officers and men travelled up to the Commando Group camp at Petworth for a parade and inspection by King George VI; they all sensed that the day the free world was waiting for must be near at hand. They were right, for three days later the Commando left its base at Bexhill and travelled to Camp 18 in Southampton, where on arrival the camp was sealed and detailed briefing for Overlord begun.

Bill Bidmead, who was in A Troop, provides a pen picture of those days in Camp 18.

We arrived in Southampton where we were taken off to a huge marshalling area. It looked like a large park surrounded by barbed wire. Once inside we were not allowed out. 'Like being in nick', said Frankie Ives. The weather was quite pleasant, which was just as well as we were under canvas.

Security was tight. Marches were organised outside the camp. We were closely guarded. Taff Isherwood organised our PT, also numerous football matches. The camp was staffed half by British and half by Yanks.

TSM Bill Portman, MM (left), supervises the priming of the Mills (36) grenades on the open deck of the *Maid of Orleans* on the evening of D-1. (*Courtesy of the Imperial War Museum, London* – B5099)

Bill and his mates were introduced to the American game of 'horseshoes', but just as he was finishing one such game, his troop leader, Capt Alastair Thorburn, returned from a Commando 'O' group.

'This is it, lads,' said Thorburn. 'We are going to invade France.' Cheers rang out. 'Where it takes place you will be told later.' He went on to describe the Commando's role, as outlined in Lovat's summary above. Then he gave some details of the assault on the 'town' – no name given: how the two French troops would attack and destroy a strongpoint dominating the beaches, known as the 'Casino', followed by the five British troops, backed by the heavy weapons' troop, who were to push on further into the 'town' to destroy a coastal battery. Thorburn explained that companies of infantry would land before the Commando to clear the beach of obstacles, knock out four strongpoints and lay white tapes for No. 4 to go through on their way to the objectives in the town.

Bidmead emphasises the thoroughness of this and subsequent briefings with photos and maps, with the intelligence officer going round each sub-section to ensure everyone was fully 'in the picture'. He adds: 'Nobody wanted any slip-ups. This was going to be the biggest invasion in history.'

Next day they went down to Southampton Docks and boarded their transport ships, the British troops split between the *Princess Astrid* and the *Maid of Orleans*, and the two French troops boarded their LCIs at Warsash. Bidmead records:

> We had gone aboard on the last day of May. As a couple of days went by, a huge armada of ships gathered in the Solent. Taff Isherwood gave us PT on deck and Lt Jannery gave us some weapon training at the stern of the ship. The weather didn't look too good. The date had been fixed, we were to land on 5 June. 'I hope the weather improves,' said Danny Flowers, 'it was better than this for Dieppe.' The weather got worse and the whole operation was cancelled for 24 hrs. The following day the weather had improved slightly and that evening we were told that it was on and we would be off at 2100 hrs. Big cheers all round.

General Eisenhower, from his Headquarters on the Portsdown Hills, overlooking Portsmouth, had given that famous short order, 'Okay, let's go.' Operation Overlord was launched.

CHAPTER EIGHT

To Normandy – 'The Longest Day'

Operation Overlord was carried out by the greatest amphibious invasion force the world has ever seen. On that one day alone, 'D-Day' – 6 June 1944 – over 176,000 men, 3,000 guns, 1,500 tanks and some 11,500 other vehicles were put ashore, under enemy fire, on the beaches of Normandy. Nearly 11,000 ships and naval craft were committed to the task of carrying and escorting the huge Allied landing force, while overhead the Allied air forces flew over 10,000 sorties.

The Allied commanders knew, and secretly predicted, that the cost in human lives and material to establish a foot-hold on the enemy-held coast would be high. They even forecast that as many as 10,000 men might lose their lives on the single day; thankfully they were unduly pessimistic. Nevertheless, about 2,500 Allied servicemen were killed and a further 12,000 became battle casualties.

It is against this awesome background that the story of No. 4 Commando's action on 6 June must be put into context. Although the story here is devoted entirely to this single British-French Commando, one should be mindful of the others involved and acknowledge the sacrifices made by all who fell, whether sailor, soldier or airman. They must not be forgotten – and they are not.

With this in mind, we take up the story of No. 4 following their embarkation, with Commando HQ and the six British troops, aboard the LSIs *Princess Astrid* and *Maid of Orleans* and their French comrades, the two French troops, aboard the LCIs, Nos 523 and 527.

It was the evening of 5 June. The weather was anything but ideal for the month and, more importantly, for the crossing. 'The wind was keen and the sea was lumpy', is how the Commandos' naval flotilla commander, Lt Cdr Curtis, described it.

No. 4's medical officer, the chirpy Scot, Capt Patterson, was more graphic: 'The wind howled and it rained in vicious scuds. The skipper [presumably Col Dawson] had said in his talk, "The Allied High Command must be heavily counting on surprise, for the Germans must surely think that not even Englishmen could be fools enough to start an invasion on a night like this."'

As the great convoy of ships and craft left the Solent to start their cross-Channel trip, the Commandos busied themselves with the usual pre-operation preparations. But for Patterson these preparations were different. He recalls, first, splicing his identity discs to 'gloomily hang' them round his neck. This somewhat morbid necessity completed, he went around the mess deck 'dishing out' sea-sickness tablets and morphine phials, and also ensuring that the troops were fully aware of the final medical arrangements once they had landed.

It wasn't until the invasion armada was well on its way down the Solent that all ranks were finally told the place-name of their objective on landing – Ouistreham. Although this didn't mean much to the British Commandos, it did to the French troops, Maurice Chauvet recorded his feelings on being told the name of this little seaside town which they had to assault: 'instead of the Anglo-Saxon codename', now he felt 'that this time it was for real'. Up to this moment for Chauvet and his countrymen, indeed for all in No. 4, the landing beaches and objective in Normandy had been 'nothing more than snaps, models and maps . . .'.

For twelve days all of the Commando had been learning by heart the minutest details about the roads in the area they were about to invade, but for all, especially for Chauvet and his fellow compatriots, it had been rather abstract: 'It had not sunk in that we were actually landing in France. I needed to see those proper names on the map, then the operation meant something – liberation!' 'With the maps we had been given Montgomery's message: very English, but very friendly', commented Chauvet.

Reveille on board the *Astrid* was at 0330 hrs, followed by breakfast, a hearty one for most, but not all, on that 'lumpy sea'. According to Pte Bill Bidmead, 'the fish did well too'. Then came the customary banter and basic soldiers' humour that accompanied the 'dressing up for the Show' – plus the traditional, strictly supervised, 'tot of rum'. Surprisingly a lot of the men, especially the younger ones, didn't like – or drink – rum.

All were heavily laden; every man carried a rucksack which in the words of one wit 'contained everything but the kitchen sink!' and weighed up to 80 lb. In addition to his own weapon and ammunition, every man carried extra ammunition for various troop weapons, Brens, mortars, K guns and PIATs. Signallers and medical orderlies had extra supplies for their specialist needs too. And under all the equipment was worn the inflatable 'Mae West'. Little wonder, therefore, that Capt Donald Gilchrist aptly commented: 'We were festooned like Christmas trees!'

In spite of Lovat's declared abhorrence of steel helmets, it had been decided that the men could wear them if they preferred, because as the adjutant, Gilchrist, said, 'There will be plenty of jagged metal flying around.' In the event No. 4 landed with some still sticking to their favoured green berets – 'Green for Go' was their reckoning. Others wore the steel helmet for the initial landing and the assaults into Ouistreham, then swapped, and discarded, their 'steel topees' for their green berets. That is why in the many pictures and films of the landings one sees the Commandos in a mixture of steel helmets and berets. The choice was made by the men themselves.

The heavy and bulky items to be carried ashore, such as stretchers, the 3-in mortars, Bangalore torpedoes and telescopic ladder, had been pre-loaded in the LCAs before setting sail.

A grim sight awaited the troops aboard the *Astrid* and *Maid of Orleans* as they came on deck to go to their boat stations. McDougal, much moved, wrote:

There was a loud explosion on the port quarter and in a lurid orange glow one of the escorting destroyers broke in two. We later learned that it had been struck by a torpedo. It was the most depressing sight imaginable. The two halves of the stricken ship slowly reared out of the water like an inverted 'V' and gradually sank into the leaden waves.

Bill Bidmead also recalls the tragedy as he moved to his LCA and commented: 'Poor blighters, they didn't have a chance.' He describes the scene in those tightly packed LCAs:

The rattle of rifle bolts and cocked actions could be heard as rounds were pushed 'up the spouts' of personal weapons when the Navy lowered the LCA into the choppy sea. They cast off too soon, the craft crashed into the sea. It was only by a miracle that we did not spill out. . . .

Gilchrist recalls looking round in the grey pre-dawn light at the others in his LCA and felt reassured to be in such company. 'There were some old soldiers in our boat. McCall was one. He was sitting comfortably behind me, looking as if he was to enjoy a trip on the *Jean Deans*, the Clyde steamer, to see the Rothesay illuminations. . . .'

Gilchrist continues in his own irrepressible style: 'now all of them were about to see illuminations that would make the efforts of Blackpool and Rothesay look like a dinner by candlelight, and fireworks that would make a Guy Fawkes enthusiast give up his trade . . .'.

In a more subdued and factual style McDougal records:

On the run in, it was impossible not to be thrilled by the happenings round about. Aircraft scurried to and fro in the lightening sky, all independent – and all beautifully ours. Shells from the warships HMS *Warspite* and *Ramillies* were screaming overhead, destroyers fired salvo after salvo, and soon we heard a new sound – the roaring swish of missiles from the rocket ships. The whole coastline was now under a thick pall of smoke. . . .

Unfortunately, the choppy seas had not subsided, and, in spite of 'Doc' Patterson's tablets, several were sea-sick. Pte Glynn Prosser was one of those suffering: 'I was heartily sick, but as we neared the beach I felt excitement and was then relieved to hear the skipper of the LCA announce, "It's a dry one . . .".'

However, it was anything but a dry one for Pat Porteous, VC, and his D Troop:

> There was a hell of a chop in the sea and as my landing craft was lowered, she hit a very big wave and we took in a lot of water. There was a handpump to pump out the bilges, but it wasn't working very well, so we all started baling like mad. We managed to keep the water down, but every time a big wave came along we took in a bit more water. So we were baling all the way in. It was very cold, very miserable and I was afraid that the thing [LCA] was going to go down when we were still miles off the beach. . . .
>
> Anyway we got to within sight of the beach and there was a hell of a lot of smoke, and muck, and stuff flying about . . . when we were still, I suppose, about sixty yards out our poor landing craft finally gave up the ghost and sank in about three feet of water. We waded ashore. It wasn't too bad, but there was a lot of stuff flying about from some big German pillboxes just to our left.

This was to be expected, and they were prepared for such a reception, but it was the scene on the beach itself that was disarming. In the overall plan for the landings the leading battalions of 3rd Infantry Division, supported by the tanks of 27th Armoured Brigade, with their specialised beach-clearing equipment, had been allotted the task of clearing this beach of the many obstacles, wire and mines, then neutralising the enemy defences on the sand dunes, to enable the Commandos to dash ashore and speedily make straight for their objectives in Ouistreham.

But as they touched down on the beach the situation was vastly different to that expected. Ahead of them, on the beach, were some six rows of stakes and obstacles, only partially cleared, some of which still had mines attached to them. However, more grisly and alarming was the sight of scores of the dead and wounded of the East Yorks – 'just swilling about in the water', recalls Porteous.

McDougal was more explicit:

> Twenty yards up the beach we reached a line of men without the distinguishing rucksacks. They were the assault troops whose task had been to clear the beach and the immediate defences. At the moment they were committing suicide by trying to dig in where they were. Over to my right I saw one of their officers get to his feet, wave his men forward, run two or three paces and then crumple to the ground. No one else moved. As we drew level I kicked at the feet of the nearest man. 'Get up, you idiot, keep going.' The man made no move. He was dead.

So was the man next to him, while a third lay writhing on the sand, clutching at a shoulder that had been shattered by machine gun fire. They all looked like young troops and I thought that the man who had taught them to dig in on an open beach ought to be with them now. . . .

In direct contrast, Commandos had been drilled, since 1940, to get out of their landing craft quickly and go 'split arse' up and off the beach, even if the landing was opposed. Survival depended on adhering to this drill. There on the beaches of Normandy was proof of its validity.

It had become second nature to all in No. 4; indeed, L/Cpl Frank Farnborough, a veteran of Dieppe, recalls the final briefing from his troop leader, Capt Len Coulson, on the *Astrid* just the night before the landing. He writes: 'It all boiled down to this. Nip off the LCA a bit lively. Get off the beach a bit sharpish, and then go hell for leather for a place called Ouistreham to destroy the battery there.' One couldn't ask for a more direct and succinct instruction than that.

On the day Frank started to do just that too. 'The ramp went down and out we poured. I've never moved so fast in all my life.' He cleared the beach, but in the dunes, moving to the assembly area, he was hit: 'a burst from an automatic weapon of some sort made a mess of my left arm. It spun me round and down I went. Later when my Mae West was taken off me, there were bullet holes along it. So I was lucky to get away with that one.'

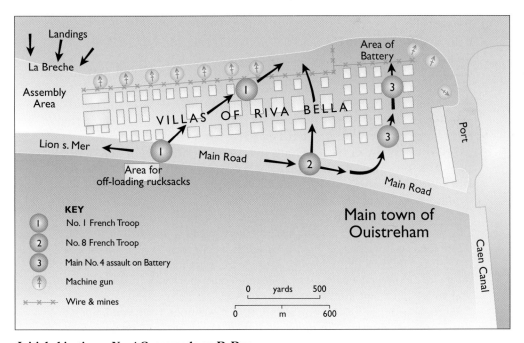

Initial objectives – No. 4 Commando on D-Day.

Frank was later evacuated through 'Doc' Patterson's Regimental Aid Post (RAP) back to England. He ends his personal experiences of D-Day on a laconic note: 'That's the story of my day trip to France.'

Mention of Patterson brings us to his account of the landing:

> We touched down, bumped and slewed round. Then the order, 'Ramp down!' The boat began to empty, and being in the stern, we 'Medics' were the last to leave. I seized a stretcher . . . staggered to the bows and flopped into the water. It was thigh deep. . . .
>
> There were many bodies in the water. One was hanging round a tripod beach obstacle. The water was churned with bursting shells. . . .

The first wounded man of No. 4 that Patterson saw was little Cpl Mullen, the popular intelligence corporal, unit inventor and 'unofficial war artist'. A little man with a very big brave heart – he was submerged up to his chin. Patterson and one of his orderlies, the stalwart Pte Hindmarsh, cut away Mullen's rucksack and dragged him to the water's edge. Then Patterson felt a smack across his bottom, as if someone had hit him with a big stick. It was a shell splinter; fortunately it hit nothing important. Less fortunate was Mullen; he died there and then, he was beyond help.

Sgt Linham, of Capt Burt's E Troop, recalls his landing. He left the landing craft, together with one of his Bren groups, L/Cpl Jennings, the No. 1, and Pte Youngman, the No. 2. They found the water waist deep and started to wade, but almost immediately Youngman was hit and sank under the weight of his rucksack. He never came up to the surface.

The story of Youngman's death, so early on D-Day, is made more poignant because his son, Ronald, has for the last seventeen years been the General Secretary and Treasurer of the Commando Association, and in that capacity organises and accompanies Commando veterans and families on the annual pilgrimages to Normandy, which include visits to the well-kept War Graves Commission's cemetery at Hermanville-sur-Mer, where Ron's father and other comrades who fell on 6 June are buried.

L/Cpl Gerry Swailes of A Troop still retains vivid memories of 'all those poor East Yorks who never got off the beach, and those beach stakes, some still with mines on them . . . and all that wire too'. He was one of those detailed to deal with the wire near the dunes. He gave his rifle to one of his mates while he started to cut the wire; unfortunately that 'mate' dropped his rifle in the sand which fouled and clogged the breech, making it useless. They tried to brush and wipe the sand off, but to no avail. Then decided to try another method. Unperturbed, 'we stood up and pissed on it . . . but still no good'. However, nearby was a dead soldier, 'so I took his Tommy gun and ammo, and kept it for the rest of my War . . .'.

Arguably, the men of Capt Carr's heavy weapons troop had the most gruelling task, clearing the bullet and shell-swept beach, carrying all their weapons, equipment and ammunition, because their jeeps weren't due to land until D + 1, plus their rucksacks and personal weapons. Pte Joe Burnett reckons that all those speed marches with full kit, weapons and ammunition in Sussex during the build-up for the invasion certainly paid off.

One of the bravest actions of the landing occurred when Capt Carr managed to get through a gap in the final wire fence on the dunes, and single-handed set off to deal with an enemy machine-gun post – hardly the job for the heavy weapons troop leader. He succeeded, thanks to some supporting fire, to scramble, still wearing his rucksack, up the small mound of the MG post and lob a grenade over the top and into the pit. It silenced the gun.

After the blast, Carr stood up, then slipped down to the foot of the slope underneath the MG post. Just then a stick grenade, thrown from the enemy position, landed between Carr and the gap in the wire. Amazingly, he got up unharmed and rejoined his men. A group of follow-up Commandos swarmed over the wire, worked their way round the back of the enemy post and finished off the crew before going on to deal with another enemy position.

Just beyond the dunes, amid some half-demolished buildings, was the Commando's assembly area where they regrouped and reorganised for the next phase of their operation – the twin assaults into Ouistreham.

Having described the landings of the Anglo (A to F) Troops of the Commando who landed in LCAs from the *Astrid* and the *Maid of Orleans*, it is now time to relate the exploits of the two French troops of No. 4 who landed separately, on the port side of the rest, from their LCIs, Nos 523 and 527. Unlike their comrades landing from the two LSIs, the French did not have to transfer from parent ship to smaller craft to land, but could do so directly, down the awkward ladder/ramps flanking the bows of their craft.

Although both LCIs beached, more or less, at the right place on the beach and at the right time, they had problems. (Incidentally, there are excellent models in the No. 4 Commando Museum in Ouistreham depicting, in detail, the landings and subsequent actions of No. 4 in Ouistreham.) First, because the beach obstacles had not been adequately cleared, No. 523 crashed into one of these obstacles and hit the beach so hard that it was stuck, but the French troops were able to use the laddered ramps to get ashore and charge off up the beach through little water.

No. 527 was not so fortunate. Her propellers were fouled on beach obstacles, then a direct hit from enemy fire smashed her ramps and some of the crew were wounded. Scrambling nets were hastily lowered over the sides and the Commandos started to swarm ashore. Some, too impatient to wait their turn to go down the nets, jumped down into the water and waded ashore.

In common with their other comrades in No. 4, the French too were appalled at the awful sight of floating bodies and the wounded soldiers of the H-hour assault troops in the water, and also those on the sand trying to dig in.

A dramatic drawing of the French Commandos' landing from their two LCIs, 523 and 527, on the beaches of La Breche on the morning of 6 June. (*Reproduced by courtesy of Ivor J. Pook, from papers etc. of his uncle, the late Lt Cdr Jack Berry, who commanded 523 on D-Day and was subsequently awarded the Légion d'Honneur for his part in those landings.*)

However, despite these initial setbacks, the French, with typical élan, dashed on up the beach. Guy Vourch, OC No. 1 Troop, one of the first of his countrymen to land on French soil – albeit sand – was caught up in the fever of the moment and yelled with the rest of his men as he stumbled in the wet sands inland towards the dark lines of the dunes and the assembly area. He had only gone a few yards, however, when there was an ear-splitting explosion immediately behind him. He felt numbing blows in his back and right arm as he was hurled forward on to the sand. For a moment, he lay dazed, scrambling weakly. He saw his men pressing on ahead and he felt bitter to be left behind. For him the battle was over almost before it had begun. He got rid of his heavy rucksack and eventually managed to get off that deadly beach without further wounding. Evacuated and then 'patched up', he was able to return to his troop some two months later, at which time they were only about six miles inland, still committed to their original task of holding the left flank of the invasion beach.

Enemy mortar fire, in particular, took a heavy toll of the French troops as they rushed up the last stretch of the beach and through the final wire – and a minefield – to the assembly area in the dunes.

Only 114 men (including 6 British signallers and medical orderlies) of the two French troops, out of the total of 177 who had left the LCIs such a short while before, made it to the assembly area. Fortunately, nearly all of the casualties were only wounded; but nevertheless they were now 'out of battle'. One of the wounded was Capt Kieffer, hit in the thigh by a mortar fragment, but he insisted on carrying on. Indeed, he played a crucial role in the subsequent action.

In the joint assembly area both elements of the 'Franco-Britannique' Commando got ready for the next, all-important, part of their operation. Troop leaders prepared for the next phase of the operation: they checked numbers and, where necessary, reorganised, all under the protective cover of Bren gunners who had been posted in the area to cover any likely landward approaches by the Germans.

McDougal had this to say about the assembly area.

> Here, a little off the beach, things were unnaturally quiet, after the chaotic din of the beach, which had been almost numbing in its intensity; it seemed extraordinary that we should be able to speak in a normal tone of voice here. Maybe the dunes were acting as a sort of baffle wall as we could still hear the thump of mortar bombs.

Col Dawson had, with typical inter-Allies' diplomacy, decided that the Commando two-prong assault into Ouistreham should be led by the French, although the six British troops had further to go to their objective. However, allowing Kieffer and his men to lead these assaults, in their own homeland, greatly appealed to their Gallic pride – and was much appreciated. It was a nice gesture.

So off the French went down the pre-selected route using the main road from Lion-sur-Mer to Ouistreham, past the fashionable pre-war villas of Riva Bella, followed by the rest of the Commando.

Dawson had planned that all in the Commando would offload their rucksacks at a certain spot, by the war-damaged holiday homes on the side of the road, soon after leaving the assembly area. Glad to be rid of these burdens, the men of No. 8 Troop, led by Lt Alex Lofi, set off to attack their objective. Sticking to the pre-selected route along the main road until reaching the side road that led to the objective, Lofi first encountered a 'signed minefield' which was crossed without any trouble; then they bypassed several machine-gun emplacements, which were unmanned. So far, so good.

Then their luck changed, for nearing their objective, they came under mortar fire which inflicted several casualties, including the wounding of Lt Hulot, who was in charge of the leading section. Nevertheless, they

Battle-weary: the strain of D-Day and the first few days of fighting in the Hauger area is clearly seen here on the face of Sgt Louis Lanternier, a member of one of the two French Troops of No. 4 Commando. (*Courtesy of the Imperial War Museum, London* – B5282)

continued down the road until almost on their objective, when they were held up by machine-gun fire. Notwithstanding, Lofi ordered his men to take up fire positions on the first floors of surrounding houses, which commanded good fields of fire on to 'the complex of very well hidden trenches in the middle of which stood the blockhouse, "Casino", still intact'.

From the houses No. 8 Troop engaged the enemy positions with every weapon, including their two K guns and the PIAT. Although the latter had very little effect on the concrete strongpoint, it inflicted casualties on the enemy in the open trenches. Under covering fire from within the troop, an assault was put in, but was repelled, so Lofi's men continued to keep up their fire on the enemy strongpoint.

F Troop making their way along the main Lion-sur-Mer to Ouistreham road, after having dumped their rucksacks, and heading for the road junction that led to the battery. The Commando carrying the mortar bombs is Rowland Oliver. (*Courtesy of the Imperial War Museum, London* – FLM1866)

Meanwhile, Kieffer and the other French troop, No. 1, were on their way to attack the Casino strongpoint from the rear. Taking the pre-planned route, No. 1 Troop moved down both sides of the road in their rehearsed tactical formations, until they were confronted by a formidable obstacle blocking the road. It was a large concrete anti-tank wall, which had not been identified in the pre-operation studies of aerial photos. It was over six feet high, but there was a small gap in the middle just wide enough for a man to squeeze through. Fortunately for the Commandos, this very same wall denied the enemy in Casino, fifty yards away, a clear view of anyone approaching from this direction, so they quickly made their way through the gap – one at a time.

Once past the anti-tank ditch the men of this troop, like their comrades in No. 8 Troop had done, took up fire positions in the villas overlooking the strongpoint, but from the rear. Then they too started to engage the enemy, but the Germans' reply was equally effective, especially their fire from an 88-mm gun, which destroyed one of the houses, which only a few minutes earlier had been evacuated by a group of this troop.

The momentum of the Commandos' attack had slackened and for the time being they had to be content with just engaging the enemy with fire.

It was at this stage that an aged Frenchman, a veteran of the First World War and a member of the local Resistance, appeared and offered his assistance with the expressed wish that he wanted to fight. So he was given a rifle. More importantly, he told one of the French warrant officers, Faure, where some telephone cables were which linked the enemy observation posts in the Ouistreham area to their fortifications and artillery emplacements inland. This gallant old Frenchman then led Faure and one other to where the cables were buried, a hole was dug, the cables located and successfully severed.

But as Kieffer subsequently reported, 'This vital piece of information and action to disrupt the enemy's lines of communication didn't solve the problem of capturing the "Casino" strongpoint.'

Kieffer, who had been worried about Lofi and his troop, had only just arrived at the No. 1 Troop position and, finding them pinned down too, was in the act of mounting a desperate attack when he happened to hear a message on his radio that some British amphibious tanks, having cleared the beach, were in the Ouistreham area. So, with his batman, he went back to the main road to see if he could find one.

His luck was in. He returned soon afterwards riding on the top of a tank. This chance acquisition made all the difference. Kieffer guided the tank to a position just in front of the Casino strongpoint and directed its fire. The results were dramatic. The enemy guns were silenced and No. 1 Troop stormed in to mop up. In less than thirty minutes after the 'godsend' arrival of the tank, the Casino objective had been taken. The capture of the Casino and the subsequent action brought in No. 4's first batch of prisoners – some eleven of them.

This symbolic monument by the site of the Casino strongpoint in Ouistreham is dedicated to the members of the French troops of No. 4 Commando, who were the first French troops to fight in Normandy for the liberation of their country. Each French Commando who was killed on D-Day is remembered on a single granite stone, like those on the left of the picture. The cupola at the base of the monument was one of the revolving turrets of a machine-gun emplacement that covered the beaches. (*Author's Collection*)

The French Commandos had achieved their mission and were now in control of the western end of the Riva Bella surburb of Ouistreham, but their success was at a cost, for casualties had further depleted Nos 1 and 8 Troops.

While they had been involved with the capture of the Casino, the rest of Dawson's Commando were fighting their way to the battery at the eastern end of the invasion beaches, near the entrance to the port. And we follow them as they left the assembly area in the wake of the two French troops.

C Troop, led by Capt David Style, was the advance guard as they proceeded down the main road into Ouistreham as planned. They were responsible for dealing with any enemy opposition en route. Next in the Commando advance was Porteous's D Troop, who had the task of securing the entrances to the battery, but first they had to cross the wide and challenging anti-tank ditch, for which they had initially brought a specially designed telescopic ladder, but this had been damaged beyond use during the landing.

Following D Troop was A Troop, who with their K guns were to provide close support fire from the first floor of the houses overlooking the battery. Finally came the two assault troops, E, under Capt 'Hutch' Burt, who were to destroy the right-hand guns, and F Troop, under Capt Len Coulson, who were to deal with the left-hand guns.

Commando HQ, of Col Dawson and his little group, following up behind the leading troops, were to establish themselves at a suitable place halfway between where the French troops left the main road to attack the Casino strongpoint and where the main Commando force was to leave the main road for its assault on the battery.

Capt Carr's heavy weapons were to follow up in the rear of the other troops and take up firing positions for their mortars at the road junction where the rest turned off the main road.

All these troops, like their French comrades in front, were – thankfully – to dump their rucksacks at the same pre-selected place. The Commandos would collect their rucksacks later, after dealing with their two respective objectives – 'or at least some of us would', commented Gilchrist rather morbidly. 'Meanwhile it was a load off our backs, if not our minds. We were now lightly equipped, spartan like', he added.

C Troop got off to a good start and made rapid progress, but the following troops had casualties from sporadic shelling and the odd 'Moaning Minnie' oil bomb. Such casualties were dragged to ditches at the side of the road to await medical treatment, while the rest pressed on.

As they went along, another tank, a stray, like the one commandeered by Kieffer, lumbered up and attached itself to the Commando column. It wasn't long before it was in action to deal with a house in which some enemy snipers had been firing on E and F Troops.

By now C Troop were successfully penetrating further and further towards the road junction that led to the battery. The rest were only able to

No. *DIW/III/CAS/RNF*
(If replying, please quote
above No.)

Army Form B. 104—81.

Infantry Record Office,

York

27 June 1944

~~Sir, or~~ Madam,

I regret to have to inform you that a report has been received from

the War Office to the effect that (No.) *142402* (Rank) **FUS**

(Name) *MAHAN   Robt McKenna*

(Regiment) ROYAL NORTH'D FUSLIERS ....was wounded
but remained at duty.

on the .... *6* ....day of .... *JUNE* 19 *44*

It has not yet been reported into what hospital he has been

admitted, nor are other particulars yet known, but directly any

further information is received it will be at once communicated to you.

I am to express to you the sympathy and regret of the Army

Council.

Yours faithfully,

Officer in charge of Records.

This was the sort of official notice that next-of-kin dreaded coming in their post, the curt
formal notification that a member of the family had been wounded – or even worse. However,
in this case, the Army Form B104–81 states that although Bob Mahan had been wounded on
6 June, he had remained at duty. Indeed, he was much involved in the fierce fighting at Hauger
on D + 4. (*Bob Mahan*)

progress by making a series of short dashes, for they now came under mortar fire in addition to the odd sniper's fire. However, with the assistance of the tank they were able to maintain the momentum of the advance, but not without some further casualties.

Notwithstanding their steady, unhindered progress so far, C Troop came under heavy machine-gun fire as they left the main road and turned down towards the battery. 'It was here', wrote Pte Bob Mahan, one of that splendid intake of policemen, 'that Sgt Martin [another of the same police intake] and I got through some defensive wire, when we were both hit by mortar fragments. Martin was badly wounded, but I only suffered minor wounds and was able to carry on towards the battery area.'

Having reached the planned area to take up their positions to cover the arrival of the Commando, Style sited his men and the troop weapons according to their prearranged plan. One of the troop's snipers, Sgt 'Paddy' Byrne, had the satisfaction of seeing two of the enemy fall to successive shots, while L/Cpl Gerry Lynn, with the troop's PIAT, scored a couple of direct hits on the observation/control tower that dominated the area. Like his French comrades with their PIAT, however, he found that these bombs had little effect except, in his own words, 'to produce a flurry of enemy grenades'.

About this time, A Troop arrived on the scene and, moving further towards the battery, dashed into the nearby houses to take up fire positions on the first and second floors, to cover the approach of D, E and F Troops.

Bill Bidmead (A Troop) wrote:

> We were soon installed in one of the top rooms of a house. The rest of the Troop were in other nearby houses. What a marvellous view we had of the battery position. But in the midst of it was a 60 ft observation/control tower, which we were told, in our briefing, would be a pile of rubble. It still stands today and is a museum. The Germans were throwing grenades from the top at our men getting in position for the assault. Then all hell was let loose as our K guns opened up.

Pte Alex Morris, also in A Troop, was No. 1 on a K gun and well remembers their time in those houses overlooking the battery; he adds:

> The K gun was a magnificent gun, but because of its unreliable sights, tracer rounds were loaded on a ratio of one tracer to five ball rounds . . . I directed my fire to the top of the tower hitting the wall and just over, trying to keep the Germans' heads down and stop them from lobbing grenades down on our chaps. . . .

Next to arrive, after A Troop, in the area was D Troop, responsible for securing the crossing of the anti-tank ditch. To Porteous's utter surprise and relief he found planks across it, which, he later admitted, 'was just as well as one of the blokes who was carrying the specially made ladder had been killed on the beach, and this substitute bridge had been smashed to pieces'.

TSM Bill Portman reckoned that the planks had been positioned over the ditch for the convenience of the 'Jerries' stationed in the battery; this was no doubt the case, and in particular when they returned from 'a night out on the town'. Be that as it may, those planks were much appreciated – and well used – by Porteous's men, who rushed over to attack the enemy in the gun pits protecting the gun emplacements. They were most successful and took several prisoners.

Hard on the heels of D Troop's success, E and F Troops crossed over the anti-tank ditch and made straight for their allotted gun emplacements, only to find, to their utter amazement – no guns! Instead, all they found were telephone poles cut to size to represent guns and mounted on improvised carriages. They later learnt from a local resident that the guns had been removed some three or four days earlier and resited a couple of miles inland.

Nevertheless, Burt's and Coulson's troops started to mop up the whole of the battery site with considerable success. They had a number of prisoners at the end of the operation. There followed a short period of taking stock, having 'a breather', seeing to the wounded and reorganising for the next phase of the operation.

The assault on the battery had not been without casualties. The walking wounded were led back to 'Doc' Patterson's RAP, which he had established in the area where the rucksacks had been dumped. Bidmead recalls collecting the dead together to await burial parties.

Among those wounded in the attack were veterans Bill Nabbs and Gerry Lynn, both with serious eye injuries. Bill lost the sight of one of his eyes, but that didn't deter him from being the Commando's standard-bearer for many years at the annual Normandy pilgrimages, while Gerry, although also blinded in one eye, devoted many years, postwar, to voluntary service with the cadets, for which he was awarded the British Empire Medal (BEM). Sadly he died while I was writing this book.

Back at the RAP Patterson had established, casualties were coming in, but German mortar fire on the area forced Patterson to move all his stretcher cases to the cover of a house, which like many in the area was empty. Later he was able to evacuate the badly wounded down to field ambulances in the beach-head for transfer back to England. But many, including Farnborough, Lynn, Hooper and Tyreman, had to spend the night in the RAP, during which time the immediate area was strafed by a lone enemy aircraft.

Having completed the first phase of their D-Day missions, the Commando started on the next, the link-up with the Airborne troops and the rest of Lovat's brigade on the far side of the Orne, about six miles away.

After a quick 'O' group at Commando and Troop levels, and having – reluctantly – collected their rucksacks, No. 4 set off on their 'forced march'. Early on, as they left the coastal area and got into the farming hinterland, Joe

Burnett, one of the mortarmen, and his mates – in true Commando style – 'took over' a horse and cart to carry their mortars, equipment, ammunition and their rucksacks.

About the same time, Maj Menday, the second-in-command, who had temporarily taken over from Dawson, who was being treated for his wounds, decided to send the adjutant, Capt Gilchrist, ahead to liaise with Lovat's HQ and find out what was expected of No. 4 on arrival over the Orne. 'Get information and be ready to meet us', he instructed Gilchrist.

'I was to be the advance party of one . . . a man nearby had a folding parachute bicycle, we had managed to bring a few of these light-weight machines ashore, just in case – I was the case', recalled Gilchrist.

So off he rode, leaving his rucksack in the care of his batman, McCall, and Menday's batman, Macaulay, who had volunteered to take it along – 'carrying it between them like a baby's portable cot'.

Compared with that previous march to the Casino and the battery, this one across open farmland was comparatively quiet, except for some unwelcome mortar fire and shells whistling overhead, destined for those still on the beaches.

There was plenty of evidence of the fighting waged by their comrades of No. 6 Commando who had previously passed through on their way to the bridges. Bill Bidmead wrote:

> Quite a bit of opposition must have been encountered by the Brigade, judging by the carnage we met on our way. Many dead Germans lay on the side of the road. Further on we came across some chaps of No. 6 who must have been ambushed on their bikes. Dead Germans and Commandos lay all over the road.

Now, more concerned with his own progress, he comments: 'As we marched on, the sun got hotter and hotter, and our rucksacks got heavier and heavier. . . .'

John Skerry, then a sergeant in E Troop, is well able to recall the names of the villages they passed through, for he still has his mud-stained map of the area, carefully kept for nigh on sixty years. Colleville-sur-Orne (after the war it was renamed Colleville-Montgomery, in honour of 'Monty'), St Aubin-d'Arquenay, Bieville-Beuville and, finally, Benouville, where the Commando closed up, rested for a while and prepared for that dash over the Orne Bridge, soon to be known for evermore as 'Pegasus Bridge'.

A couple of hours earlier Lord Lovat and his piper, Bill Millin, had staked their claim in history when they crossed over the bridge – 'two minutes late', apologised his Lordship – to join forces with the Airborne troops. However, contrary to many subsequent accounts and the scene in the epic film, *The Longest Day*, Millin did not play as he went over. Neither he nor Lovat had time. Like the rest, they were running as fast as they could, to avoid being hit by sniper fire.

When Gilchrist arrived, still on his bike, at the bridge, he managed to get a tow across by hanging on to the back strut of a jeep. He quickly found Brigade HQ, where he reported on No. 4's actions in Ouistreham and obtained details of Lovat's intentions for the deployment of the Commando on the ridge of high ground on the eastern side of the Orne, before returning to the bridge to await the arrival of the Commando.

During that brief rest in the area of Benouville, before crossing the bridge, they could hear machine-gun fire and the single shots of the snipers, so they knew what to expect. They split up into small groups and dashed over the bridge as fast as their legs could carry them, with bullets hitting and ricocheting off the metal sections. Halfway over, one of F Troop's popular officers, Lt Peter Mercer-Wilson, was killed outright by a sniper's bullet. It was a bitter blow to his two fellow officers in the troop, Coulson and McDougal; they had been together for some time, had shared the same billets and were likened to 'The Three Musketeers'. McDougal, who saw Peter fall, silently vowed he would return to the bridge area as soon as he possibly could to ensure that he had been properly buried.

Meanwhile, he had a job to do. Greatly saddened, he stumbled up the lane beyond the bridge with the rest of his section. The war had to go on.

F Troop, No. 4 Commando, at Breville, July 1944. 'Big Mac' McDougal is on the extreme right of the back row. (*Roland Oliver*)

Reaching the far side of the Orne and linking up with the Airborne troops meant that No. 4 had completed the second phase of their D-Day mission. Now for the third phase: to take part in the defence of the high ground and deny it to the enemy, thus securing the left flank of the Allied invasion. It was a vital task and much depended on it.

Having cleared the two bridges over the canal and the river, the Commando halted in the cover of a shady road, and in tactical troop groups, with all-round protection, 'gratefully sank down into the luxury of dusty grass by the roadside. . . . Aching shoulders were eased from biting straps, and cramped limbs stretched to the comfort of the prone position. . . .'

'Down in the dip beyond the roadside hedge one sub-section began a "surreptitious brew up" . . . the whole thing suddenly took on the aspect of a successful completed scheme', wrote McDougal.

But the welcome rest didn't last long, for while the troops were relaxing the troop leaders attended a Commando 'O' group, when they were given a brief résumé of the overall situation in this sector of the invasion. On the whole, things were going quite well, although some of the paratroopers had been dropped in the wrong places, and as yet there was no news of them – this last item of news applied to No. 4's own Lt David Haig-Thomas and his batman, Ryder, of C Troop (the parachute troop), who had dropped with 6 Airborne Division. There was much sorrow a few days later when Ryder turned up at No. 4's position and reported that Haig-Thomas had been killed in an enemy ambush soon after landing. It was a sad loss; he was a very popular and respected, fun-loving, Commando officer.

The enemy had been mounting counter-attacks on the Paras' positions around the bridges, and as a result of this pressure Gen Gale and Brig Lovat had decided to modify their original plan and limit their next phase to holding a tighter and more compact perimeter on the high ground to the east of the Orne.

This meant that No. 4 didn't have much further to go to take up their newly allotted defensive locality. It was absolutely essential, however, that they got dug in in their positions by dusk, as the enemy would almost certainly counter-attack in strength, as soon as they knew where the Paras and Commandos were. So it was 'Up on your feet' once more, and, shouldering those heavy rucksacks, they trudged off to what would become their 'battle stations'. Along the main road that runs parallel to the Orne and leading towards Sallenelles and the coast, they marched in tactical groups ready to meet any opposition en route.

After nearly two miles they left the main road and took a minor one that led to the château of Hauger, an impressive building in the style of the Napoleon III period. There in the grounds Maj Menday, still 'holding the fort' for the wounded Dawson, allocated troop areas, with the short overall order 'not to yield an inch'.

Troop leaders then led their men to their areas or, rather, 'Troop Blobs', as they were called; for in this close countryside of small fields marked with hedgerows and sunken tracks, small woods, orchards and farm outbuildings, aptly called 'bocage' country, linear defence was out of the question, and little islands of all-round defence, with extremely limited fields of fire, were the only answer.

As they took up their positions and started to dig, all were greatly encouraged to watch the spectacular arrival of 6 Airborne Division's reinforcements of glider-borne troops descending on to the ground behind them, in the Paratroopers' close perimeter guarding the bridges.

Commenting on the forward position of his A Troop, Bill Bidmead had this to say:

> We arrived at our allotted position well in front of the rest of the Commando . . . it seemed to be a death trap of a place . . . a corner of a wood with a cornfield on our right flank . . . practically no field of fire because of the woods . . . we could be approached by the Germans with little difficulty and no warning, if we didn't watch it.

He continued: 'After a little thanksgiving get-together by Ted Lewis [the TSM] we started to dig the best positions for ourselves and our "K" guns.'

In every troop locality the men went off in their usual pairs, although some had to pair up with a new mate because of casualties, and started to dig those all-important slit trenches, as they had done so many times before on exercises back in England, Scotland and Wales over the last four years. This time it was different: their lives depended on them, not just their prestige; however, there was some consolation in that they wouldn't have to fill in the trenches afterwards as they did at the end of all training exercises.

On pre-D-Day exercises Lovat's brigade had experimented in digging defensive positions and had decided that the standard infantry entrenching tool was not up to the job. So they had come ashore with decent tools – miners' picks and 'G.S. shovels', which had been specially foreshortened to make carriage and digging easier.

Initially, the men worked in pairs, but as progress was made one of them started on a most essential morale-boosting chore – 'to brew up' and get something to eat, while his mate carried on digging.

In every man's rucksack were rations for forty-eight hours and a little 'Tommy' cooker; the latter was ideal and quite efficient for boiling water and heating pre-packed and tinned foods.

As darkness fell and the trenches were being completed, there was a general quietness on No. 4's front, although enemy shells did whistle overhead on their way to the Airborne perimeter and there was also some ominous enemy air activity, as well as machine-gun and mortar fire, on the Commando's right flank. With the trenches dug, all settled down in them to watch and wait, expecting an enemy attack at any time from any quarter.

But according to McDougal it was not just quiet, but 'menacingly quiet'. There were suspicious sounds of the enemy nearby, but it had been laid

This large modern stone memorial has been erected to honour all those of the British-French No. 4 Commando who landed on the beaches at La Breche to assault the Casino strongpoint and the German battery at Ouistreham. (*Author's Collection*)

down, as Commando policy, not to fire or make contact with the enemy at this stage unless directly attacked. They were to lie 'doggo', so that the Germans had no idea of their strength or their positions. Coulson's instructions to his men were typical: 'We are here to stay, so if we can keep quiet till we're properly dug in and properly ready, we'll be able "to sort them out" if they do attack.'

Thus it was as night fell and midnight came to bring to an end the momentous first day, the men of No. 4 Commando were firmly dug in around the château of Hauger on the ridge beyond the Orne, having achieved all that had been demanded of them on the historic day.

Capt Carr later wrote of that day: 'I was one of the luckier ones [although he had been wounded on the wrist and hand by shrapnel] to be around at the end of D-Day. . . . So ended the greatest day of my army career, a day on which I am proud to have been of service to my country, a day for which I give thanks to God for my survival, and to my wonderfully brave comrades who fought with me.'

Those sentiments, so aptly expressed by Knyvet Carr, would seem to be an appropriate place to conclude this chapter on what was for all who took part 'The Longest Day'.

CHAPTER NINE

The Long Stint
(7 June to 9 September)

The night of D-Day/D + 1 was quieter than anticipated; there was no enemy counter-attack. Nevertheless it was a night all remembered for a variety of reasons as they waited and watched in the darkness. A darkness 'when every sound was questioned, for even the rustle of the corn sent chills up and down the spine'.

A system of sentries was established in every troop locality whereby one man of each pair, or threesome (as in the case of the Bren team), in a slit trench would be awake at any one time. But on the whole there wasn't much sleep for anyone; they were all concerned and determined to remain vigilant.

There was an element of mild excitement in the F Troop position at about 0200 hrs when three miserable-looking and terrified Germans, who were unarmed, literally bumped into one of the sub-section's positions and gave themselves up. They had no alternative. Apparently they had fled from the fighting at Ouistreham. They were taken to Commando HQ for interrogation by the Intelligence Section, which had been supplemented by two German-speaking Commandos from X Troop of No. 10 Commando. This was the only excitement of that long night.

As dawn rose, the Commando 'stood to' at 0430 hrs, with the expectations of some form of enemy attack, but nothing materialised, and with strict instructions from Brigade HQ not to make contact unless directly attacked, No. 4 just sat tight. There was some isolated and ineffective enemy sniping during the morning, but this gave way to heavy shelling and mortar fire on both E and F Troops in the afternoon.

By the afternoon most of the slit trenches, which had all been sited to provide close all-round protection and to give the occupants sufficient proximity to be in audible contact with each other in the dark, had some form of overhead cover. In addition, signallers had been laying line to augment the wireless and runner communications between all the Troop and Commando HQs.

One interesting feature of the defended localities was the use made of the walls around the château, in which holes were made to provide fire breaches – these can still be seen today. Small 'potholes' were also dug to meet the demands of 'bladders and bowels'.

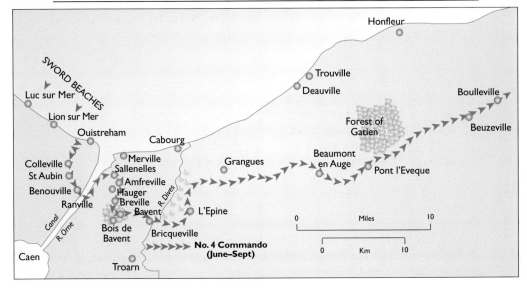

The Normandy Campaign. No. 4 Commando – 6 June–6 September.

In the two French Troops' area there had been far more enemy activity, so much so that Maj Menday, still commanding, instead of the wounded Dawson, reckoned that the enemy interest in this sector could indicate an attack from the Sallenelles direction, so he ordered Kieffer to send a reconnaissance patrol to that village to assess enemy presence and strength. An enterprising Sgt-Maj Lardennois managed to enter the village unseen, and by questioning the villagers obtained much useful information before returning. In the event, because of increased sniper and heavier mortar fire, Kieffer decided to postpone any offensive action at this stage.

In the early evening a group of enemy dive-bombers suddenly swept the whole of Le Plein ridge, occupied by Lovat's brigade, 'filling the evening with shrill horror, they didn't stay long, though they swooped overhead and machine gunned the whole area before they returned to their base'. Thereafter enemy air attacks were sporadic and mostly confined to single plane attacks, usually in the late evening.

On the main No. 4 Commando front the night of D + 1/D + 2 was again a quiet one in that there was no enemy attack, but the woods immediately in front of the German positions were frequently lit by illuminated flares and red Verey light signals, and all wondered if the enemy was preparing an attack. However, on the French troops' front, at about 0200 hrs (now D + 2), Kieffer received a message that some German tanks were approaching his positions, so he sent out a patrol to investigate, but it returned with a negative report. Nevertheless, he sited his PIATs to cover any likely tank approaches, and at dawn a single tank was spotted moving towards a small hill, but then it suddenly disappeared and was not sighted again.

Back in the main Hauger position, after 'stand down' that morning, some arrangements were made to try to let the men get some sleep, on a rota basis. Bidmead wrote:

What a heavenly relief, I wrapped myself up in my blanket and lay by the top of my slit trench. I had not been there long when I heard, 'f—— hell! Germans!!' Looking up, coming through the woods, silhouetted in the early morning mist, came hordes of Germans. They must have crept up on us during the night. But they hadn't seen us yet. It was then that 'Taff' Isherwood picked up his K gun and emptied a full magazine into them. . . . The rest of the Troop added their fire power. The screams and cries of the dying and wounded Germans on that June morning were terrible.

Alex Morris, another K gunner, who for the past thirty-six hours had been patiently waiting to fire his lethal weapon, remembers the moment he took up his gun and, taking aim, delivered burst after burst through the trees. 'It was a hell of a racket, tracers ricocheting in all directions in the wood.'

But the enemy weren't just in that one wood. A Troop now found itself coming under fire from three sides, yet in spite of the casualties being inflicted on the enemy, they were forced to withdraw. The position was untenable because it was out of sight from the main Commando position, could not be supported by direct covering fire and didn't have a gunner forward observation officer (FOO) to call for direct artillery fire. Accordingly they were compelled to pull back through the fourth clear side to the main Commando position, in a phased withdrawal, sub-section by sub-section, as best they could, bringing all their weapons and their wounded with them.

Morris continues: 'It was while we were still firing that the order came down to leave our rucksacks behind and pull back to the main position . . . to withdraw in the best possible way to keep our K guns intact . . . it was an order so well carried out that not a single man nor gun was missing when we finally arrived at F Troop lines.'

On arriving there, Alex Morris dropped into a trench occupied by Pte Ernie Ostick, 'an old colleague of mine from the Manchester City Police'. Morris told Ostick what had happened, and the latter wondered if the enemy would follow up. Then, apparently, Morris reminded Ostick, 'Don't forget, Ernie, you are supposed to be looking after me.' This was a standing joke between the two ex-policemen, as Ostick had promised Morris's father that he would keep an eye on his son when they had volunteered to join the Commandos.

Morris and the rest of A Troop reckoned that their treatment of the enemy with their K guns 'made them think twice about making another attack that day, as there wasn't one'.

He added this final note about their action that morning:

one thing that did upset us about the withdrawal was the loss of our rucksacks, which contained all our personal belongings, extra clothing and cigarettes etc. However, a couple of weeks later, a daytime patrol discovered our rucksacks still in the ditch at the edge of the wood and many of them were found to be intact, apart from a bullet hole or two. It would seem that the Germans had been suspicious of any booby traps and so had fired a few rounds into them.

That morning also saw 'Hutch' Burt's E Troop, whose position was bedevilled by a narrowing cornfield that terminated only about fifty yards in front of them, subject to considerable shelling, mortar fire and some sniping. This, together with widespread enemy movement in front of the whole brigade front, seemed to indicate that the enemy were making reconnaissances for a major attack. But it didn't come that day.

However, the enemy shelling and mortar fire did – and it never let up. It continued to be the bane of the Commandos' existence for the next three weeks. The Commandos labelled these times 'hate sessions'. Gilchrist recalls: 'At every meal time, almost without fail, a bomb would whine overhead and crash down somewhere in the unit area. Sometimes a single bomb, sometimes a concentration over a period of two hours.'

No. 4 wasn't alone in these 'hate sessions'. Col Mills-Roberts, commanding No. 6 Commando, alongside No. 4 on the ridge, experienced similar treatment:

our chief trouble was the rising number of casualties from enemy mortars – every day the toll of these mounted. The Germans used mobile mortar teams, some of these were horse drawn. They would move into a certain place, fire a number of rounds and then move on to the next position, so that retaliation was difficult.

As the days went by and the Commandos got wise to these tactics, they developed warning procedures. Look-outs, with whistles, would be posted forward, and as soon as they heard the 'phut, phut, phut' of the mortars, they would blow their whistles as a warning to take cover. This worked to a degree, but the casualties continued.

Back to that evening of D + 2, after 'standing down', as darkness fell, they all prepared for their third night of waiting and watching. As yet they hadn't had the opportunity to get some proper sleep or rest, or the chance to take off boots or even have a wash or shave.

Soon after dark the enemy made a sudden and sharp attack on C Troop's position, but it was beaten off. Some of this German force, who had not taken part in the attack, however, appeared to be taking up positions in the cornfield, staying there while their comrades retreated. They started to open fire on C Troop. Capt Style decided to send a party to deal with them; they were successful, forcing the enemy to withdraw, without loss to themselves. Later that same night, there were sounds of a battle from the direction of Sallenelles – much automatic small-arms fire and the thumps of grenades. A short time afterwards a group of Commandos from 45 RM Commando staggered into F Troop's locality. They were breathless and distressed. They told Capt Len Coulson that the enemy had broken into their position and were established on the road leading into No. 4's position. This could be serious. Coulson immediately contacted Maj Menday at HQ. His response was instant.

Gilchrist records the action that followed:

Within a matter of minutes, following a hurried 'O' Group, Pat Porteous was leading his men down the road. They charged into the enemy and got to grips with them with their automatic weapons. Although outnumbered by at least two to one, Porteous's men routed the Germans, killing several and putting the rest to flight.

They had restored the situation, but suffered casualties, depleting D Troop even more. But there was no further enemy attack that night.

Next morning, D + 4, all in the unit, after another sleepless night, were, in the words of one, 'almost at the end of our tether for want of sleep'. They were utterly exhausted, yet all knew what was ahead. Capt Coulson expressed this general 'gut feeling' and belief when he told his men 'I think it's bound to come today.' His hunch was proven correct.

At about 0930 hrs the whole of the main No. 4 locality was heavily shelled and mortared for about half an hour. But they weren't the only ones. The Germans had been plastering No. 6 Commando for a couple of hours beforehand, and had followed it with a heavy attack against their positions on the extreme right flank of Lovat's brigade. Like the other Commandos, No. 6 had been instructed, in the event of an attack, to hold their fire until the last possible moment.

Now they did just that, as Mills-Roberts describes:

The Germans entered our defensive rectangle, two sides of which bristled with rifles and Brens. Not a shot was fired until the massed enemy was about sixty yards away. Then all weapons opened up. There was chaos in the orchard, killed and wounded lay still; the rest came on, but the attack had lost its impetus. . . .

Thanks to the presence of a forward officer bombardment (FOB), No. 6 was able to call for artillery support from the heavy battleships offshore. Their fire was almost immediate and hammered the roads where enemy reserves were being moved up from beyond Breville.

The attacks on No. 6 continued until nearly midday, before they were finally repulsed and the enemy withdrew completely. Meanwhile, it had become the turn of No. 4 to bear the brunt of another determined full-scale German attack.

It was during the early barrage of enemy mortar and artillery fire that the first sighting of any enemy on the No. 4 Commando position was made by F Troop, who up to this stage had not been subject to any enemy attacks or incursions, apart from some odd sniping. They had, of course, been harassed by the universal mortar and artillery fire.

They spotted a couple of Germans with wireless equipment, apparent observers for the German mortar/artillery batteries, walking along in such a casual and nonchalant manner as to suggest that they were unaware they were practically in F Troop's territory – in fact, only about twenty yards from a forward slit trench. Needless to add, they didn't survive.

But oddly enough their hasty demise coincided with intensified shelling: 'the noise in the orchards and wooded areas was deafening . . . trees resounded to explosions and the rendering of timber . . . descending shrapnel rattled on the buildings . . . it reached its peak in the afternoon'. It was later reckoned that this increased bombarding was the enemy's revenge for their thwarted attacks on No. 6 Commando.

At about 1700 hrs F Troop saw the enemy massing directly opposite their positions, so Coulson sent his 2-in mortar men, 'Jock' Dale, who had been on the 'tube' at Dieppe, and L/Cpl 'Rollie' Oliver, to take up a firing position in the orchard to engage them with HE. This they did, with success, until all their bombs were expended, when they returned to their slit trench.

At this moment the FOB, the one who earlier had been with No. 6, arrived and reported to assist Coulson. The latter was not altogether happy about 'friendly' naval fire from offshore warships; he was a bit sceptical. However, he agreed to have a sample 'stonk' on the wood in front of his position, where the enemy were obviously forming up and preparing to attack them. The FOB sent off the relevant map references and fire details over the wireless to the battleships, and after a while yelled out: 'Shot one!'

For a moment nothing happened as the troop waited expectantly and apprehensively in the safety of their slit trenches. Then suddenly there was an almighty explosion, not on the wood, but in the corner of the orchard where just minutes before Dale and Oliver had been with their mortar. Showers of stones, earth and tree debris splattered down on the area, then the 15-in naval shell buried itself before exploding, leaving an enormous crater. It was a narrow escape for those two mortar men.

An embarrassed and apologetic FOB assured Len Coulson that the next rounds would be all right; however, at this rather delicate moment another artillery expert arrived on the scene. This chap was from a 25-pdr regiment, which was in support of the Airborne Division. He immediately impressed Couslon, who decided to accept his offer of help, while the FOB left quietly.

After being 'put in the picture', this gunner officer clambered up a nearby wall, reviewed the situation, and commented, 'There're quite a lot of the bastards, aren't there? Not much point giving them one or two rounds, might as well shove about twelve rounds in right away.' Coulson agreed.

After checking range, map references and the like, the gunner officer transmitted these details and the number of rounds to his battery, located to the rear of No. 4 down in the area of the bridge.

Meanwhile, all of F Troop, wisely, after the previous experience of 'friendly' fire, slid deep into their slit trenches. 'There was a whistling overhead and the edge of the wood disappeared in clouds of black smoke. The gunner officer whooped in triumph, and F Troop's look-out man up in a tree, shouted, "Just the job, send some more!"'

Another salvo was fired and then the airborne gunner officer declared, 'It's no use asking for more. We're rationed until they get more ammo ashore, so that's your lot for today', and he departed.

The artillery fire on the Germans in the wood certainly broke up their planned attack for the time being, but in retaliation their shelling and mortar fire was stepped up. Much of this increased fire fell on E Troop, where in the space of a few minutes they suffered several severe casualties. Sgt Ernie Brooks recalls that he and Sgt 'Jock' Laing were conferring with their troop leader, 'Hutch' Burt, when they were all three hit by shrapnel. Laing, one of the Commando's best footballers, was killed instantly, Hutch was badly wounded, as was Ernie Brooks; both had to be evacuated back to England, via the bridgehead.

In a matter of those few minutes, E Troop, already depleted of both section officers and TSM Heaynes, as casualties on D-Day, were down to fewer than twenty all ranks, with a section sergeant temporarily in charge.

In spite of the bombardment in their forming-up area, the Germans were determined to remount their attack on F Troop and used their MG 34 machine-guns to provide immediate close support across the open ground.

But F Troop had been prepared and patiently waiting for this moment for three days. With well-controlled fire from all their troop weapons, including the 2-in mortar, they took a very heavy toll of the initial attack. But the enemy re-formed and started again, only to meet another fusillade of sustained and accurate fire. This time the attack melted away, and those still alive retreated, taking their wounded with them.

'We've done it, we've done it! They've gone for good!' shouted a jubilant Coulson, and for good measure he got Knyvet Carr to range on to the retreating Germans, with his 3-in mortars, as they withdrew via the wood. It was a significant victory, with hardly any casualties.

Elsewhere both C and A plus the French troops became heavily involved in enemy attacks on their positions too. On the left flank C Troop fought off a heavy German attack, having previously accounted for a number of the enemy with an ambush sited on a highly likely line of approach. The fighting then continued at short range. Cpl Bob Mahan wrote, 'Capt Style had ordered me to knock out a machine gun which had been set up and was firing from the embankment of a sunken track/road. I crawled through the corn and was able to knock out the crew with a couple of grenades.'

He continues: 'I then heard Capt Style calling me from the roadway. When I reached him, he was standing with his Colt covering about twelve Germans, with their hands in the air, apparently surrendering, but refusing to lay down their weapons.'

Unbeknown to Mahan at the time he was on his way to deal with the machine-gun, a group of Germans, under the cover of a white flag, had started to approach Style's position. So the troop leader, with some of his men, went forward to accept their surrender; this had been about the same time that Style had shouted out to Bob Mahan. When he joined Style, the latter told him not to shoot the Germans, although Mahan writes: 'I was inclined not to obey, with so many of my comrades casualties.'

Then it happened. Unseen by any of C Troop, a German had crawled, under the cover of a hedge, to a position where he was able to throw a stick grenade and then open fire with his Schmeisser automatic. The stick grenade burst beside David Style's leg and shredded his calf; it also killed one of his men, who was beside him. A burst from the Schmeisser caught Style as he fell, hitting him in the chest and shoulder, and killing yet another man of Style's group.

Mahan and L/Cpl George Jones (who had been with Style from the earliest days, on the Lofoten Raid, then had gone to West Africa and was at Dieppe with him) were both unscathed. The Germans ran off.

Style ordered Mahan to go back and warn the troop that the enemy might try to attack through the left flank. Then Style injected himself with morphine. Jones applied a field dressing, but, unable to move Style by himself, tried to make him comfortable before going back to get further help. Meanwhile, those of the troop in a position to do so took their revenge on the fleeing Germans. As soon as it was possible, L/Cpl Joe Walsh, another veteran of Style's troop, and Pte Sievewright volunteered to go forward to bring back their 'Skipper'. This they did, although Sievewright, sadly, was killed on this mercy mission.

As Style had predicted, the Germans did renew their attack on the troop's left flank, and bitter hand-to-hand fighting followed. Sgt-Maj Peter King, now in charge of the troop, set an inspiring example when he picked up and returned a couple of German stick grenades to their original owners. Eager for revenge, the men of C Troop followed King's example and the Germans were forced back, with heavy losses.

Such was his display of leadership and heroism that day that King was subsequently honoured with the rare distinction of being granted an immediate commission in the field, becoming '2/Lt Peter King'.

A Troop was also under attack, but just before the main attack on their position the Germans were seen entering a large house, near the cross-roads, which they had under observation. Their crack marksman,

Sgt George Fraser, was soon in action. Although the enemy were now known to be in the house, they were not visible and so presented no proper target for the eager Fraser. However, he decided to make life uncomfortable for those inside by firing into each window, in turn, with the hope that the rounds would ricochet inside the room. He also fired at the door, with a similar idea in mind.

But Fraser's hour of glory came soon afterwards, when the enemy made their assault on the troop's locality. From his position covering the middle of the crossroads, he coolly directed and encouraged his section to repel the attack, which they did, and then he led a bayonet charge to rout the enemy, capturing prisoners and leaving many Germans dead. It was a fierce, but very successful, action. The success was due, in no small measure, to Fraser's leadership and example; he was truly outstanding, but he paid the ultimate price. He was struck down and killed, just before the conclusion.

After the action Fraser was recommended for a well-deserved decoration and was subsequently awarded a posthumous Military Medal.

The two French troops, now under the command of Capt Lofi, who had taken over from Kieffer when he, much against his will, had been evacuated back to England for treatment, were also heavily involved that day. They too came under a heavy enemy bombardment from mortars and artillery early on the morning of D + 4. It was general all along the eastern flank of the Allied invasion, so the Commandos weren't alone. The scale of the continuous bombardment on his two troops left Capt Lofi in no doubt that this was 'le jour' – the day – the Germans would try to dislodge the Commandos from the ridge.

Sure enough, the enemy attack came as expected, except that on the French position the enemy infantry was supported by tanks, one of which – 'a loner' – managed to penetrate their rear position, but was eventually knocked out by a PIAT.

The massed German infantry made the grave mistake, for some unknown reason, of deciding to halt their initial advance on the French positions in order to extend to an assault formation. The French had also been trained, like their British comrades, to wait and hold their fire. But now Lofi's men had an extra bonus – this unexpected halt by the enemy. It was a God-sent opportunity for the French K gunners; and they took full advantage of it. The results were devastating for the enemy.

However, a further tank managed 'to fire with everything it had', according to 'Sgt Gray' (another of the German Commandos from No. 10 attached to No. 4, his real name being Manfred Gans). He also recalled: 'I saw the courageous L/Cpl Geysel, one of the K gunners, fall instantly killed by a bullet in the forehead . . . then a shell from the tank tore off the lower half of the face of poor comrade Bagot.'

In Ian Dear's book, *Ten Commando*, Gray continues to relate further stories of individual bravery in this bitter battle which ultimately ended with some very fierce hand-to-hand fighting. Sgt de Montlaur, for example, 'raced forward to take over a Bren, when both of its crew became casualties, before calmly shooting the German who had accounted for the Bren couple'. There was also L/Cpl Laot, 'attacked by three Germans, he killed two of them before being bayoneted by the third'. Years after this battle, one of the French Commandos told Ian Dear, 'That day of 10 June, D + 4, was lived by all with such intensity that we lost all sense of time.'

Back in the Hauger enclave, the situation in the E Troop area had become so critical that Maj Menday was compelled to seek assistance from his neighbours, No. 3 Commando, who were on the eastern flank of E Troop. So it was a sound and logical request and Col Peter Young, commanding No. 3 Commando, fully agreed. He responded with the offer of a troop, suggested that it should take over from the sorely depleted E Troop, who could then be released to become an immediate reserve force. This arrangement was agreed and acted upon.

This, however, was not the end of Menday's worries that hectic day. No sooner had he sorted out the problems of E Troop when Pat Porteous's D Troop were in trouble and needed help. This brought into action the staff of Commando Headquarters; Maj Menday grabbed hold of Jimmy James, the Welsh transport officer, who, taking all the men in the HQ area, rushed off to help out in D Troop's locality.

They had success and Gilchrist recalls, after their foray, that he saw 'Elliott, Beacall, Marsden and Bagnall, all of the Orderly Room, now smirking, cleaning and handling their rifles, the way that Dad tenderly baths the new baby . . .'

By late afternoon the enemy attacks petered out, and the Germans had withdrawn. The Commandos' positions had been held. They hadn't yielded an inch, and the enemy's efforts to dislodge them from the ridge had failed.

As a finale, No. 4 Commando had the satisfaction of seeing Allied fighters strafing the forming-up locations of the enemy infantry reserves who were to follow up the original German onslaughts, which had been repulsed. The enemy had suffered heavy losses. No. 4's casualties had mounted too. It seems that the Commando strength was down by about 50 per cent from the original numbers that sailed from the Solent on D − 1, but accurate figures are not available and subsequent estimates have varied.

It was later confirmed that the German forces involved in the attacks on Lovat's brigade that day consisted of battalions from both the 744 and 857 Infantry Regiments, elements of the 21 Panzer Division, all supported by self-propelled guns, other artillery and heavy mortar units.

Lovat, in his memoirs, summed up the outcome of that eventful day in these words:

If the Germans had suffered a bloody nose, then the [Commando] Brigade has also taken a severe hammering. Nos 4 and 6 Commandos had borne the brunt of the fighting, but mortaring and counter battery fire had taken its toll all through the Brigade. As the battle turned (in our favour) and the Germans broke, No. 3 and 45 RM Commando, with strong fighting patrols, routed out the forward areas up to and beyond no-man's-land, where the enemy sustained heavy casualties – the bodies of their troops lay everywhere.

The battles won by the Commandos on that day represented a crucial turning point in their campaign in Normandy. Thereafter, the initiative passed increasingly to the Commandos.

In the failing evening light Lovat made a tour of all his units and he recorded his feelings and thoughts arising from his rounds.

Like the still air that follows the impact of a hurricane, the severity of the last attack left a hushed silence over the field. There was no question of a truce to bury the dead . . . the first elation of the winning side was outweighed by a deeper sense of loss. The aftermath was desolation. The survivors, as always, rose magnificently in the dark hour; stretcher-bearers moved up to the front line, doctors and the walking wounded, helped by medical orderlies, came and went. Burial parties performed their appointed duties: 'The Band of Brothers' were very close that day.

And so we dug the Commandos' graves, lowering them away in groundsheets in long neat rows, then set about making wooden crosses to mark each spot.

Lovat was there in the orchard at Hauger when Fraser and his fallen comrades were buried. René Naurois, the French warrior padre of No. 4, said a Requiem, and Lovat ended his description of the burial: 'The whole performance was carried out swiftly in respectful silence, in keeping with the hush of a golden evening. We left the battlefield, as it were, on tiptoe.'

The battle was over, but the war had to go on.

The next day, D + 5, was a Sunday, and it may seem odd, but Capt Len Coulson, a firm believer and Covenanter, in spite of the possibility of further enemy attacks or skirmishing and the predictable harassing mortar fire, decided that he would hold some sort of church service, not in the open, but with his men still in their trenches – those same trenches from which they had repelled the enemy's attacks just twenty-four hours earlier.

With only head and shoulders above the ground, they listened to Len Coulson, their Troop Leader, read the lesson, and silently bowed their heads to hear the words of prayer, with the faith of the Covenanters.

From that day onwards life began to improve; no longer were their positions subject to daylong – if erratic – sniping and the odd sharp skirmishing attack, although they still had to endure ceaseless shelling and mortar fire, augmented on occasions by a marauding enemy SP gun. Consequently, the Commando started to exploit this changed situation by preparing and effecting a policy of 'offensive defence', with a programme of, mainly, sniping by day and fighting patrols by night.

There was a general pattern to the Commando sniping programme, common to all in the brigade. It was carried by a pair of men, the marksman sniper and his 'pal', the observer and cover-man. Both would wear improvised camouflage clothing and, covering each other in turn, they crept and crawled, using the cover of hedges, ditches and the 'the lie of the land', to a position as near as possible to the enemy to make 'a kill'.

In the initial training of the snipers in No. 4, which went way back to the time the Commando was at Inveraray, the emphasis was mainly on individual marksmanship, but after Dieppe and the arrival of the ghillie/stalker Sgt Fraser more and more importance was placed on fieldcraft and working in pairs.

Each troop had its own team of snipers. Lt McDougal describes in some detail of how he and Guardsman Spearman operated as a team. But he makes no mention of another sniping star, Paddy Byrne of C Troop. He became almost a legend in the unit for his efforts, which were acknowledged with the well-deserved award of a Military Medal.

Peter Masters, another of the German Commandos from No. 10 attached to No. 4, in his book, *Striking Back*, aptly subtitled *A Jewish Commando's War against the Nazis*, recalls (Paddy) Byrne's expertise and skills not only as a sniper, but also as a guide to lead FOBs, listening and standing patrols through No-man's-land to suitable places for their allotted tasks. He accompanied Paddy on several such expeditions, and writes admiringly of his stalking prowess as well as his deadly sniping – with 'his telescopic sniper's rifle with the notches on the butt signifying kills'.

Masters wasn't the only No. 4 soldier to record Byrne's coolness and ability in action. Glynn Prosser was another. He accompanied Paddy on a non-sniping mission when he volunteered to go in a small party to bring back an officer who had been badly wounded on a patrol. Prosser writes: 'There was some urgency as the naval FOB had arranged for a bombardment to come down on the area we were going into.' He continued:

> Paddy was cool and I could see for myself how much he was at home in 'his territory'. I didn't feel happy about the prospects of being shelled by the Navy, and also felt uncertain of what kind of welcome we might get from the Germans, who had shot the officer we were going to bring back. . . . But the operation went smoothly, as Paddy had expected it would. . . . We found the officer, he had died of his wounds. We carried him back to our lines, just before the warships' guns opened up, Major Menday thanked us, and I counted it a privilege to have been with Paddy Byrne.

Those last few words provide a praiseworthy tribute to a very brave and capable soldier, who, after the war as a regular, swapped his green beret for a red one and became a member of the Parachute Regiment, was commissioned and had a full and distinguished career with the 'Red Devils' before retiring.

Before D-Day, all the Commandos had been told that their stay in Normandy would be short; they would be pulled out as soon as the Allies broke out of the invasion beachhead, which was planned and expected to be just a matter of days, but it didn't work out like that.

In the original Overlord plan Montgomery had hoped to capture Caen, the focal point for the breakout, on 6 June, but the effort failed. Three subsequent attacks were launched, but they failed too. It wasn't until 20 July, forty days after D-Day, following the heaviest air bombardment of the whole campaign, during which the RAF dropped 2,500 tons of bombs – the Commando had a grandstand view of the awesome raid – that the ancient city of Caen was eventually captured.

Consequently, the Airborne forces and the Commandos were committed to holding the left flank of the Allied beachhead, while Montgomery built up his forces for the capture of Caen (codename Operation Goodwood) and thereafter, until the threat of an enemy flank attack had been eliminated.

As a result of this hold-up and delay in the development of the invasion, instead of holding the ridge for a matter of days, the Commandos' stay there lengthened into weeks and eventually two and a half months – eighty-two days to be precise. It was a very long time to be in the line without relief of any kind, but No. 4 met the challenge with typical Commando resourcefulness, not only operationally, but also administratively.

During those days and weeks, following the 'do or die' battles of D + 4, the Commando developed a routine and pattern of life in the line to meet their tactical policy of 'offensive defence'.

On D + 6, as a result of intensive enemy shelling, Lord Lovat was badly wounded, and had to be evacuated; so bad were his wounds that for him the war was ended. Before being evacuated he called for Col Mills-Roberts and handed over to him. Thus command of the brigade passed to yet another ex-No. 4 officer.

For all his apparent 'Bull', Mills-Roberts was highly respected, and certainly very popular with the troops. He was, after all, a fearless leader, who inspired all ranks under his command and led by example. As Bidmead said, 'He was one helluva man', and was to lead the brigade after Normandy – and after No. 4 had left it – across the Rhine and into Germany to final victory and VE Day.

Settling down to their trenches in the Hauger location, the troops began to organise their own 'domestic' arrangements. Feeding was one example. Each troop had its own cooks; they set up their 'cookhouse' in a suitable place, farmhouse, barn or 'outhouse' in the rear of the troop position, where the men would come, on a relief basis, for their grub, just as they had done on those 'On Commando' training jaunts back in the UK. They also took advantage of any local produce to supplement their Army rations. Somehow, they acquired cooking utensils, the odd domestic pots and pans – and even crockery!

All troops had their fair share of foraging for the local produce. Sometimes these expeditions were carried out when returning from a patrol. There was one occasion when a F Troop patrol, which had gone out to cover the withdrawal of a couple of their snipers, acquired a stray calf, which they killed, and then in a deserted farmyard they found a lonely old sheep, which was also killed. To overcome the problem of bringing their supplementary meat ration back to their troop location, they took over a 'deserted' farm cart. All that training in 'living off the land' was paying off. According to McDougal, for the next few days all in F Troop 'lived like kings. The war seemed to have taken on a less grim aspect. Holiday was in the air.'

Capt Eric Cross, the Commando admin officer, responsible for resupply of ammunition, equipment, rations and reinforcements from the beachhead stores and transit depot, was kept busy with his jeeps and trailers. He became the toast of the unit one day, when he delivered a supply of *white* bread. Apparently he had made contact with the supply officer of HMS *Astrid*, the landing ship that had brought No. 4 over to Normandy on D-Day, which was berthed in the Mulberry Harbour, and their cooks baked a special consignment of bread, albeit rationed to a slice or so per man. But it was like 'manna from heaven'. Up to then the staple starch diet was the Army's hard-tack biscuits, so much like dog biscuits that one wag reckoned that many more and they would soon be sprouting 'wagging tails'. Cross wasn't so popular with his first supply of NAAFI beer; for some reason it tasted like vinegar – and had to be dumped.

On 14 July the Commando moved from Hauger, not the hoped-for move back to England, but just down the road about a mile or so to the little village of Breville, which had been the scene of bitter fighting between the Germans and Airborne forces. There was much evidence of this fighting in the village when the Commandos arrived. Today a memorial in the centre of the village, erected to honour the fallen Paras, serves as a permanent reminder of their heroism and sacrifices.

The village stands on a slope in a commanding position overlooking the valley below that stretches towards Caen. On the other side, facing where the enemy were, the rolling woods and bocage presented a similar sort of terrain that No. 4 had grown used to, respected, but mistrusted in the Hauger location.

The layout of the Commando defences in Breville was somewhat different to that at Hauger. Headquarters was, initially, located in the biggest house in the village, with Menday still in command. F Troop became the reserve troop, and was dug in around the village green. The remaining 'fighting' troops were also dug in, but spread out on a semi-circular perimeter, facing the enemy, around the village, thus protecting their front and exposed flanks. C Troop was on the left, then D and A

Troops, with E Troop, once more, on the right flank. B Troop, with the heavy weapons, was positioned in a small wood some way behind A Troop, prepared to support the forward troops in defence and also to provide counter-battery fire. This was increasingly brought down on the enemy thanks to the information provided by listening posts sent out daily, with relative impunity, now that the Commandos were dominating no-man's-land. However, sporadic enemy shelling and mortar fire continued to inflict casualties, with – on average – two or three men having to be evacuated each day for treatment.

On 16 July Gen Montgomery visited the Commando position to compliment all ranks on their 'splendid performances' and to decorate those who had been outstanding on D-Day; these included both Col Dawson, with the Distinguished Service Order (DSO) and Capt Kieffer, with the Military Cross.

On the last day of that month Dawson received orders to move from Breville, to take over from an Airborne battalion which was holding a defensive position in the Bois de Bavent.

Next day, 1 August, No. 4 moved. Bidmead writes: 'we were told that the place [the forest] had an evil atmosphere about it, what place out here didn't?' He continues, 'The sickly sweet smell of unburied dead greeted our arrival' – apparently, not only unburied enemy soldiers, but also a lot of dead cattle, bloated with maggots and swarming with flies.

Another interesting feature of 1 August is that copies of the original War Diary reappear in their regular reference files in the PRO, having been missing from 2 June. (I eventually tracked down photocopies of the missing Diary entries under a separate War Office file reference.) It records the decision to send out 'infiltration patrols deeper into the forest to seek out the enemy's location and obtain more information about his habits'. On that day, too, was the welcome arrival of twenty-eight reinforcements.

The Bois de Bavent is remembered by all of No. 4, not only for the action there, but also for the mosquitoes. Bidmead wrote:

They made life hellish, especially at night time. . . . The forest was thick with them . . . they bred on the nearby River Dives and the marshland . . . you could see their little fat bodies filling up with your blood if you didn't swat them quickly enough. Before we moved off on a patrol we smothered ourselves in anti-mosquito ointment, but this seemed to attract them more.

While the increased programme of listening/standing/fighting patrols and sniping provided excellent results and enabled the Commando to dominate their sector, it also brought problems, for it meant extra duties and operational risks for the already 'battle-exhausted' men, and this was aggravated by the fact that the daily toll of casualties continued to drain unit numbers. As a result, reinforcements were 'blooded' almost immediately on arrival. This was not ideal, but fortunately, apart from the odd case, did work well. This was mainly due to the fact that the newcomers were accepted as 'one of us' from the start and were integrated in ones or twos into sub-sections.

Whatever the privations of the position in the Bois de Bavent, there was one consolation – a place to swim. Near to the Commando location was an old quarry which was full of water – just right for a swim. And the Commando made good use of it, swimming, of course, in their birthday suits. There was one snag, which was that the old chimney stack of the quarry was used by the enemy mortar men as a ranging aid.

While No. 4 was in the Bois they were paid a handsome compliment, when Gen Montgomery asked Brig Mills-Roberts to provide him with a personal bodyguard for his move forward in the breakout from Falaise into Belgium. It was feared that Monty's HQ might be attacked by isolated groups of Germans overtaken by the then rapidly advancing Allied forces.

As a result, first Capt Thorburn and then Capt Coulson took a party consisting of NCOs and men from both Nos 4 and 6 Commandos for the task. Alex Morris was one of those chosen for this 'perk'. He recalls this unique experience:

> The whole bodyguard consisted of two officers and 35 men. Ten men were always on actual duty, the remainder at hand, dressed and ready for action. The guard had to be discreet and unobtrusive, but at night we closed right in around Monty's caravan. At first light we withdrew quietly.

All those who were on this special task of guarding Monty during that daring and spectacular advance following the breakout from Falaise have their own favourite yarns to tell of 'guarding Monty', which over the years have earned their tellers many pints in locals up and down the country. However, what is evident from other sources is that having been warned most emphatically of the responsibility of their task, and having come straight from action in their slit trenches where the Commandos were accustomed to challenging once then firing if no satisfactory reply was forthcoming, they were in no mood to take chances. Accordingly, they were so aggressive in their guarding duties that members of Monty's HQ were almost scared to venture out of their caravans at night without hailing the nearest sentry and informing him of their intention. Monty appreciated all this, and before they left had an official photograph taken of his 'bodyguard', with himself in the centre, and presented each member with a signed copy. It has become a treasured souvenir.

On 16 August there were indications that the enemy on the whole Commando Brigade front might be withdrawing, so preparations were hastily made for the Commandos to advance in pursuit. On the move at last. . . . No. 4 Commando was chosen to lead the breakout, which they did on the morning of 18 August, advancing some three miles, unopposed, to the village of Bavent which, only that morning, had been evacuated by the enemy. It was quickly occupied by Capt Lofi and his French Commandos and they were warmly received by the local people.

Leaving Bavent behind, the Commando marched on to the next village, Bricqueville, where they took up a position awaiting the next development. By now it was becoming apparent that the Germans in the area were beginning to pull out. To exploit the situation the Paras and Commandos must react quickly and boldly.

With this in mind an audacious plan was rapidly hatched by Gen Gale to infiltrate the enemy strongpoints in a series of both day and night approach marches and attacks using both the Red Devils and the Green Berets in coordinated 'leap-frogging' actions. There was, initially, no time to be lost on careful and deliberate planning with reconnaissances. Speed in execution would be the key to success.

No. 4 Commando was selected to lead the advance with a gruelling all-night approach march to a hamlet, called L'Epine, which was being held by the enemy. McDougal describes the march on a night of 'Stygian darkness', which included the crossing of tributaries of the main river Dives. It was a harrowing experience.

Eventually the Commando arrived in the area of L'Epine and prepared to launch a night attack at 0145 hrs. It was most successful and the War Diary records that a number of enemy positions, occupied by supply personnel from various units, were attacked in the area of the crossroads. 'A total of 43 prisoners were captured, several enemy were killed and among the enemy weapons captured was one 75mm and two 81mm guns, with ammunition', which Capt Carr added to his troop's armoury. In this action the Commando lost one man, killed, and five wounded.

No. 4 held this position while the rest of the Brigade passed through to attack the enemy positions on the high ground towards Grangues, but came under very heavy enemy shelling and mortar fire in the afternoon, which wounded a further fourteen. And to add to the misery it started to rain, damping not only skins but also morale. Fortunately the next day, with the Commando still in the same position, the rain stopped and the sun shone. McDougal writes: 'We spread our kit out to dry and went about our duties with fresh heart. The previous day was at last behind us.' The rest of that day, 20 August, they were able to rest, and, because the brigade attacks had gone well, the enemy shelling and mortaring had stopped too. So they made the best of the lull, but not for long. . . .

Next day they were on the move again and marched all day, finishing in an orchard, just off the road that leads to Beaumont-en-Auge. There, very tired, they were able to get a well-deserved good night's rest, free from enemy fire – and mosquitoes. On the 22nd they resumed the pursuit; the unit Diary records:

We entered a part of France which had not been a battlefield and for the first time were among undamaged houses and in a habitable area. The French people everywhere accorded us an enthusiastic welcome, complete with flowers and cries of 'Vive l'Angleterre' – and the odd bottle of wine – as we marched through.

It was now obvious that the enemy was in full retreat and the joint Para/Commando force made every effort to bring them to battle, but apart from mopping-up operations were unable to do so – in spite of long all-night marches made in the hope of catching the enemy before they pulled out from their positions at first light.

Bill Bidmead sums up the frustration suffered: 'The long slog went on. We would march all night and in the morning the artillery [they were motorised] would be in front of us. It would all be in vain – the Germans seemed to be one step ahead all the time.'

Hopes were raised when the Commando was briefed for a combined attack with the Paras on the medieval town of Pont l'Eveque, but this operation was cancelled almost as soon as it was announced because, once again, the Germans had withdrawn following air strikes on their positions in the town.

Following another all-night march, 25/6 August, the Commando entered the recently liberated town of Beuzeville, where, in brilliant sunshine, the Commando marched through the main street: 'people were cheering and waving and thrusting bottles into ready hands. Most of these folk were genuinely delighted to see us,' recalled McDougal, 'particularly the older generation, many of whom stood with tears of joy coursing down their furrowed cheeks, saluting as we passed. They were saluting us not as men, but the return of their respect.'

In a side-street as the Commandos marched by, some French men were forcibly shearing and shaving the hair off a young woman, paying the price for collaborating with the Germans. This was the other side of the 'coin of liberation'.

The Commando marched on for a further three miles to some orchards in the area of Boulleville, where they halted. Troops were allocated barns and outbuildings to 'bed down'. For the time being their fighting was over. It was 26 August.

Weary and battle-exhausted, they rested and slept for the next three days. 'It was just like heaven', was the universal recollection. Apart from guard and security duties, all ranks had time off. Some visited the local shops, only to find that the prices had shot up. This infuriated the French Commandos of No. 4, who expressed their disgust by wrecking one or two of the offending shops. Dawson and Kieffer allowed some of the French Commandos to go off on leave to Paris and other nearby liberated towns where their families lived. But a few longed only to return to England where they had girlfriends.

The Commando remained in this location – enjoying the sunshine and generally relaxing after that 'long stint' which had started three months earlier on 6 June. Then, on the morning of 6 September, they were on the move again. But this time it was the move they had long awaited – back to Blighty.

A convoy of transport took the unit back to the D-Day beaches and to Arromanches where they all, including Coulson's party who had been guarding Monty, boarded the *Ulster Monarch* at the Mulberry Harbour to take them back to England. Lord Lovat, then convalescing, had a military band to greet his old Commando at Southampton. Then it was off to Petworth, to collect railway warrants, money and that all-important fourteen days' leave pass.

CHAPTER TEN

Walcheren – Perfect Little Campaign

Those fourteen days of leave just flew: the first few days were spent in resting and 'drawing breath' after being so heavily committed in Normandy, although some, returning to their families in the Home Counties, had a taste of the dangers and trials that had beset the civilians who lived in those areas during the past weeks as Hitler responded to the Allied invasion with his latest weapons – the V1 ('Doodle Bugs') and V2 (rockets) – which took their daily toll of lives and properties.

All ranks duly reported back to Petworth in Sussex, which was the base for the Commando Group. There was an air of uncertainty about the future of the Commando. It seemed likely that Mills-Roberts's No. 1 Commando Brigade would be going out to join No. 3 Commando Brigade in the Far East. This possibility was reinforced when the emphasis on training switched to jungle warfare, but this was short-lived. For within days it was announced that No. 4 Commando was leaving Mills-Roberts's command to replace No. 46 Royal Marine Commando in Brig Leicester's No. 4 Commando Brigade in Belgium.

It was not popular news. No. 4 had been happy, under Lovat and Mills-Roberts, in Normandy, alongside their comrades in the other two Army Commandos (Nos 3 and 6) and No. 45 RM Commando. It seemed a pity to break up a winning combination, but the decision had been made. Now No. 4 was to be the only Army Commando in a hitherto all-Marines Brigade. Sgt Rowe, the MT sergeant, cheekily, maybe pointedly, told his section, 'After all, someone's got to stimulate the Marines.'

On 4 October, just before No. 4 Commando was due to sail from England and join the Commando Brigade in Belgium, the newspapers came out with an interesting headline, 'RAF SINKS ISLAND'. Heavy bombers had blasted gaps in the dykes at Westkapelle on the island of Walcheren, and torrents of sea water were flooding through into the centre of the island.

Col Dawson and others in No. 4 read this news without any special interest, though there were already some who had looked at the map of the western coast of Europe and thought that Walcheren might prove of particular interest to them when they joined their new Brigade. And they were right.

When the Commando arrived in Belgium they found that the Brigade was already training for a combined operation of considerable magnitude, and there were rumours that the experiences of D-Day were to be eclipsed in the new proposed assault landing. Planning was going ahead for an invasion of Walcheren, although the actual destination of the Brigade was a secret jealously guarded, with all the paraphernalia that had preceded Operation Overlord.

At this stage it is necessary to outline the strategic background for this proposed invasion of Walcheren. By September 1944 the Allies had swept up through Belgium and had captured the major port of Antwerp, reckoned to be one of the finest in Europe. They had seized it with all the dock facilities intact. With its capture the Allies had an ideal seaport and supply base to further their intended deep thrust into Germany itself.

Unfortunately, although Antwerp was in Allied hands, it could not be used as a supply base because the port lies some forty miles from the mouth of the Scheldt, and all the water approaches were covered by enemy coastal defences, thus denying its use to the Allies.

Nevertheless, Montgomery had declared that 'The Allies' need to use the port of Antwerp was imperative', and Admiral Ramsey, Eisenhower's naval chief, was convinced that the opening up of Antwerp could only be achieved by an amphibious assault to capture Walcheren. Accordingly Monty had issued orders for the clearing of the western coastline of the Scheldt before an amphibious operation on Walcheren. Towards the end of October the situation had been reached whereby Operation Infatuate, the invasion of Walcheren, could go ahead.

During the planning stages three different plans had been prepared, which in turn demanded three different roles for No. 4, for which they trained in the sand dunes around Den Haan where they were billeted. In fairness to the planners, it must be pointed out that the changes in plans were mainly governed by the changes in the flooding conditions on the island, caused by devastating bombing by the RAF. So widespread was the flooding that there was even water in the streets of Middleburg and Flushing.

Dawson commented:

It was frequently debated whether this violent and extensive flooding might not be playing into the enemy's hands by limiting the possible avenues of advance. In the event the Germans never seem to have considered the water as a potential ally. The fantastic flooding mesmerised them into a fatal inactivity, destroyed their communications and sapped their morale to an incredible extent.

Even so, the Germans, tunnelling and boring with their usual industry and ingenuity, and employing masses of reinforced concrete, had turned the dykes into an almost continuous fortification, bristling with guns of every calibre, especially in the Westkapelle area on the western side of the island.

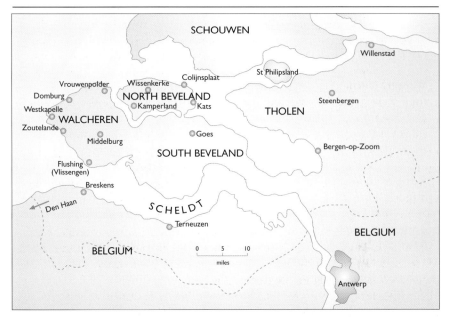

No. 4 Commando Operations, November 1944 – May 1945.

At Flushing, where it was eventually decided No. 4 would land, the defences were equally formidable, the waterfront was wired and mined, and the beaches screened with anti-landing stakes, some with shells fixed to them. All these devices were covered by pillboxes and strongpoints. In addition the flak guns had been so sited to fire in a dual – air-and-ground – role; finally, the artillery batteries located in the hinterland had pre-arranged anti-invasion fire programmes.

The initial training of the Commando after arriving in Den Haan concentrated on getting the reinforcements, who had brought the Commando up to strength after the Normandy campaign, settled into their new sub-sections and carrying out plenty of field firing. This was immediately followed by the arrival of 'some weird tracked vehicles that made their appearance on the streets of Den Haan'. These were the amphibious Weasels and Buffaloes (classified as landing vehicles tracked – LVTs), with which No. 4 became very familiar before the operation ended. It was originally intended that the Commando would use them, so a considerable number of the MT drivers were turned over to training on the Weasels, and a great many hours and much hard work were put in on very uninviting terrain, experimenting on these unfamiliar amphibians. Although Weasels were not used for the operation on Flushing, the Commando was allocated eighteen. It was intended that these LVTs, under the command of Sgt Rowe, would be taken from Ostend by LCTs later on D-Day and help the Commando in their follow-up operations.

Bill Bidmead, who had by this time transferred from his old troop to the MT section, and was a jeep driver, was one of those who went on the Weasels. He wrote:

> We were learning to drive some amphibious 'tin cans' called Weasels . . . they were tracked vehicles, light and amphibious . . . the training consisted mainly of driving into a nearby reservoir and out the other side . . . it resembled a boat lake at Southend. I expected any minute for someone to shout through a megaphone, 'Come in, Number Seven'.

Some of those MT drivers undergoing training on the Weasels had a year previously been up in Scotland training as 'muleteers' with real animals – mules – and here they now were on Weasels. Such was the unpredictable and varied training of the Commandos.

After the drivers had been trained to use, land and fight from the Weasels, the final plan three, Operation Infatuate, was produced. The main features of this plan were that the three Royal Marine Commandos – Nos 41, 47 and 48 – plus two troops from No. 10 Commando would land in the Westkapelle area, while No. 4 Commando, with their French troops still with them, would cross over from Breskens to assault and capture the town of Flushing in a frontal amphibious attack. This new plan necessitated a very detailed study of Flushing and, of course, a revised training programme with the emphasis on street fighting and house clearing.

Although No. 4 Commando did not use amphibious LVTs (Buffaloes and Weasels) for their assault on Flushing, they were equipped with the smaller Weasels, seen here centre foreground, and used them later in the Walcheren campaign. (*Courtesy of the Imperial War Museum, London* – B11646)

Lt McDougal recalls those days after arriving in Belgium:

Initially we had no idea of our next task. The fact that we had been so hastily brought back to Europe indicated that something was afoot, but so far our orders had been merely to get fit. So to start with, we played football every day and had plenty of cross-country runs, and carried out innumerable field firing exercises. This training could be quite realistic as there were strong ex-enemy defence works still remaining in the area. So, under cover of smoke and HE from the mortars, we put in attacks on these pill-boxes, gun-pits and emplacements. . . .

About the third week of October, the first inkling of our task reached us. It seemed that we were to be given a direct assault on some heavily defended area, as yet unnamed. Troop Leaders were warned that street fighting would almost certainly be necessary, and were told to prepare their troops accordingly. An area on the outskirts of Ostend was set aside for us. We went there, Troop by Troop, to spend days clambering up and down walls, moving through rows of houses, using smoke grenades to cross open squares and using toggle ropes to scale the walls of houses.

There, as so many times before, it was the old soldiers and old hands who led the way, 'Old Donkin and McVeigh, both of whom loathed marching, were as nimble as cats in nipping up the side of a house.'

At this stage it was decided that No. 4 would cross over to Walcheren in LCAs and not in Weasels. They were to be taken ashore in LCAs; they were not sorry. They preferred the flat-bottomed landing craft.

Dawson and his intelligence officer, Capt Wright, started a detailed study of the town from air photographs and in cooperation with selected locals,

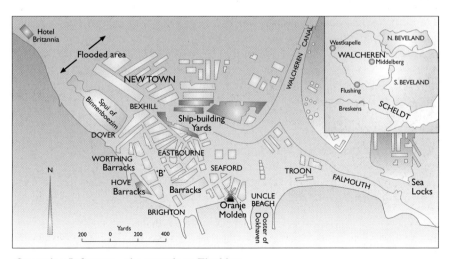

Operation Infatuate – the assault on Flushing.

including Capt P.H. Van Nahuijs of the Dutch forces. Up to a month previously Van Nahuijs had been the Police Inspector in Flushing and as such had been in constant touch with the German authorities in the town, while himself being all the time a member of the local Resistance movement. It was he who, when Col Dawson was considering where to land (he had the unenviable task of selecting his own landing beach) had suggested a promontory of rubble and rubbish by the Ooster of Dokhaven.

As for the battle plan, it was governed by the topography of the town and the dispositions of the enemy. Flushing falls into two distinct parts – the old dock area and the new residential area. These two areas are separated by a neck of land about four hundred yards wide, upon which are two main crossroads connecting the two parts of the town. These two crossroads are 'bottlenecks' – seize and hold them and you have complete control of the town, also denying the enemy access to reinforce their troops in the old town. They were the key to success.

When formulating his plan Dawson wisely chose, considering the tongue-twisting nature of Dutch place-names, to give all the salient features, tactical bounds and objectives codenames after towns in Britain where the Commando had been billeted – a sort of billet honours list and easy to remember.

Those two bottlenecks were thus known as Dover, on the promenade between the sea and a large sunken lake, called Spui of Binnenboezem, and Bexhill between the lake and the shipyards, where incidently a large liner was still in the process of being built.

Dawson's outline plan was simple enough: to land on the promontory to the west of Ooster of Dokhaven and secure a beachhead – Uncle Beach – then push straight through the old part of the town and seize and hold Dover and Bexhill, then clear the old town up to these two key positions to enable the follow-up troops of an infantry brigade from the 52 Lowland Division to pass through and clear the new town. By one of those ironic quirks that so often happen in war, this division had trained for years in Scotland specifically for mountain warfare, but was never employed for that task. Now here they were, after all that training, going into battle in the low and flooded island of Walcheren in Holland. No. 4 had been involved with some of this division before when they, too, had been training for mountain warfare in the Cairngorms in 1943.

The major problem was that of getting ashore with all those defences and obstacles outlined above. Information about the garrison was sketchy. The main battery and positions were pinpointed from air photographs, but the identification and detailed positions of the troops were difficult to confirm. The overall strength of the German forces on the island was reckoned to be in the order of some 9,000 troops, of which about one-third were thought to be in Flushing itself.

The Commando was strengthened by several detachments, including a section from the Dutch Troop of No. 10 Commando, a small group from the Special Boat Section, an RA group to call for artillery support, some sappers with LVTs for moving stores, ammunition and so on in the later stages of the operation, and also some Pioneer Corps troops for the same purpose. There were also detachments of medical, signals and beach-clearance specialists, all under Col Dawson's command, a total of just over 550 – a formidable and balanced amphibious assault group.

By this time No. 4 Commando had been reorganised and the troops redesignated. Out went the old alphabetic titles and in came numbers. The Commando now consisted of No. 1 Troop, commanded by Capt Alastair Thorburn; No. 2 Troop, commanded by Capt 'Tug' Wilson; No. 3 Troop, commanded by Maj Gordon Webb, MC; No. 4 Troop, the heavy weapons troop, commanded by Capt Knyvet Carr; No. 5 Troop, one of the previous French troops, now under Capt Lofi; and the other old French troop, now No. 6 Troop, commanded by Capt Guy Vourch. Maj Kieffer was still with No. 4 and he acted as the link between Dawson and Nos 5 and 6 Troops. In spite of these changes, the officers and NCOs all retained their previous ranks and, by and large, other ranks were not split up from their mates.

Dawson's plan for the assault on Flushing was simple, but the most difficult part, he admitted later, 'was finding a suitable place to get ashore, and consequently it was this aspect which received the most elaborate treatment'.

The SBS detachment, codename Keepforce, was to lead the way from Breskens to Flushing and find a suitable place to land. They were to be accompanied by Capt Rewcastle and a section from No. 1 Troop, whose task it was to secure the 'beginnings' of the beachhead – codename Uncle.

The beachhead party 'proper', under the command of Maj 'Bill' Boucher-Myers (who had returned to the Commando after an extensive course at the Staff College, and was now Dawson's second-in-command), consisted of the remainder of No. 1 Troop, the whole of No. 2 Troop plus Commando HQ, and the RN detachments, who were to supervise and coordinate the landing of the rest of the Commando and subsequently that of the follow-up detachments and the 155 Infantry Brigade of the 52 Infantry Division.

The tasks of Boucher-Myers's party were as follows: to secure the beachhead through which the main body of the Commando would pass to assault the town itself. After this No. 1 Troop were to be responsible for the left flank, with the ultimate objective of Arsenal Barracks. No. 2 Troop were to clear the right flank and seal off the enemy on the Falmouth spit. The main body, consisting of Nos 3, 4, 5 and 6 Troops, were to pass through the beachhead, secure the two vital bottlenecks at Bexhill and Dover, clear the various barracks along the main road, marked 'A' on the map, and also seize the municipal buildings in area 'B', also on the map.

In more detail, the objectives allotted to No. 3 Troop were the small harbour at Brighton and the barracks at Hove. No. 5 Troop, following close on the heels of No. 3 Troop, were to deal with any enemy en route, but their priority objective was Dover. No. 6 Troop, with the Vickers MGs of No. 4 Troop with them, would capture the post office and adjoining municipal buildings before going on to their main objective, Bexhill. No. 1 Troop, after dealing with Arsenal Barracks, would clear Seaford and No. 3 Troop would mop up the Eastbourne area after finishing their tasks at Brighton and Hove.

With this plan in mind it is easy to appreciate Dawson's directive to his troop leaders in the third week of October to focus their training on street fighting and house clearing. That training was to pay a dividend on 1 November in the old town of Flushing.

The assault was to be supported by massive air and artillery support. In the event the heavy bombing to soften up the enemy defence at Flushing had to be cancelled because of bad weather, but the artillery support programme was increased to include super-heavy and heavy guns in lieu.

So much, then, for the background and plans. Troops were briefed and their billet area sealed as they made their preparations in gloomy, wet and miserable weather.

Early on the last day of October an advance party of Capt Cross, the administrative officer, and his men moved up to Breskens, the jumping-off point for the operation, to recce some houses for the overnight stay. Bidmead was with Capt Cross and records:

> We were to grab billets, if habitable, for the rest of the Commando who were to arrive later. Absolute devastation greeted our arrival, bomb craters twenty feet deep, pill boxes literally lifted out of the ground by bombing and hardly a building was intact. The Canadians had a terrific battle to capture this place. Capt Cross had a near impossible task to find billets for the Troops. There was also the smell of dead bodies.

Dawson, describing the journey up to Breskens, writes in a similar vein.

> The journey was made through desolate and devastated countryside, roads visibly sinking into the mud and water which lay on each side . . . villages smashed to ruins by the heavy fighting that had gone on for so long in these parts . . . as we drew near to Breskens we passed the artillery positions occupied by the heavy guns that were to give us support in the landing. . . . Breskens was an indescribable shambles of shattered houses . . . no building had escaped damage . . . the harbour had suffered severely from the pounding it had received when it was used for evacuating the Germans . . . the enemy had mined and booby trapped parts, but fortunately one wooden jetty was in full working order and our twenty LCAs were moored alongside.

The Commando arrived in Breskens in time to have a practice embarkation. Across the water from their LCAs they could see their destination for the next day, the town of Flushing, but visibility through the misty drizzle was so poor that all they could really identify was a forest of tall dockside cranes.

Later that afternoon a small naval craft sailed down the Scheldt laying a smokescreen to cover the LCTs swimming down from Terneuzen. Unfortunately, the smokescreen stopped immediately opposite Breskens. The Germans took the hint and started to shell the harbour, and although the shelling was accurate and heavy, causing some casualties to the RN personnel in the harbour, the LCAs were undamaged, but a dory planned to be used by the SBS team was written off and had to be replaced by an LCP.

The Commando returned to their bomb-blasted billets to grab some food – including some self-heating cans of soup, hard-tack biscuits and, of course, hot sweet tea, plus anything else that was going. McDougal recalls that the mail had caught up with them and one of his stalwarts, Guardsman Percy Toombs, even received a birthday card. Meanwhile, the fighting padre of the French troops, Father René de Naurois, gathered his fellow compatriots together in the ruins of a local church and held mass. Glynn Prosser was one of the English-speaking Commandos who also attended. He recalls: 'Our Protestant padre had been wounded before this, so I knelt down with the Catholics and took Communion.'

The rest of the Commando settled down to make their final preparations and get a couple of hours' sleep. There was an early reveille and just after 0300 hrs the Commando were on their way down to the docks; an hour later the embarkation was completed and they were ready.

The landings were phased into three flights – the initial recce-cum-landing party of SBS and one section of No. 1 Troop, then Maj Boucher-Myers's group, and finally the main body of assault troops.

At 0440 hrs the first little flight of landing craft slipped their moorings and nosed their way out of the harbour. Because the weather had 'closed in' and was unsuitable for the heavy bombers, the additional heavy artillery bombardment started at 0445 hrs (H-hour minus 60). The results were spectacular and awesome. Fires were soon ablaze in the town and then suddenly the troops in the leading craft could see the silhouette of the windmill, the Oranje Molen, thrown into relief against the glare of the burning buildings, providing an unmistakable guide to the planned landing point – the groyne by Uncle. 'We could not have had a clearer indication of our chosen landing point', Dawson later reported – bringing back memories of a similar guiding light provided by the lighthouse for No. 4 on the Dieppe Raid.

Meanwhile, the rest of the landing craft were cruising around in the channel between Breskens and Flushing waiting for the call to go in – and watching the 'fireworks'.

At 0545 hrs the recce group of the first flight closed the beach and a landing was effected, but only after a couple of mishaps. However, Capt Rewcastle managed to land right on the tip of the promontory by the windmill and happily succeeded, more by luck in the darkness than by judgement, in avoiding the anti-landing stakes with the shells attached and any mines. He and his men were able to winkle out the Germans there before a shot was fired.

The wire on the dyke was quickly cut and Rewcastle's men laid down white tapes to mark the gap and also to indicate the path leading inland. Lt Hargreaves, who was the naval officer in charge of the flotilla and an old friend of No. 4 – he had been at both Lofoten and Dieppe – then sent the lamp signal for the second flight to come in to Uncle beach.

It was at this stage that some of the enemy started to respond and the LCAs came under enemy cannon fire from the Brighton area, but it was too high and all the landing craft of Boucher-Myers's group landed without any casualties.

Capt Rewcastle succeeded in clearing the whole of the promontory; indeed, by the time the beachhead party 'proper' had landed, Rewcastle had some twenty-odd very scared Germans kneeling in the mud near one of their own pillboxes with their hands clasped behind their heads. The prisoners had been taken from a strong pillbox containing a 75-mm anti-tank gun. Rewcastle and his section then rounded up a further batch of Germans in a big underground shelter towards the back of the promontory. Dawson subsequently used this underground shelter as his Commando HQ. His initial task well and truly accomplished without loss to his section, Capt Rewcastle and his men took up a defensive position covering Uncle.

On landing it was the turn of No. 1 Troop's other section to go into action; they cleared the area between the windmill and the barracks, then found that the barracks they were to clear were empty. So they went into Commando reserve.

Lt P. King with his section attacked two enemy machine-gun posts which were firing on the incoming craft to Uncle beach. They knocked out both posts, taking ten prisoners in the process.

While all this was going on, Capt Wilson's No. 2 Troop had turned right after leaving Uncle and, bypassing Troon, had run up against a 50-mm gun in an emplacement. One section, under Lt Hunter-Gray, using a pre-arranged plan of attack, assaulted and captured this defence work, together with twenty prisoners and the gun! Covering each other in turn, Wilson's two sections under Hunter-Gray and Lt Albrow stormed along the waterfront from pillbox to pillbox, ably supported by fire from their newly captured 50-mm gun. Sgt Mullard and his sub-section had been delegated as the 'winkling-out' party and at the end of this little operation had a total of no less than eighty-one prisoners. Wilson's men had also captured a 75-mm field gun and a 5-cm flak/anti-tank gun, both intact and with ammunition, which they later used to their advantage – thanks to the knowledge gleaned on those courses on 'Foreign Weapons'.

By now the enemy were thoroughly aroused, and when the third flight came in at about 0630 hrs, it encountered considerable opposition from

Members of No. 2 Troop take over a captured German gun position at Flushing on 1 November 1944. (*Joe Spicer*)

machine-guns, a 20-mm cannon and other small-arms fire. Les Lilley, who was in a 3-in mortar section of No. 4 Troop, takes up the story:

> the run up to the actual landing was very noisy indeed . . . our landing craft took God knows how many small arms hits as it was approaching our touch-down point . . . we were under heavy fire from the Hotel Britannia complex . . . just as the ramp went down we either had a direct hit low down or ran over one of the steel sea defences.

As their LCA started to sink, they scrambled ashore, but some of the heavy weapons and equipment were still on board. Lilley and his comrades got as far as the windmill – all except one. He records, 'My long term friend, Gnr Hill, was shot dead on the beach.'

Meanwhile, Capt Carr, assisted by Sgt Lloyd and Pte Leyland, waded out to the sinking LCA and, under continued enemy fire, salvaged one mortar and four cases of bombs, the other mortar having already been got ashore. On rejoining the rest of his men Carr gave the order to clean and prepare the 'casualty' mortar for action. Half an hour later they were all ready to engage the enemy. The time was 0715 hrs.

With all the main body ashore, the major task of clearing the old town began. No. 3 Troop were the first through the beachhead and quickly reached the area marked 'B' on the map. But their movements were curtailed by a considerable number of enemy in the area of Brighton – in fact, this area was not finally cleared of the enemy until the next day. Some bitter street fighting ensued.

McDougal, who was commanding one section of No. 3 Troop, wrote 'As we ran on, threading our way through the dim streets, every man was probably going through in his mind the details of the route we had memorised from the aerial photographs. In the lead was Lt Nick Barras, a tall, quiet spoken policeman, who had played football for Gateshead.' He had joined the Commando in the final stages of the Normandy campaign; McDougal continues, 'it was not until we started training for the Flushing operation that we really got to know him. He and his men hurried towards his objective; a terrific crash from time to time denoted the odd 'short' from our artillery, while chunks of a house frequently toppled down simply as a result of the vibrations of the explosions.'

McDougal and Barras with their respective sections had two different objectives, both involving house clearing. Barras and his men forced an entry into their block of buildings (in the Brighton area) and began to clear them, working their way quickly from room to room upwards. Near the top was a spiral stairway. Barras and Sgt Fraser made their way upwards, covering each other. They got almost to the top when Barras was shot at short range by a sniper firing from a house opposite. He died immediately.

Meanwhile, McDougal's section ran into trouble too. On the way to their objective, Hove – a naval garrison barracks stretching the length of a street – they met a group of enemy. In the encounter old Pte Donkin, who at forty-one was the oldest man in the Commando, ex-miner, old soldier and father of nine children, was killed. McDougal's account of Donkin's death is one of the most graphic and dramatic accounts in his book. He wrote:

We were heading for our barracks on the seafront, with McVeigh in the lead. We dashed down an alleyway, at the foot of which we found a row of little houses. Beyond these was the back of what appeared to be a garage . . . quite close to the barracks . . . there was a hole in the back wall of this garage, which McVeigh quickly enlarged . . .['mouseholing'] and one by one the leading group swung into the darkness of the building itself.

The other walls were wooden and flimsy, as was the door which was ajar. The leading man reached the door and almost ran into a body of German soldiers beside the flank wall of a bunker. The Germans immediately opened fire into and through the walls of the garage. I was just coming through the hole . . . saw the disadvantage and roared 'Back out – this way!'

It was then that Donkin jumped into the doorway and stood there framed, with both feet planted firm, stocky body balanced on slightly bandy legs, and methodically started to tommy-gun from left to right the fifteen or so Germans visible to him by the concrete bunker. He reached the right-hand end of his swing and was starting the return, when one man on the left, whom he had missed at the start, got in a quick shot. It took him straight in the throat, killing him at once. McVeigh, who was beside him with a rifle, made no mistake with his shot, then doubled back through the now empty garage, through the hole in the wall and joined us in the alleyway.

So ended one of the longest and best-known 'Me and My Pal' friendships – McVeigh and Donkin – in No. 4, one that started even before the early Weymouth days when they were both in their parent regiment, The Loyals, on the beaches at Dunkirk.

No. 3 Troop tried an alternative route through the back gardens, but found the enemy too numerous to tackle with the numbers at hand, so it was decided to wait for reinforcements from the Commando reserve.

No. 6 Troop, under Capt Vourch, had landed according to plan on Uncle, sustaining two casualties, but set off with all speed with the Dutch Capt Nahuijs as their guide, first to the immediate objective, the post office. There, Lt Senee's section stormed it and took nearly fifty prisoners – Vourch in his report wrote 'some German soldiers and one officer refused to surrender and were dealt with by a grenade'.

At the post office one of Carr's Vickers MG sections joined up – as planned – with Vourch and they all made their way to Bexhill, their ultimate objective, at the extremely early hour of 0745 hrs, and what's more, wrote Dawson, 'They kept a firm hold on this important bottleneck throughout the whole battle.'

No. 5 Troop, under Capt Lofi, on landing, made for Worthing, but after some street fighting on the way, found the enemy there too numerous and too alert to permit penetration into the barracks; fortunately one of the infantry companies of the follow-up brigade relieved Lofi and his men, so that they could press on to their objective at Dover. Here a Flakvierling (a four-barrelled 20-mm AA gun) and a machine-gun post opened up on them, 'causing trouble'; however, with the support of the mortars and by firing their PIATs at both these enemy positions No. 5 Troop gradually neutralised them. But they failed to establish themselves at Dover, so they took up positions down the road from it, and, supported by No. 3 Troop, were able to deny the enemy any use of the road from Bexhill.

In the early afternoon Thorburn's No. 1 Troop, now Dawson's reserve, was ordered forward to assist No. 3 Troop clear the barrack buildings. Thorburn later wrote:

By the time we had cleared half of the building, which was a slow and arduous task, the light was beginning to fade and we were having trouble from snipers. They caused two more casualties in quick succession, so I decided that it was suicide to carry on that evening in darkness, so I took up a position of all-round defence, and there we stayed for the night, keeping in close touch with No. 3 Troop – and ready to resume the attack at first light in the morning.

Just before I had decided to halt for the day, Lt Peter King was responsible for saving further casualties by dashing across thirty yards of open ground in order to throw a grenade through the window from which snipers were firing; we later discovered that both snipers had been wounded by his grenade. A very noisy night was spent by us, very cold and uncomfortable too; however we were not worried by snipers at all, and the shell fire missed us.

Glynn Prosser remembers that night:

Some of us were just about to settle down in a garage or shed of one of the houses, when Capt Alastair Thorburn suggested that about eight of us go with him to surprise the Germans who were in a neighbouring house. There was an air-raid shelter in the next garden which would accommodate us for an hour or so, and then we would attack. After a very short while rifle grenades began to burst around the shelter. We had obviously been spotted. The firing suddenly stopped, so we made a quick getaway. The following morning we started to move on and, a few feet away from the air-raid shelter was a German lying in a shell hole – dead, but still clutching an automatic weapon.

Prosser reckoned that the dead man had been sent to deal with them, but had been hit by one of his comrade's rifle grenades, and concluded, 'I even felt sorry for him.'

During the day there had been much activity on the beach at Uncle too. This had included clearing the obstacles, landing the reinforcement troops of the leading battalion of 155 Brigade (who gave some stout and welcomed support to No. 4 throughout the day by taking over various positions that had enabled the Commandos to press on to their main objectives in the old town), and the all-important task of unloading stores and the provision of a POW cage for an ever-increasing number of prisoners. Apropos the latter, it is interesting, indeed almost amusing, to read:

It was important to get the stores unloaded quickly, and for this the prisoners were pressed into service. Without their invaluable contribution the usual chaos on the beaches would have been inevitable, and these prisoners undoubtedly did more for us in the battle for Flushing than they did for the Third Reich.

That night Col Dawson had good cause to be satisfied with the outcome of the day's fighting. The main old town area was securely in the hands of No. 4, although one enemy strongpoint still remained to be mopped up in daylight on D + 1. But more importantly, any possibility of an enemy counter-attack via Bexhill and Dover had been thwarted by the Commando's firm grip on those two vital bottlenecks.

On the whole that night passed quietly enough, but not without one incident. A determined attack by two Germans with a flame-thrower on Bexhill was foiled by some accurate fire by Vourch's men.

Early on D + 1 Lofi set off with his troop to capture the concrete strongpoint that dominated Dover and which had halted their progress the previous evening. They couldn't advance down the road so, instead, they had to 'mousehole' their way through the walls of the back gardens. Lofi managed to get one of his section into a cinema and the PIAT team on to the roof, where they were able to provide some covering fire for the other section to cross the road to the far side, where they entered a building. Both sections then continued moving forward by 'mouseholing' once more through garden walls, clearing any Germans in the houses as they went – often in hand-to-hand fighting. They were making slow but steady progress and were about to prepare for the final assault when they were ordered to withdraw so that a strike of six Typhoons could attack the strongpoint and other enemy positions beyond Dover.

However, in the afternoon Lofi continued his advance, clearing the houses until he finally reached the corner overlooking the strongpoint. (Dawson tells how Lofi, en route, came across an appalling example of the ruthless manner in which the Germans behaved towards the local Dutch people. He discovered that a comrade of No. 6 Troop had been cut off during the previous day's fighting and been compelled to take refuge in a house, which the Germans later retook. When they found some British equipment lying in it, they had taken the entire family, who lived there, outside and shot them in cold blood.)

As a result of Lofi's advance the Germans were now confined to the strongpoint itself and to a house on the opposite side of the road. The Germans in the house decided to make a bolt for it, but unfortunately for them they met the concentrated fire of No. 5 Troop's small arms and suffered several casualties.

Then one of Lofi's groups made it to the anti-tank wall at the crossroads and started to engage the strongpoint with PIAT bombs. However, as there was still no sign of surrender from the occupants, Lofi decided to blow an entrance with a made-up charge. Cpl Lafont volunteered to carry out this daring task and was all set to dash forward when a white flag on a long stick appeared from an embrasure.

Moments later three officers and about sixty soldiers stumbled out of the strongpoint, with their hands on their heads. The battle for Dover had been won.

While Lofi's troop was thus involved, Vourch's No. 6 Troop was well established at Bexhill and in such control of the area to enable the road there to be used as an entry point for the battalion from 155 Brigade to pass through to start their mopping-up operations in the new town.

No. 1 Troop was at the same time mopping up in their area and by midday had cleared it with just a few casualties.

Away to the east Capt Wilson's No. 2 Troop, patiently holding on to their gains of the previous day, began to clear the whole of the promontory of Falmouth. Apart from attracting enemy mortar and some artillery fire from the northern side of the harbour, they encountered little opposition and so completed their allotted task. They had captured, in all, well over a hundred prisoners, who were despatched, under TSM Bill Portman, to Uncle beach to help with the unloading and other chores there.

It so happened that Capt Wilson discovered that some of the troublesome machine-gunners firing on his positions were established on the highest cranes over in the shipbuilding area, but they were dislodged by some very effective and spectacular shooting from the 3.7 in Mountain Howitzers (of 52 Division) from a gun position established near Uncle.

By late afternoon No. 4 Commando had successfully carried out the first direct assault on the waterfront of a strongly defended port since the raid on Dieppe. It was a major success.

In a special training pamphlet published later by the War Office in which it analysed Operation Infatuate, it attributed the outstanding success of No. 4's operation to the following factors.

First, although it had been difficult to select and find the most suitable landing point, especially in the dark, the decision to make the initial assault landing and surprise the beach defences before first light had resulted not only in minimising casualties but also in completely surprising the enemy.

Second, it emphasised the thorough training that had been undertaken before the operation, especially in street fighting and house clearing, pointing out that Dover was reached by 'mouseholing' the entire length of the street and that each man had been trained for this task and carried a small made-up charge for the purpose. It also laid stress on the value of the traditional training of the Commandos for night operations, which gave them such confidence that it became 'second nature' to do so and in the event, as at Flushing, 'darkness was a good friend to them'.

Third, it stressed the importance of every individual soldier being thoroughly briefed on maps and air photographs, and pointed out how essential it had been for the sub-units to adhere strictly to their orders and pre-selected tasks and not be diverted. As a result enemy pillboxes and other defences had been by-passed by troops in the dark because their priority was to press on to more distant objectives, with mopping up a second priority to be tackled subsequently.

Other interesting points were brought out in the list of key factors, but suffice it here to mention the above, which were the main ones.

Throughout their battle for Flushing the Commando had excellent artillery support plus daylight air support, both of which were 'on call'.

Invaluable, too, was the attachment of Dutch Commandos from No. 10, assigned to each troop leader. They were able to get a great deal of useful information 'on the ground' from the locals. This included details of alleyways, houses, gardens, garages and the like, all invaluable in the street-fighting scenario.

As darkness fell on D + 1 No. 4 Commando, having completed their initial task of securing the old town, began to consolidate, reorganise and prepare to hand over to the battalion of 155 Brigade who were to take over their positions. In the midst of this Col Dawson was ordered to speed up the handing-over tasks and embark on LVTs, as soon as possible, and go to assault two formidable coastal batteries, situated north-west of Flushing.

Dawson considered that such an operation, at this time and without proper preparations, was not feasible and stood little chance of success. After he had made his case against this operation at short notice, Brig Leicester agreed to postpone the operation for twenty-four hours, to allow time for all the necessary preparations to be made.

Next day (D + 2), having handed over to the relieving battalion of 155 Brigade, No. 4 Commando was able to 'pause for breath' in the beachhead area of Uncle. At this stage those badly wounded were shipped back by LCT to a field ambulance in Breskens and subsequently evacuated to a Canadian hospital established in Bruges.

Peter Lambert, of the heavy weapons troop, writes: 'I was a Vickers machine-gunner, carrying the 56 lb tripod on my back.' His section was with No. 6 Troop. On arrival at Bexhill, Carr told him to return to the beachhead to get medical help as they had some casualties. He was in a shop doorway. Just as he set off he was hit in the stomach by a sniper's bullet, but a cigarette tin in his trouser pocket saved him from more serious wounding. He fell down, in agony.

> Some Dutch people came to my aid and put me on some sort of stretcher. They were taking me to get some help, when a German officer came to the 'stretcher' with a Luger [pistol] in his hand and appeared about to shoot me. The Dutch remonstrated and seemingly said I was going to die anyway and persuaded him to leave me.

Fortunately for Lambert, some Dutch Resistance members took him to a nearby monastery where he was looked after until next day, when he was taken to the beachhead at Uncle.

He continues:

> There the Medics were wonderful . . . I was shipped over the Scheldt estuary to Breskens, where a school had been taken over for a Field Ambulance, and operated on about 36 hrs after the incident . . . I came to in a ward of British, Dutch and German casualties – male and female. A few days later I was taken to St George's Hospital in Bruges. . . .

Peter did make a full recovery, but his Commando days ended on that street in Flushing on 1 November 1944.

This striking action monument was erected by the people of Flushing in memory of all ranks of No. 4 Commando who fell during the Second World War, and to the loyal citizens of Flushing who were killed during the occupation and at the hour of their liberation. It is located on the open space by Uncle beach where No. 4 landed in the dark on 1 November 1944. It was unveiled in an impressive civil ceremony on 31 May 1952 which was attended by a large number of No. 4 veterans who sailed over from England on a RN destroyer. (*Author's Collection*)

Another casualty at Flushing was the highly respected RSM, 'Jumbo' Morris, who was very badly wounded in the lower leg and foot, and, like Lambert, his Commando days were also ended with the assault on Flushing. TSM 'Taffy' Edwards, of No. 3 Troop, was later appointed to succeed Morris, and he, too, proved to be a much-respected and popular RSM.

As regards the proposed new operation, because the RM Commandos made such good progress against the enemy in the battery area where it was intended to deploy No. 4, this new attack was considered unnecessary and was cancelled.

Nevertheless, No. 4 were ordered to move north from Flushing to link up with the rest of the Brigade. They were to move towards Westkapelle by sea in LVTs, but the weather and sea conditions ruled this out, so they started to march along the coast to Zoutelande, where Brigade Headquarters and Nos 47 and 48 RM Commandos were resting and reorganising.

Dawson describes that march:

It was an extraordinary experience. On the left of the track the dunes of loose, shifting sand, rose to heights of ten feet or more. There were shelters and pillboxes everywhere, all with an indescribable amount of

German equipment, food, clothing, and personal effects – especially letters. The track itself was narrow and our marching column had to move in single file. The track was pitted with bomb craters. On the right of the track lay the flood waters, stretching away inland as far as the eye could see in a smooth sheet, broken here and there by the upper storeys of houses or tree tops. No words or photographs can adequately convey the utter desolation of the scene. . . .

The Commando had to be ferried across the flooded waters at this stage by Weasels. This would be an appropriate place to mention the adventures, exploits and fate of the eighteen Weasels that had been allocated, back at Den Haan, to No. 4 for this operation.

Under the light-hearted heading of 'Pop Goes the Weasel', Dawson recounts their story. The following is a brief summary. Loaded aboard LCTs, the Weasels, left behind, set sail from Ostend at midnight on 1 November, but a series of incidents, some incurred by the enemy and some by nature – weather, high seas and flood torrents – prevented them from rejoining the Commando until the morning of D + 5, when only nine surviving vehicles arrived at Domburg. On the first attempt to land at Walcheren their LCT was hit by enemy gunfire and one of the Weasels set alight, but Sgt Rowe and his men managed to put out the fire and, indeed, Rowe drove his Weasel off, but it got impaled on one of the anti-landing devices. However, he got free, got back aboard and the LCT returned to Ostend, minus one Weasel. On a subsequent attempted landing at the 'gap' at Westkapelle in a heavy sea that tossed the tiny amphibians 'like straws', five were swamped and lost. Fortunately the LCT crew came to the rescue and after a violent battle with the raging flood torrents and storm winds all the No. 4 drivers were rescued.

Dawson had this to say of these drivers:

> Of all the troops in the Commando, few can have had as unpleasant a time as the drivers of these vehicles, and few can have worked harder throughout the operation than they did . . . working in difficult conditions and not infrequently under conditions of real danger . . . their skill and endurance was recognised and appreciated by all. . . .

The Commando remained at Zoutelande for two nights, and it was not until D + 5 (6 November) that sufficient stores had caught up and the unit was fit and ready for further action, and so marched on to Domburg to prepare, with the three RM Commandos, for the final push to clear the enemy from the northern coastal strip.

On D + 6, as the result of a very successful operation by No. 41 (RM) Commando, information was gleaned from German prisoners that most of the enemy were located in hastily prepared defences in a wooded area between Domburg and Vrouwenpolder. A plan was made for No. 4 to advance during the hours of darkness early next day and, under cover of a heavy artillery barrage, start to clear this area.

Leaving Domburg of 0345 hrs, with No. 3 Troop in the lead, the Commando made their way towards the enemy positions. By 0445 hrs they had reached the start line to begin their mopping-up operations. At this time the artillery barrage began to bombard the area where the main numbers of enemy were thought to be dug in. Only one solitary enemy gun fired in reply.

When the barrage lifted, No. 3 Troop moved off down the line of the light railway, with one French troop on its left to deal with any enemy in the dunes, and the other French troop and Capt Wilson's No. 2 Troop clearing the woods on the right flank of the advance.

Then events took place with dramatic rapidity. All the troops became involved in minor skirmishes, which were invariably overcome by small sub-section rushes and attacks, once or twice with the bayonet. The Germans simply gave in. Prisoners were being brought back to Commando HQ, which was close at hand, with the main body.

At 0815 hrs, while a batch of prisoners was being searched in the Headquarters area, four Germans were seen walking through the undergrowth nearby. They were challenged by RSM Edwards, who thought they were a new batch of POWs, although they were armed. On being interrogated, however, they stated that they had been sent forward by their officer with a view to making a formal surrender of all the remaining German troops in the area.

Capt Ken Wright and his runner accompanied the Germans back to their headquarters, where the local commander telephoned his superior and it was confirmed that the Germans were ready to negotiate a surrender.

The German regimental commander sent a car forward from Vrouwenpolder for Col Dawson. Accompanied by Wright, sitting on the bonnet of the German staff car, Dawson set off, but not before he had cancelled an air strike and artillery bombardment due to be brought down on Vrouwenpolder at 0900 hrs.

In his final report Dawson describes in some detail the elaborate exchanges of salutes and formality of the official surrender. It was, apparently, a very emotional affair in that the German commander, with tears in his eyes, declared that the disorganised state of his troops and their lack of ammunition compelled him to take this step. He also asked that his men be treated properly, that the dead be honourably buried and the wounded well cared for. Following assurances by Col Dawson on all these matters, the surrender was officially concluded. A total of just over 900 German prisoners marched into No. 4 Commando's cage, while many others surrendered to No. 41 RM Commando. Dawson records that in this final episode of the battle for Walcheren, which ended with such a conclusive outcome, 'No drop of British blood was shed.'

With the surrender of Vrouwenpolder, all organised resistance on Walcheren was at an end. The sea passage to the important port of Antwerp had been cleared and the supply base for the final push into Germany secured.

In his summary of the operation Dawson commented, '4 Commando, the first to land on Operation Infatuate, had the unique distinction of being also the last troops in action, and the recipients of the final surrender'.

In the whole operation, No. 4's casualties amounted to one officer and twelve other ranks killed, and one officer and twenty other ranks wounded. But the Commando had taken, in all, no less than 1,200 prisoners and inflicted probably some 200 casualties on the enemy, besides capturing and destroying large quantities of weapons and equipment of all sorts and sizes.

Little wonder Dawson concluded: 'It had been a perfect little campaign.'

CHAPTER ELEVEN

It All Ended in Germany

No. 4 Commando remained in the Vrouwenpolder area with their haul of German prisoners, although they also escorted many of them back to proper POW cages on the mainland via Flushing, until 14 November when they returned to Den Haan. There, the officers were surprised to learn that the owner of the Hotel Coq d'Or, where they had been billeted before Operation Infatuate, together with his wife, had been arrested by the security forces for spying. However, there was no suggestion that they had been thus engaged while the Commandos had been under their roof.

The few days spent at Den Haan were devoted to reorganising, re-equipping and resting after the operations on Walcheren. One Commando wrote of their state on arrival back in the rest area: 'we presented the classic sight of soldiers returning from the front. Our clothes stiffened by dried mud which was glued to them, we bent under the load of our rucksacks filled with so many memories. Our eyes were reddened by lack of sleep . . . but in spite of our tiredness we had the feeling of having accomplished something.'

Indeed they had, for after a massive mine-sweeping operation the first cargoes began to be unloaded in the great port of Antwerp by the end of November. The Allies now had the port they needed for the next phase of the war in Europe.

Once rested and reorganised, No. 4 were on the move, this time for a short stay in Blankerburge, on the western outskirts of Zeebrugge – where some reinforcements joined the unit – before crossing over to Walcheren once again, where they were ordered to prepare the defence of the coastal strip of North Beveland.

Opposite this coastline was the island of Schouwen, slightly smaller than the Isle of Wight, which was still occupied by the Germans. Their estimated strength was in the order of 5,000, including artillery units. They posed the threat, admittedly only a small one, of a counter-thrust from the north-west against Antwerp. It was much more likely that they might try to infiltrate small parties to carry out sabotage missions.

This, then, was to be the main task of the Commando, succinctly stated in six words: 'to prevent enemy infiltration and sabotage'. Thus committed, it meant that No. 4 were destined to be, in McDougal's words, 'in the backwater of the mainstream of the War'.

Nevertheless there was a job to be done, and Col Dawson appreciated that it was best done by allocating stretches of the coastline to individual troops to defend by patrolling, and also by initiating an offensive policy with a programme of small raids on Schouwen to gather information about the enemy there and keep them on the defensive. At the same time he was also responsible for the internal security of the region and for assisting in the smooth running of local civil affairs. Accordingly, he based troops on the centres of Wissenkerke, Colijnsplaat, Kats and Kamperland. He also managed to get a small flotilla of six LCAs for raiding and the support of field artillery detachments.

Dawson's Operational Orders for the Commando and detachments under command are still available for viewing at the PRO, Kew, and are a model of the type of comprehensive orders necessary for a force that has the complicated role of being operational – defensively and offensively – yet also has the added tasks of an occupational force responsible for internal security and civil matters as outlined above.

In the midst of these orders, which cover training, operational and administrative instructions plus those on curfews and 'Fishing Passes', it is amusing to find under the subheading of 'Baths' the instruction that all ranks 'have one shower per week' followed by a typical Commando rider, namely, 'Improvisation is the answer'.

In the various detached troop locations all ranks were accommodated either with local families or in requisitioned buildings. Capt Alastair

Members of No. 2 Troop, OC Capt Wilson, pictured here before their successful raid on Schouwen, 18 January 1945. Although they killed several of the enemy and brought back eight prisoners, they did lose one of their most popular long-serving members, Cpl Maybury, seen here in the back row, marked with an X. (*J. Spicer*)

Thorburn, whose No. 1 Troop was based in Wessenkerke, was 'billeted with a very nice family called Van der Maas'. He continues: 'Our job was to patrol the north shore to prevent enemy attempts to land. This was a cold, wet and rather dull assignment, but there was always a tot of rum after the patrol. We also did raids on the island of Schouwen.'

Dennis Cooper, who was in Thorburn's troop, also writes of his time on North Beveland.

> The Commando was billeted in various villages and hamlets with their respective Troops. We were at Wesserkerke, the French were nearby. We used what had been the Old People's Home for HQ, there we had the Troop kitchen and various rooms for use by the Sections. Behind in the yard was a German horse-drawn Field Kitchen, which the French used and they also had a large wire mesh cage for trapping wild birds to supplement the issued rations. Like us they were always hungry.

Cooper goes on to describe the method of nightly guard duties and patrols along the dykes and coastline. A hut was used for the section post and a 'tortoise stove' installed, which was fuelled by driftwood, which they collected either during the day or just before going on duty. Their particular post was:

> a mile or so away from Troop HQ on the main dyke, looking over to Schouwen. Leaving the post each morning we humped all our gear to the jeep and trailer parked on the inner dyke. There was a Bofors gun emplacement, built into the outer sea dyke, where we turned inland and we always got a load of stick from the gunners, telling us to keep down or we would be seen from Schouwen and the Germans there would shell us. . . .

It was advice they ignored until one day, after they had returned to the hut to tidy it, restock with wood, and carry out the odd recce, they passed the gunners' position to the customary shouts to keep down. Instructions they continued to ignore, as usual, but this time the gunners were right. Cooper and his mates had to make a dive to the nearest – albeit waterlogged – ditch to survive a nasty stonk of enemy fire. Cooper recalls: 'We took care never to walk on the top of the dyke in daylight again.'

A programme of raids was started in early December, but one of the early ones, on 8 December, had a tragic and cold-blooded outcome. A Commando party was to land on Schouwen to bring back a small group of Dutch Resistance patriots. The landing went well, but owing to a misunderstanding over the rendezvous, the Commandos never made contact with the Dutch patriots; instead they bumped into an enemy patrol who turned about and fled in the darkness. By now, because of the factors of 'time and tide', the Commandos had to withdraw and they returned empty-handed. The War Diary added this macabre postscript: 'It was subsequently learned that the enemy patrol captured the Dutch patriots and ten civilians were hanged next morning.'

One of the most successful raids was carried out just after Christmas in January 1945. It was one of several mounted that month, arguably in response to reports received that the garrison on Schouwen had been reinforced by about 1,500 troops, and these included 'some fanatical Nazis'.

Intelligence sources considered that an enemy offensive against North Beveland was a 'definite possibility'. So Dawson not only improved the defensive positions on the dykes and stepped up the coastal patrols, but he also increased the number of seaborne raids.

On the night of 18 January a large-scale raid led by Maj Boucher-Myers was a resounding success. They killed three of the enemy, wounded two and brought back eight prisoners – the last ably guarded and shepherded by the Commando's giant ex-policeman, Sgt McCubbin. Unfortunately, one of No. 4 was killed, the popular Cpl Maybury, an ex-Guardsman and one of the Commando's star footballers, who had been with the unit from its earliest days.

With the aid of the Dutch Commandos and interpreters attached to No. 4, the 'I' Section was able to amass a considerable amount of information from the eight prisoners. In fact, as a result the intelligence summary produced runs to several pages of close typescript and covers a wide range of civil information, including the names and other details of collaborators, as well as intelligence on the enemy forces on Schouwen.

However, in spite of a busy and demanding programme of commitments, training was not neglected, for it was laid down that 'the emphasis for the training of those not on coastal watch duties is to be on physical fitness and field firing'; there were also some amiable extra-mural activities. A rota of short local leave passes (forty-eight to seventy-two hours) was initiated in December to Brussels, Antwerp and Ghent, while the French troops made it to Paris – as did some of the others.

But the undoubted highlights of the social calendar were the Christmas parties organised by troops for the children in their locations. These were a great success, and troop jeeps with their trailers made runs to Brussels to buy 'goodies' and toys for the children, while their parents were treated to some NAAFI 'luxuries' – even bars of soap were regarded as luxuries! A simple delight for the children – and not a few mothers – was a ride in the Commando jeeps.

Les Lilley well remembers that Christmas Day:

It was a particular 'hoot' because we had promised the Dutch children a jeep ride, but all the parents turned up too, so I almost required a periscope to see where my jeep was going.

In gratitude for what we were doing to make the kids happy, the locals donated all kinds of fowl, but they were all 'on the hoof' and very much alive, and this was at the time of Von Rundstedt's offensive in the Ardennes, when we were always 'On the Alert'.

Throughout their stay in North Beveland an important feature was the daily artillery duels, but this time – in contrast to the Normandy campaign – it was the Germans who were mostly on the receiving end. The Allied gunners had the services of a very brave Army sergeant who flew, almost daily, over Schouwen, in a flimsy Auster aircraft spotting for his gunner comrades below. Cooper writes: 'We used to stare in disbelief as he circled over the Germans with shells bursting all around . . . then he would slowly turn around and retire to a field behind us where he parked his plane.'

On North Beveland, as elsewhere in the war – and subsequently in post-war confrontations – our own troops were sometimes the innocent victims of 'friendly fire'. Peter Snook, who joined No. 4 in December 1944, was a signaller, and after taking part in several raids, was wounded by 'friendly fire'. He was just one example, however, and although he had to be evacuated to England for hospitalisation, he returned to No. 4 later when it was in Germany.

Further small raids to gather information or to select targets for the artillery units were made throughout February. Lt Peter King, his section sergeant, Don Martin, and a signaller successfully carried out one such raid on the eastern end of Schouwen. Their main aim was to identify new enemy targets and signal back to the artillery HQ the details for opportunity shoots. For three days this patrol, moving by night and observing and relaying

During February 1945, while billeted in Willemstadt, No. 2 Troop trained for further small boat raids using canoes and inflatable dinghies. The warm sunny weather that spring allowed the Troop to enjoy some recreational moments too. (*Ken Stoakes*)

information by day, was able to direct fire on selected enemy targets, all without detection, before finally returning to North Beveland. It was no mean feat, although all three had many apprehensive moments with fingers crossed, hoping – and praying – they had provided correct map references and coordinates and there would be no problems with the 'friendly fire'.

The War Diary reports that 'during this period the patrol managed to cover most of the area allotted to it, artillery fire was successfully directed on to certain targets and on groups of Germans when seen grouped together in the open'. As a result of their success, Peter King was awarded a Military Cross, and although Don Martin was unsuccessfully recommended for a Military Medal, he was Mentioned in Dispatches.

What is significant about this raid, one of a series appropriately bearing the overall codename Inquisitive, was that it was a new type of operation unforeseen in the early days of the Commandos, but after the war, in particular, it became an accepted and normal task for Special Forces, carried out with success in both the Gulf War (1991) and in Afghanistan (2001/2), using long-range wireless sets and guiding in bomber aircraft instead of directing artillery.

In mid-March, after nearly three months' continuous duties on coastal defence and small raids, No. 4 was relieved by No. 47 RM Commando, and moved to the Middelburg area on Zeeland.

For Ted Brewer the relaxing, but brief, stay is best remembered for his success in an Inter-Services Athletics Meeting held there, when he won the long-distance race – and he still proudly cherishes his winner's medal.

On 30 March the whole Commando moved to the Bergen-Op-Zoom area, with HQ in Halsteren, and became responsible for security on Tholen and St Philipsland, plus a continuing programme of small reconnaissance raids on the coast of Zuid Holland.

At this stage the Commando's fleet of small boats included not only dories but also some two- and four-man canoes, and the handling of these small craft was a high training priority. Now that the weather was warmer and the sun shone – in striking contrast to those cold, wet and windy days on the water in North Beveland – training on these craft was most enjoyable and regarded as almost 'recreational'. For many of the 'old hands' it brought back memories of days on the Norfolk Broads in 1943. But there was an operational purpose for the smaller craft and, under Capt Wilson, commanding No. 2 Troop, together with Lt Hunter-Gray, who had won a Military Cross at Flushing, a series of successful small raids was carried out between 10 and 20 April from Willenstad. The aim of these small raids was to gather information on the enemy, for as the Diary records: 'One of the problems is that practically nothing is known of enemy strengths or identifications.'

Meanwhile, on the main battle front the Allies were nearing the end of their campaign in Germany. On 2 May the Russians finally completed the capture of Berlin and next day Gen Montgomery accepted the unconditional surrender of the German forces in Denmark, Holland and North Germany.

Locally on No. 4 Commando's front, the French troops went across to Schouwen and Col Dawson crossed over to Overflakke on the island to receive the official and unconditional surrender of the enemy forces in the region.

The long-awaited day of victory – VE Day – came on 8 May. It is on record that the Commando on that historic day 'celebrated in traditional Commando style'. No need to add more.

A few days later there was a tragic incident which marred an otherwise happy stay in the Bergen-Op-Zoom area, recalled by Bill Johnson. It happened on a warm Saturday evening when off-duty Fusilier Ball of the Commando was fatally shot by a 'trigger-happy' Dutch soldier in the town. A near-riot was quickly averted by confining all the Commando to their billets while investigations went ahead. The incident was made even sadder because up to that point relations with the Dutch, military and civil alike, had been friendly and cordial. Fortunately, this happy relationship was re-established, but the sad death of Fusilier Ball remained. He was to be the last Commando soldier of No. 4 to die 'on active service'.

Although the fighting was over in Europe, the war was still being fought in the Far East and many in No. 4 wondered if they would join their comrades of the four Commandos already involved out there; meanwhile, they were treated to the 'fruits of victory' in Europe. One came when Col Dawson, Maj Kieffer and a party of officers and men from both the British and French troops of No. 4 Commando were called to Paris.

Robert Dawson tells of this unique occasion:

A large detachment of No. 4 Commando, including all those who had been awarded French decorations, travelled to Paris and were invested with their medals in the courtyard of the Ministry for the Navy, followed by the traditional 'vin d'honneur'. Then we received perhaps the most gracious compliment the French nation could pay; we marched as a unit and alone (apart from the French naval band which led us) from the Ministry in the Place de la Concorde to the Arc de Triomphe, where Philippe Kieffer and I laid a wreath on the Unknown Soldier's tomb and relit the flame. I doubt if any other British Regiment has ever been honoured in this way.

It is a pity, in the light of the slow and sad demise of this splendid unit, that this magnificent occasion was not its final act. But it was not to be; within days No. 4 was transferred to Germany as part of the occupational force. Sgt 'Mac' Parr of the heavy weapons troop was sent, with Capt 'Sandy' Carlos-Clarke, on the advance party to Recklinghausen in the Ruhr, to arrange for the arrival of the rest of the Commando. They travelled by road in jeeps, with trailers.

Sandy had been wounded in Normandy, but had rejoined the Commando for Flushing. He was colourful character and had joined No. 4, via

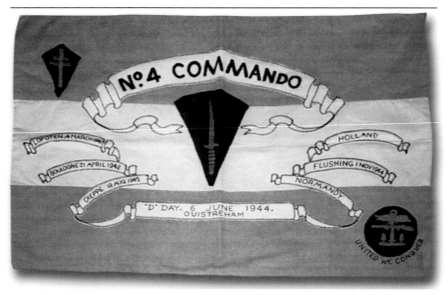

This souvenir flag was made locally, after VE-Day 1945, when the Commando was stationed in Recklinghausen, Germany. It displays the Croix de Lorraine (top left), honouring the French troops, the centre badge is the famous Commando fighting knife – still the badge of today's Royal Marine Commandos. In the bottom right-hand corner is the original Combined Operations Badge. Emblazoned on the flag are seven outstanding Commando actions. (*Author's Collection*)

Achnacarry, where he had instructed for a while, from a cavalry unit. He was 'a horsey' man, and after the war a very successful racehorse owner/ trainer. He had a string of horses, many of them with names associated with the Commandos, including one – appropriately – called 'No. 4 Commando'. It had quite a few wins and 'places', and many of Sandy's ex-Commando mates had winning 'flutters' on it during the 1960s.

Mac's description of the road journey from Holland into Germany and through the war-devastated industrial region of the Ruhr provides a stark reminder of the effects of the Allies' air raids. But he also recalls the pathetic sight of thousands of homeless people taking to the roads to find shelter and food. They included displaced persons (DPs) and other refugees, but 'the most pitiful were some hapless ex-inmates of the concentration camps, still in their "stripey pyjamas". . . . It was an unforgettable experience', recalls Parr.

In Recklinghausen the town mayor and civil authorities had moved the residents out of a large block of well-appointed and undamaged flats, much to the chagrin of the owners, for occupation by the Commando. The quarters were, in the words of many, including Charlie Jacobs, 'Quite posh, in some rooms chandeliers were still hanging and we slept four to a room.'

The Commando's task in Recklinghausen was hardly commensurate with their purpose and role in war. They had to take over from a US unit which had been guarding 91 Civilian Internment Camp (CIC) which housed several thousand Nazis – all civilians, as opposed to prisoners of war. They ranged from suspicious characters who had no identification cards to known Nazis with records of service with the infamous SS or with concentration and internment camps, and included 'hard-case' women.

The Commando was responsible mainly for guarding the camp and for escort duties; they were not involved in the investigation/interrogation process, although Capts McDougal and Wright were detached for two months to help in the detailed interrogation and sorting of some 250,000 POWs. In his book McDougal describes what a depressing job it was, as 'for two months we worked every day in this sickening mass of festering humanity . . .'.

Soon after their arrival in Recklinghausen, the French troops went back to France for demobilisation. It was the end of their participation in No. 4. Many firm and enduring friendships had been forged with these gallant Commando allies, during the fighting in France and in Holland – friendships that have survived even to the present day and are still renewed annually in Ouistreham on the anniversary of D-Day, thanks to the joint efforts of Ron Youngman and Leon Gaultier.

The duties at the camp were not arduous, basically '24 hrs on and 48 hrs off'. Accommodation was good, as were the food and rations, but the job itself was depressing and irksome. However, as No. 4 was not the only British Army unit in the area, there were others whom they could challenge at both football and rugby, and for those not good enough for the unit team there were facilities at hand for seven-a-side and inter-troop matches. Drill parades were held too, and a feature of the stay at Recklinghausen was the weekly 'spit-and-polish parades' held every Saturday. According to Peter Snook, 'we were a very smart Commando on parade', which no doubt impressed the local Germans.

On 24 June Col Dawson left No. 4 and was posted to the Holding Operational Commando – on paper – as he was standing as a parliamentary candidate in the first postwar General Election. In the event he was unsuccessful and returned to resume command of No. 4 at the end of July.

Apropos the General Election, it is pertinent to remind readers that although all servicemen overseas were able to vote through proxy or postal arrangements, the legal age to be able to vote was twenty-one years; this meant that many of the younger members of No. 4 were ineligible – in spite of having fought for their country! George Bridges was one of these youngsters, but reckoned 'it was a good laugh'.

In the meantime the strength of the unit was reduced to just 188 all ranks, when at the end of June 233 other ranks were posted to Nos 3 and 6 Commandos back in England, who were earmarked for the war in the Far East, which had yet to be concluded.

However, the dropping of atomic bombs on Hiroshima and Nagasaki on 6 and 9 August respectively virtually brought that war to an end and, with the Japanese signing of the instrument of surrender on 2 September, the Second World War was over.

Notwithstanding, No. 4 Commando continued its guard duties in Recklinghausen, but about this time the unit also became involved in the ironic situation of having to mount mobile patrols in the surrounding countryside to prevent marauding bands of refugees and DPs from raiding and attacking local German farmsteads and their occupants.

Offering some relief from the garrison duties, Dawson was able to take parties off in August for civic commemorative parades in Flushing and Dieppe. A detachment of the Commando also gave a demonstration of 'Commando Tactics' and provided a Guard of Honour for the Queen of the Netherlands in Rotterdam during the month.

By now, with the war over, the main concern for most, other than regular soldiers, was their 'demob', so arrangements were put in hand to provide various courses and advice for their resettlement back in 'civvy street'.

In September No. 4 Commando was reinforced by officers and men, with high release numbers, from Army Commandos in England which had no operational role or commitments. No one knew that a decision had been made to disband Army Commandos, and no official nor public announcement to that effect had yet been made.

On 10 October Col Dawson left the Commando for demobilisation and eventual employment in the Foreign Office. Command of the unit was delegated to Lt-Col B.G. 'Puggie' Pugh, an original member of No. 1 Commando and latterly the Brigade Major of 4 Commando Brigade in the Walcheren campaign, so he was no stranger to No. 4. His name will, however, be forever linked to the Commando's Green Beret as he was instrumental, back in 1942, when he was adjutant of No. 1, in bringing to fruition the idea of this distinctive headdress for the Commandos and arranging its manufacture.

It was while he was commanding that Gen Sir Robert Sturges, GOC, Commando Group, visited the Commando on 25 October and announced that all Army Commandos were to be disbanded, the coveted Green Beret was to go and all ranks in the Army Commandos not due for demob would be posted back to their parent regiments or corps. It was a sad day, especially for those who considered No. 4 Commando was their regiment – they had known no other. At home when the news broke, many newspapers had editorials condemning this 'shameful decision'.

In the event No. 4 Commando remained in Recklinghausen and carried on its guard duties and countryside patrols until mid-December, when it was relieved of the guard duties on the CIC, but remained in the area to carry on the mobile patrols and other occupational duties over the Christmas period.

In spite of a paucity of entries in the War Diary from that fateful day in October, there is one cryptic one for 25/6 December. It reads: 'Christmas Holiday – all ranks commiserate with their unfortunate companions who are forced to spend Xmas in the UK' – the Commando scribe still had his sense of humour.

It was the last entry for 1945, and four weeks later the Commando was officially disbanded, with all ranks being posted back to the UK and dispersed to their regimental depots for demob or further postings. No. 4 Commando, a proud fighting unit with a record second to none, was no more.

Although all ranks of the Commando had been dispersed and scattered to either civilian life or continued service in the Army, the fighting traditions of the Commando and its influence have lived on as part of the legacy handed down to its successors, the Royal Marine Commandos.

In this respect it is relevant to recall that a postwar Commando training manual of the Royal Marines states:

The Commando must firstly be a highly skilled infantryman. Secondly he must be expert in his own branch of infantry work. He must:

a. Be able to move fast across any country and be independent of roads.
b. Be happy to fight at night.
c. Be ready to work in small parties or on his own.
d. Be able to land on coasts impracticable to normal infantry and follow up climbing leaders in cliff assaults. . . .

And these tactical characteristics are followed by the assertion that more important than anything else is the inculcation of the 'Commando spirit', which is made up of:

a. Determination.
b. Enthusiasm and cheerfulness, especially under bad conditions.
c. Individual initiative and self-reliance.
d. Comradeship.

Surely anyone having read through the story of No. 4 Commando might be excused for thinking that the above quotation was a summary of the background training and characteristics of all those who had served in the Commando. Indeed, it could well make a suitable epitaph for the unit.

The bravery and deeds of those in No. 4 were recognised during the war by the award of all the possible types of medals then available to soldiers of the British Army. These were headed by that award of the Victoria Cross to Pat Porteous; other awards included Distinguished Service Order (DSO), Distinguished Conduct Medal (DCM), Military Cross (MC), Military Medal (MM) and numerous Mentioned in Dispatches (MID). In addition, officers and other ranks of the Commando received the French awards of Légion d'Honneur and the Croix de Guerre. One must add that all these awards included British decorations to French members of the Commando and, vice versa, French awards to the British members – emphasising that bond of mutual respect and comradeship that was a feature of this unique Commando. However, it must be remembered and appreciated that many sacrifices and acts of bravery went unnoticed or were not rewarded – and many of the recipients of the above awards would be the first to acknowledge this.

Finally, it is fitting to mention specific memorials and museums that are dedicated to No. 4 Commando, and others that remember and honour all

Commandos. In Westminster Abbey a statue of a Commando soldier stands in the cloisters. This was unveiled by Winston Churchill on 21 May 1948. The Commando Battle Honours Flag, with thirty-eight battle honours (including 'Norway 1941', 'Dieppe', 'Normandy Landing', 'Dives Crossing' and 'Flushing') emblazoned on it, and the Roll of Honour are located by and in the St George's Chapel respectively.

In Scotland, at Spean Bridge near Fort William, is the magnificent Commando Memorial, unveiled by Her Majesty, Queen Elizabeth the Queen Mother on 27 September 1952. Nearby in the local Spean Bridge Hotel is housed a permanent Commando exhibition, which includes an illustrated potted history of No. 4.

Further afield in France, at Ouistreham, is the splendid No. 4 Commando Museum, the only museum devoted entirely to one Commando. It contains weapons, pictures, models and other memorabilia of the British-French Commando. Open daily from mid-March to the end of October, it is supervised and run by the capable 'offices' of French Commando veteran, Leon Gaultier, and his daughter. There are other impressive monuments dedicated to No. 4 on the beaches and in the town of Ouistreham, the details of which are available in the museum, as are details of the No. 4 Commando monument at Hauger.

In Ste Marguerite, near Dieppe, the centre of the village was named 'No. 4 Commando Square' following the fiftieth anniversary of the raid. On

In September 1952 Her Majesty Queen Elizabeth, the Queen Mother, unveiled the Commando Memorial at Speen Bridge, near Fort William. She is seen here with Lord Lovat (kilted) at the memorial, the central figure of which is a sculpture of Sgt Lewington of No. 4 Commando. (*Author's Collection*)

Today, the Musée No. 4 Commando in Ouistreham – the only museum solely dedicated to a single Commando – stands opposite the site of the Casino strongpoint attacked by Nos 1 and 8 Troops on D-Day. Inside, the museum has a fascinating collection of weapons, models, memorabilia and pictures connected with No. 4 and is open daily from mid-March to the end of October. (*Author's Collection*)

the wall of the old *mairie* is the Roll of Honour and a plaque describing No. 4's action, in French and English; in the modern *mairie* is a collection of exhibits about the raid. A further memorial plaque can be seen on a bunker at the site of the German 'Hess' battery at Varengeville, while on the beach where Lovat and Group 2 landed on 19 August 1942, a new commemorative stone monolith was unveiled on the sixtieth anniversary in 2002.

At Flushing, near where No. 4 landed, in the dark, in the early hours of 1 November 1945, is a striking monument erected by the people of that port to honour all those of No. 4 who liberated their town on that day. A large party of No. 4 veterans attended the civic ceremony on 31 May 1952 when it was unveiled.

In England, at the birthplace of No. 4 Commando in the Pavilion of Weymouth has been installed a large illustrated potted history of the Commando; a replica of this illustrated display is also an exhibit in the Dieppe Raid section of the museum at Fort Newhaven in Sussex.

Finally, in addition to the memorial at Svolvaer in the Lofoten Islands, mentioned in Chapter 3, there are exhibits concerning the raid of March 1941 in the local museum.

So, all in all, the deeds, successes and sacrifices by the Commandos of the 'Fighting Fourth' are, deservedly, well commemorated and it is hoped that this book, in its own modest way, will provide an added record of the whole lifespan of No. 4 Commando from 1940 to 1945.

Bibliography

Dear, Ian, *Ten Commando 1942–45*, Leo Cooper, 1987.

Dunning, James, *'It Had To Be Tough'*, Pentland Press, 2000.

Dunning, James, 'Commando Trail', Lochaber Tourism, 1996.

Durnford-Slater, John, *Commando*, William Kimber & Co., 1987.

Fowler, Will, *The Commandos at Dieppe – Rehearsal for D-Day*, HarperCollins, 2002.

Foxall, Raymond, *The Amateur Commandos*, Robert Hale, 1980.

Gilchrist, Donald, *Don't Cry For Me*, Robert Hale, 1982.

Hunt, Sir John, *Life is Meeting*, Hodder, 1978.

John, Evan, *Lofoten Letter*, William Heinemann, 1941.

Leasor, James, *X Troop*, Corgi Books, 1982.

Lovat, Lord, *March Past*, Weidenfeld and Nicolson, 1978.

Masters, Peter, *Striking Back: A Jewish Commando's War against the Nazis*, Presideo Press (USA), 1997.

McDougal, Murdoch, *Swiftly They Struck*, Grafton Books, 1989.

Messenger, Charles, *The Commandos 1940–1946*, William Kimber & Co., 1985.

Mikes, G., *The Epic of Lofoten*, Hutchinson & Co., 1941.

Miller, Russell, *Nothing Less Than Victory*, Michael Joseph, 1993.

Mills-Roberts, Derek, *Clash By Night*, William Kimber & Co., 1956.

Parker, John, *Commandos – The Inside Story of Britain's Most Elite Fighting Force*, Headline Book Publishing, 2000.

Saunders, Hilary St George, *The Green Beret*, Michael Joseph, 1949.

Young, Peter, *Storm From The Sea*, Greenhill Books, 1989.

Index

(The index covers the main characters of No. 4, the Commando's bases, areas of training, locations of action and other major headings. Where ranks are given they are those finally reached and not necessarily the rank of the person at the time of mention in the text.)